2015-16

40th edition

EDITED AND COMPILED BY STEWART ROBERTS

First published in Great Britain by
Stewart Roberts
The Old Town Hall
142 Albion Street
Southwick
Brighton
BN42 4AX

Cover design: Gordon Wright, Canadian Spa Company

British Library Cataloguing-in-Publication Data.
A catalogue record for this book is available from the British Library.

The Ice Hockey Annual 2015-16

ISBN 978-0-9562943-8-8

The Ice Hockey Annual's official website is at www.icehockeyannual.co.uk.

Past editions of *The Ice Hockey Annual* are archived in the Hockey Hall of Fame, D K (Doc) Seaman Hockey Resource Centre, Toronto, Canada.

CONTENTS

COVER

TONY HAND MBE decided to hang up his skates in 2015 after 34 seasons of breathtakingly skilful ice hockey. *See Editorial and special article on page 14.*

photo: Diane Davey (www.ddimaging.co.uk)

ACKNOWLEDGEMENTS

The years roll by

A warm welcome to the 40th edition of *The Ice Hockey Annual*. Who thought we'd reach this milestone when we started out in 1976? Not your editor, that's for sure.

This means the *Annual* was first published before **Tony Hand** started working his own Miracle on Ice and even before **Ken Taggart** started his miraculous reign at the English Ice Hockey Association.

Now that is a lot of years!

But, of course, none of them would have been possible without you, dear reader, our dedicated band of contributors, and the generosity of our advertisers, especially **Troy Labelle** of *Canadian Spa*.

This is the space where we take a moment to express our gratitude to all these good folk.

Here's to the next edition. (Well, you didn't think were going to say the next 40, did you?!)

Our contributors

We like to think the *Annual* is much more than just a statistical record of a season, but there's no doubt that stats are the facts that many readers enjoy the most.

So my first round of thank-yous goes to **Ronnie Nichol** and **Jim Lydon** whose excellent Elite League results service and statistical updates flood my in-box throughout the season.

All the other leagues and competitions are well served by **Malcolm Preen**, the English Ice Hockey Association's statto. Malcolm's unique stats website hasn't been going quite as long as this old tome but you can find figures going back 20 years at www.malcolmpreen.co.uk/hockey.

Writing a report on your club's season in barely 400 words is not an easy task, especially if, like many of our contributors, you're not a professional journalist. Take a bow, all whose names appear in our Club pages.

Ice hockey is a fast-paced sport often played in poorly lit buildings. So it's a tribute to the glamour of the sport that it has found some gifted folk who are also willing to make the effort required to photograph it.,

We're very grateful to all the club photographers who have provided us with team photos, to Ice Hockey UK's official photographer **Colin Lawson** for all his GB pics (we do love his one of **Ben O'Connor** in the *World Championships* section) and to **Diane Davey** whose photo of **Tony Hand** appears on the cover.

For all the other snappers, named and unnamed, please accept our grateful thanks.

Many others have contributed facts and figures about the personalities in the sport who achieved some milestone in the last 12 months, or sadly left us. There are too many of you to list here, but you know who you are. Thank you.

Our advertisers

We are indebted, as always, to the people and organisations whose products and services are advertised within these pages. We urge you to use them whenever you can.

Troy at *Canadian Spa*, suppliers of spas and saunas, has agreed to partner with the *Annual* for an eighth year. Your support is greatly appreciated, buddy.

Our friends at *Wheels (Skate Sales) Ltd*, sole importers of the world famous *Bauer* skates and equipment, have been staunch supporters of the *Annual* for many years.

Armchair fans need no introduction to subscription TV channel, *Premier Sports*, who justly bill themselves as Your Home for Hockey with their fantastic coverage of the NHL, Elite League and European games.

A new backer this year is *Gary Brine*, the former Streatham and GB junior netminder, who is now the man behind *Aspire* and *Flite*.

What is it about Streatham goalies? *Rockies Sports Bar* in Belfast's *Odyssey Arena*, is also run by a sarf London stopper **Jim Graves**.

Marketing company *Weltch Media* is another old friend of the *Annual,* as is *D&P Trophies*, the supplier of silverware to the English IHA

Ice Hockey Review provides yearly coverage of the third tier National League (NIHL), reaching the parts, as somebody used to say, that even this *Annual* cannot.

The production team

Last but certainly not least, many thanks to our printer, **Ian Watkins** at *Multi-Print Services* in Sussex, and to our designer **Gordon Wright** at *Canadian Spa*.

The Ice Hockey Annual

EDITORIAL

A once-in-a-lifetime player

Tony Hand MBE may not be the finest Brit ever to lace on a pair of ice skates. It's hard to compare different eras when you've only followed one yourself. (Even your esteemed editor doesn't go back to British ice hockey's Golden Era either side of World War Two.)

But Edinburgh's own hockey phenom is undoubtedly the most talented player that the vast majority of readers has ever seen, or is ever likely to see in our rinks.

No other player has been able to exert such an influence on so many of the games in which he played.

And that includes just about every import who has ever come here, a fact the imports themselves were always quick to acknowledge.

One of them – **Garry** (Iron Man) **Unger** – went so far as to recommend the teenaged Tony to the NHL's Edmonton Oilers, who duly invited him to their training camp in the 1980s.

Indeed, as we know, he could easily have enjoyed a high level career in North America. Instead, to our great pleasure (but to his own regret, as he admitted later), he chose to stay in the old country.

For over a third of century he has travelled the length and breadth of Britain, Northern Ireland and Europe (with GB), playing, coaching, and meeting everyone who's anyone, including Her Majesty.

Now he will concentrate on his other hockey passion, coaching. Along with all his many fans, I wish him well, especially as his club, the Phoenix, are going through very difficult times.

Our sport should hold hands

Outstanding players in any sport are seen to have a duty to speak out on important issues facing their game. This has never been Tony's way as he's not an outspoken person, rather the contrary.

Or perhaps he's just being sensible since ice hockey has so many intractable problems.

So I was pleasantly surprised when he did stick his head over the boards recently to complain about the vast number of imports in the Elite League and the poor development of local players.

These are hardly new topics but it can only be good when the best player of his generation draws attention to them.

Tony has always commanded respect among his fellow players. Can he extend this to the sport's administrators, who are, let's face it, a very different kettle of fish?

He already wields some influence in the corridors of power as his brother **David Hand** is the chairman of Scottish Ice Hockey.

Tony's great desire, he said, is "for all of us to come together for the betterment of British ice hockey."

I think we can all join Hands on this one.

Only one hand clapping

After recent events, however, it seems that Tony and David have much work to do in this area.

The good news is that our two main governing bodies each commissioned studies into how best to improve the sorry state of the game's admin. (See *Review of the Year*.)

The English Ice Hockey Association (EIHA) have followed up their expert's findings and are now actively helping their member clubs to acquire much needed funding.

The bad news is that the EIHA decided to use a different expert from the one the national governing body Ice Hockey UK hired.

This leads to the sadly inevitable conclusion that British ice hockey remains divided even as it seeks to improve its ways of working.

Enjoy your hockey and tell your friends.

August 2015   **Stewart Roberts**
email: stewice@aol.com
Follow me on *twitter:* @robers45

We can help you achieve your goals

WELTCH MEDIA

Editorial and Public
Relations Services
info@weltchmedia.com
07890 288302
www.weltchmedia.com

- Media relations
- Media training
- Social media
- Event organisation

- Publications
- Web content
- Video and photography
...and more

HONOURS AND AWARDS

HONOURS ROLL-CALL 2014-15

ELITE LEAGUE
League Winners
SHEFFIELD STEELERS
Erhardt Conference
NOTTINGHAM PANTHERS
Gardiner Conference
BRAEHEAD CLAN
Playoff Champions
COVENTRY BLAZE
The Challenge Cup
CARDIFF DEVILS

ENGLISH PREMIER LEAGUE
League Winners
TELFORD TIGERS
Playoff Champions
PETERBOROUGH PHANTOMS
English Challenge Cup
TELFORD TIGERS

NATIONAL LEAGUE
Division One Winners
South – CHELMSFORD CHIEFTAINS
North (Moralee) – BLACKBURN HAWKS
No overall champion decided
Playoff Winners
South – WIGHTLINK RAIDERS
North – BLACKBURN HAWKS

SCOTTISH NATIONAL LEAGUE
League Winners
KIRKCALDY KESTRELS
Playoff Champions
KIRKCALDY KESTRELS

WOMEN'S LEAGUE
Premier Division Winners
BRACKNELL QUEEN BEES

Top League Points Scorers
Elite League
MATHIEU ROY, Sheffield
English Premier League
PETER SZABO, Telford

Best League Goaltending Percentages
Elite League
JOSH UNICE, Sheffield
English Premier League
TOM MURDY, Telford

ICE HOCKEY JOURNALISTS UK AWARDS

ALL-STAR TEAMS

ELITE LEAGUE
First Team

Goal	KYLE JONES, Braehead
Defence	ANDREW HOTHAM, Cardiff
	BEN O'CONNOR, Sheffield
Forwards	MICHAEL FORNEY, Sheffield
	JOEY MARTIN, Cardiff
	MATHIEU ROY, Sheffield

Second Team

Goal	BEN BOWNS, Cardiff
Defence	SCOTT AARSSEN, Braehead
	JAMIE FRITSCH, Braehead
Forwards	STEFAN MEYER, Braehead
	LEIGH SALTERS, Braehead
	MIKE KOMPON, Belfast

ENGLISH PREMIER LEAGUE
First Team

Goal	TOM MURDY, Telford
Defence	JONATHAN WEAVER, Telford
	SAM ZAJAC, Telford
Forwards	PETER SZABO, Telford
	JASON SILVERTHORN, Telford
	AARON NELL, Swindon

Second Team

Goal	STEVIE LYLE, Swindon
Defence	PETER HORAVA, M Keynes
	BRANISLAV KVETAN, Guildford
Forwards	FRANTISEK BAKRLIK, M'chester
	CIARAN LONG, Basingstoke
	MILAN BARANYK, P'borough

BEST OF BRITISH AWARDS

Best Forward
ROBERT FARMER Nottingham Panthers

Best Defenceman (Alan Weeks Trophy)
BEN O'CONNOR Sheffield Steelers

Best Netminder (Phil Drackett Mem'l Trophy)
BEN BOWNS Cardiff Devils

Best Young Player (Vic Batchelder Mem'l Award)
ZACH SULLIVAN Braehead Clan

Top Elite League Points Scorer
(The Ice Hockey Annual Trophy)
BEN O'CONNOR Sheffield Steelers

HONOURS AND AWARDS

ICE HOCKEY JOURNALISTS UK AWARDS, *contd*

ELITE LEAGUE PLAYER OF THE YEAR

MATHIEU ROY
Sheffield Steelers
In his first season in Europe, the Canadian was the standout forward on the title winning Steelers, heading the league's scorers with most goals, points, game-winners and powerplay goals.

His line with **Mike Forney** and **Colton Fretter** enjoyed tremendous chemistry with the trio notching up 246 points, including 111 goals, in all official games.

Roy was previously captain of Florida Everblades of the ECHL.

ELITE LEAGUE COACH OF THE YEAR

ANDREW LORD *Cardiff Devils*
The Vancouver-born forward led his new-look team to the Challenge Cup in his first season in the dual roles of player and coach.

Under Lord, 30, the Devils only missed out on the league title by a couple of points.

ENGLISH PREMIER LEAGUE PLAYER OF THE YEAR

PETER SZABO *Telford Tigers*
The veteran Slovakian playmaker enjoyed the best season of his long career, his 59 assists in 48 games helping him to a league-leading 87 points.

The 34-year-old was in his first season with the league winners.

COACH OF THE YEAR

SLAVA KOULIKOV *Peterborough Phantoms*
After the Russia-born player-coach guided the Phantoms to one of their best league positions of recent times, he went on to upset the form book and lift his squad to the play-off championship.

He achieved this while assisting on 37 of his team's goals and scoring three himself, and often while playing against teams with deeper pockets.

This was the 36-year-old's third season as a player-coach, and his second at the Phantoms.

ZACH SULLIVAN, *Braehead Clan*

BEST BRITISH DEFENCEMAN

Alan Weeks Trophy
BEN O'CONNOR, *Sheffield Steelers*
On his return last year from four seasons honing his game in Kazakhstan, the 26-year-old Durham native established himself as probably the best blueliner of his generation. As long as he isn't tempted away again, expect him to be a shoo-in for this award for many more seasons.

BEST BRITISH FORWARD

ROBERT FARMER, *Nottingham Panthers*
Making his living in the dirty areas in front of the net and relishing physical battles with opposition defencemen, the big (6ft, 3in.), hard-working, 24-year-old was the league's fourth highest scoring Brit and the most penalised.

TOP BRITISH ELITE LEAGUE SCORER

The Ice Hockey Annual *Trophy*
BEN O'CONNOR, *Sheffield Steelers*
Those who saw Ben's 'circus shot' at the World Championships will not be surprised to learn that the defenceman's all-round skills made him the highest scoring Brit in the Elite League.

BEST BRITISH NETMINDER

Phil Drackett Memorial Award
BEN BOWNS, *Cardiff Devils*
One of the most popular men on the Devils (his end-of-game wave ceremony is a highlight of every match, win or lose), GB's number one is only 24 and has plenty of upside.

YOUNG BRITISH PLAYER

Vic Batchelder Memorial Award
ZACH SULLIVAN, Braehead Clan
The 20-year-old ex-GB junior defenceman shone in his rookie Elite League season, especially with his positioning and reading of the game.

ALL-STARS

clockwise from top left:
JOEY MARTIN Cardiff Devils
JONATHAN WEAVER Telford Tigers
ANDREW HOTHAM Cardiff Devils
PETER SZABO Telford Tigers
photos: Wales Online, Telford Tigers

QUOTES OF THE YEAR

'The Bownsy Wave'

Photo courtesy South Wales Echo

"I'm certain the Bownsy wave will be seen again next season. I don't think [manager] Todd Kelman would let me stop now because it seems to have gone down well with the fans.

"The most pleasing thing is that so many people stop on at the end of matches to join in. It's pretty tiring at times after an intense match, but the wave will be back."
Cardiff Devils' netminder **Ben Bowns** *on the popularity of his Mexican Wave.*

Concussions are serious

"Concussion is getting bigger and bigger nowadays. I think when we were younger, it was 'You've had the night off now, let's get going'. But I think it's too serious now and they don't truly know the end effects of it – it's just not worth it." **Ryan Aldridge**, *coach of Swindon Wildcats, after two of his players were sidelined.*

Desperate optimists

'Billingham Stars went some way to restoring dented confidence with a creditable 7-0 British Challenge Cup [sic] loss at English Premier League outfit Sheffield Steeldogs.' *Opening paragraph of a match report in the* Teesside Gazette.

"They caught us with a couple of goals – that's what happens when you play these teams above you. They punish you badly when you make mistakes and we made two or three." **Terry Ward**, *the Stars' coach, after the same game.*

You gotta get your minds right

"There has been a big mind-set change within the club over the last two to three weeks to the point where 'OK' isn't OK any more.

"We've been very public about that mind-set not being right for the last couple of years – from the management, through to the team. Everyone is now bought in and focused on changing that."
James Pease, *director of Coventry Blaze, after the club sacked coach* **Marc LeFebvre** *and replaced him with forward* **Steve Goertzen** *in November 2014.*

Circus

"I feel sorry for the fans that paid to watch that as you could have got that entertainment for free at the circus." **Ryan Finnerty**, *coach of Braehead Clan, somewhat miffed at the officiating in the Clan's home game against Edinburgh Capitals when his Elite League runners-up managed to throw away a 2-0 lead to the sixth placed side and lose 4-2.*

Telford Tigers and their owner

"Clubs in the English Premier League have generally been a little better with us this year, less tantrums and secret meetings apparently. Still some bitterness but we ignore that, too." **Wayne Scholes**, *the cheerfully controversial owner of Telford Tigers, in his Christmas and New Year Message on the club's website.*

"We've invested heavily in the squad, but all we've done is make it a level playing field. Before, Telford were operating on about a tenth of the budgets the rest of the league had. We've made the competition a million times more competitive..." *Scholes again.*

"We've had conversations with the Elite League before but they have to invite you. You can't approach them. It's one of those things where they want to see that you've got two or three years of really good, solid success. They want to see that it's sustainable and that you're up to a certain standard, and then they will reach out." *Scholes on the eve of the Tigers clinching the English Premier League title.*

More Quotes on page 17.

TONY HAND MBE, retired

A unique talent

Tony Hand MBE retired at the end of the 2014-15 season after a glorious career unique in the annals of British ice hockey.

An exceptional set of skills - soft hands, vision, easy skating stride, strength - enabled the 47-year-old from Edinburgh to achieve more than any other player in our sport.

From being the first Brit – and Scot – to be drafted by the NHL to receiving the accolade of his fellow players, who recently voted him the Player of the Century, he has – as our most famous sponsor might have put it – refreshed the parts of the game that other players couldn't reach.

Great Britain's all-time highest points scorer; league, cup and play-off trophies galore; and the only ice hockey player ever to be awarded the prestigious Member of the British Empire (MBE) medal by HM The Queen for his services to his sport.

Tony's haul of honours is unsurpassed, and is likely to remain so for years to come.

The tributes didn't come only from this country. *The Hockey News* of Toronto devoted a couple of pages to the news with the unblushing headline 'The Scottish **Wayne Gretzky** finally hangs up his skates'.

That must have given Hand goose-bumps.

The story recalled the famous quote by the NHL's **Glen Sather**, who coached both players, Tony very briefly at an Oilers' training camp.

"Hand," said Sather, "is the most intelligent player on the ice – bar Gretzky, of course."

Only 18 at the time (1986), he declined the opportunity to play in North America, preferring to return home to Scotland.

Just as remarkable as his talents was his longevity. To play 34 seasons in a hard, contact sport like ice hockey is rare indeed.

How did he do it? Though sturdily built, he was never a particularly physical player himself.

Like that other fellow, he usually had a 'minder', in the early days his older brother Paul.

Allied to this were his agility and his uncanny knack of being able to see what how the play was developing, which usually enabled him to steer clear of trouble.

It was perhaps his laser-like passing that made him the ultimate team player. His line-mates, whether British or foreign, invariably enjoyed a career scoring season when TH was setting them up.

The teams he played on won 15 major trophies, and his individual honours include 11 league and 13 club scoring titles. He has six Player of the Year awards and three for Coach of the Year. Though up against imports for much of his career, he was picked for 23 All-Star teams, 19 of them on the first line.

Hand wore Britain's colours in 11 World Championships and one Olympic Qualifier. He played at the top in Italy in 1994 after being the top-scoring Brit on the dual national-dominated team that won promotion a year earlier.

For two years he took on the coaching duties, the highlight of which was another promotion, this time to the final qualifying round of the 2014 Winter Olympics.

Though, like all hockey players, he almost always carried niggling injuries, he only once suffered a major one. A broken ankle early in the 2011-12 season when he was already into his 40s, curtailed that year for him and ultimately hastened his decision to retire.

This is inevitably a brief overview of a very long and star-studded career. To compensate a little, we've compiled Tony's complete statistical record on the next page.

Forgive us if we write some of the figures here again as they are frankly astounding: 1,748 games played, 1,642 goals scored, 2,992 assists, 4,634 points.

And this is just in domestic games in the major competitions. We've had to omit, again for reasons of space, European Cup games, junior GB internationals, Scottish Cups, GB friendlies, and on and on.

One honour still to come is the Hall of Fame. It's a racing certainty that the next time the Hall's committee meets they will waste little time before inducting Tony.

TONY HAND MBE

Forward (retired). Born: Edinburgh, 15 August 1967. Height: 5ft, 10in, weight 13st, 3lbs (185 lbs)

Season	Club	League	GP	G	A	Pts	Pims	Achievements
					*All Games			
1981-82	Murrayfield Racers	#	19	4	7	11	12	Age 14.
1982-83	Murrayfield Racers	British	24	20	22	42	23	
1983-84	Murrayfield Racers	British	43	74	56	130	38	
1984-85	Murrayfield Racers	British	50	99	116	215	46	League assists leader.
1985-86	Murrayfield Racers	British	47	114	121	235	68	Racers won play-offs and Autumn Cup
1986-87	Murrayfield Racers	British	43	121	131	252	94	League assists leader; Racers won league.
1987-88	Murrayfield Racers	British	47	114	129	243	76	Racers won league
1988-89	Murrayfield Racers	British	47	108	158	266	79	League assists leader.
1989-90	Murrayfield Racers	British	45	73	117	190	48	Lge assists leader; Racers won Autumn Cup
1990-91	Murrayfield Racers	British	52	85	147	232	84	
1991-92	Murrayfield Racers	British	43	69	99	168	48	
1992-93	Murrayfield Racers	British	48	90	149	239	108	League points leader.
1993-94	Murrayfield Racers	British	61	93	189	282	74	League points leader; Racers won B&H Cup
1994-95	Murrayfield Racers	British	62	101	191	292	62	League points leader.
1995-96	Sheffield Steelers	British	55	75	105	180	83	Lge & PO points leader; Steelers won triple.
1996-97	Sheffield Steelers	ISL	59	22	54	76	40	Joint top Cup scorer; Steelers won play-offs.
1997-98	Sheffield Steelers	ISL	65	22	67	89	24	League points leader.
1998-99	Sheffield Steelers	ISL	54	21	38	59	16	
1999-00	Ayr Scottish Eagles	ISL	55	11	45	56	52	
2000-01	Ayr Scottish Eagles	ISL	64	25	49	74	56	Eagles' points leader.
2001-02	Dundee Stars	BNIHL	60	39	106	145	28	Player-coach; top league and cup scorer; Stars won league and play-offs
2002-03	Dundee Stars	BNIHL	46	29	73	102	105	Player-coach; league points leader
2003-04	Edinburgh Capitals	BNIHL	59	28	90	118	56	Player-coach; league points leader.
2004-05	Belfast Giants	Elite	58	19	55	74	94	Player-coach; league points leader.
2005-06	Edinburgh Capitals	Elite	55	18	44	62	4	Player-coach; Capitals' points leader.
2006-07	Manchester Phoenix	Elite	57	18	58	76	80	Player-coach.
2007-08	Manchester Phoenix	Elite	61	24	63	87	60	Player-coach.
2008-09	Manchester Phoenix	Elite	67	21	68	89	84	Player-coach.
2009-10	Manchester Phoenix	EPIHL	59	26	100	126	56	Player-coach; league points leader.
2010-11	Manchester Phoenix	EPIHL	59	29	113	142	65	Player-coach; lge pts leader; MAN won lge.
2011-12	Manchester Phoenix	EPIHL	24	6	29	35	16	Player-coach; broken ankle
2012-13	Manchester Phoenix	EPIHL	53	14	77	91	60	Player-coach; PO pts leader; MAN won PO.
2013-14	Manchester Phoenix	EPIHL	59	19	77	96	116	Player-coach; MAN won league; joint play-off points leader.
2014-15	Manchester Phoenix	EPIHL	48	11	49	60	36	Player-coach.
34 seasons	**CLUB TOTALS**		1748	1642	2992	4634	1991	British records in points and assists.
1989-2007	**GB senior int'n'ls**		64	40	82	122	34	All-time points leader; coach 2012, 2013.

Edmonton Oilers' 12th choice (252nd overall) in 1986 NHL Entry Draft.

All games = league, play-offs and Autumn/Express/B&H/Challenge Cup. #Regional leagues.

MORE QUOTES OF THE YEAR

Pillow talk

[High scoring Lightning forward] **Milan** [**Kostourek**] *(above)* needs to bring a pillow to ... games, he spends so much time lying down and moaning." *Disgruntled Flames' fan after Guildford were knocked out of the EPIHL play-offs at home to MK Lightning.*

The joys of coaching

"Not many coaches have gone on a 23-game losing streak and kept their job. To see where we are now is kind of unreal. It feels like we've won the lottery, it feels a bit magic." *Tom Watkins (above), coach of Telford Tigers, reflecting on the team's change in fortunes.*

"Let's get one thing straight: we're not going to win games if guys don't keep to their position. We've got our right 'D' over in the left-hand corner of the attacking zone, then somebody else switches, and soon we have no one where they're supposed to be on the ice. It's so bad – it's recreation hockey stuff." *Richard Hartmann, the exasperated coach of Edinburgh Capitals after they went down 9-3 at old enemies Fife Flyers in January.*

Hip check Hendrikx-style

"There are lot of things that go into creating the perfect hip check. The biggest things are timing and knowing your opponents' tendencies. I also try to watch their eyes as they come down on me. The second he looks down at the puck, I go for my hit and catch him off guard." *Trevor Hendrikx, Cardiff Devils.*

Moranism

'[Mattias] Modig gets the lobster pot on it.' *Gary Moran, in his role as commentator on www.nottinghampanthers.tv, describing a save by the Panthers' netminder.*

A hell of a rivalry

"It's still a hell of a rivalry. 13-14,000 people are going to watch it over 24 hours. Not many sports can boast that." *Dave Simms, on the annual Boxing Day clash between his Sheffield Steelers and the Nottingham Panthers.*

On being a player-coach

"Time is the biggest factor. As a player you can focus on recovering from a tough weekend [by] doing extra things to ensure you're ready for the next game. [But] it can be tough juggling those factors with making sure there's enough time for ... video analysis, systems, game plans and anything else needed." *Andrew Lord, player-coach of the Elite League's Cardiff Devils.*

"If you're prepared and you've signed a good bunch of guys that are willing to buy into your system, how you want to run things, you don't need to coach them much on the ice." *Stevie Lyle, the new player-coach of the EPIHL's Swindon Wildcats, on how a netminder can handle both jobs. (He later appointed a bench assistant.)*

Aaron happy with 'Cats

"It was quite easy. There were no negotiations, I'm in. I'm past that now [the Elite League]. I tried the Sheffield [Steelers] thing and in the end it worked out well for me personally, maybe not professionally, but personally it was great for me.

"There's not much chance [of playing there again] unless you go to one of the top teams where you get treated as well as you do down here. You can only go to four or five teams but those four or five teams have really good imports and it's tough to get in the team. I'm here for good now." *Aaron Nell, Swindon Wildcats, on re-signing for the EPIHL club in February 2015.*

Don't tell Simmsy

"I love Nottingham, it's a hockey town. The more games you play at home the more you feel like you aren't in England, you could be in Canada. And the fans are knowledgeable. I'm not biased but this is the best rink in the league." *Nathan Robinson, Nottingham Panthers.*

More Quotes on page 42.

OFF-SEASON MOVES

A round-up of the key player and club changes during the summer of 2015:

APRIL

1st Guildford Flames release two ex-GB internationals, forward **David Longstaff** and defender **Neil Liddiard**. This heralds a string of player changes by coach **Paul Dixon** as he looks to improve the EPIHL's runners-up.

6th **Richard Hartmann**, the Slovakian player-coach of Edinburgh Capitals, parts company with the club after four seasons. He later hooks up with Braehead Clan as **Ryan Finnerty**'s assistant in time for their first venture into Europe.

9th MK Lightning forward **Jordan Cownie**, 19,

jumps to the Elite League with the Clan. The Dundee teenager was GB's Player of the Tournament at the World under-20 Championships.

10th GB's head coach **Peter Russell** leaves the Swindon-based junior school, the Okanagan Hockey Academy UK, to take the reins at the EPIHL's Milton Keynes Lightning.

It later transpires that Russell has also taken up a new position as Director of Hockey for the Planet Ice and Silverblades brands. (See *Review of the Year*.)

12th After three seasons Dundee Stars part company with their Edinburgh-based player-coach **Jeff Hutchins** as they want 'a coach who is based in the Tayside city'.

14th Edinburgh Capitals' Canadian winger **Riley Emmerson**, 29, is appointed player-coach in place of **Richard Hartmann**.

18th **Scott McKenzie**, 28, captain of Telford Tigers, quits the EPIHL championship club to become player-coach of NIHL Div Two North side, Widnes Wild. The high scoring forward (520 points in 476 EPIHL games) from Dunfermline will be responsible for ice hockey development at all levels in the Silverblades rink.

20th The hockey world is stunned when Sheffield Steelers sack their Elite League title winning coach, **Gerad Adams**. Smith tells the local paper he wants a 'full-time multi-level approach to management' as he's keen to expand the club, form an under-20 side and compete in the European CHL.

25th Sheffield's other team, the EPIHL's Steeldogs, also change coach, releasing **Andre Payette** (he later joins Whitley Warriors in the NIHL) and bringing in American **Dominic Osman** from the Elite's Hull Stingrays.

29th Another American **Chuck Weber**, 42, who led Coventry Blaze to the Elite play-off title, re-signs for the club, and says his aim is for the Blaze to qualify for Europe's Champions League.

Slovakian sharp-shooter **Rene Jarolin**, 33, the three-time leading scorer of Edinburgh Capitals, drops a league to sign for MK Lightning.

MAY

1st As widely rumoured, Sheffield Steelers' new coach and general manager is ex-GB and Coventry Blaze boss **Paul Thompson**. 'Thommo', who spent season 2014-15 as head coach of Danish side Aalborg Pirates, says: "The Champions League ... that really excites me. It's big for me. It's the future."

3rd Coventry Blaze's former head coach **Marc Lefebvre**, 32, takes over at Dundee Stars.

4th Peterborough Phantoms ink British-

Canadian winger **Craig Scott**, 23, son of **Patrick (Paddy) Scott**, who played with Milton Keynes Kings in the 1990s.

6th Sheffield Steeler and ex-GB defenceman **Mark Thomas**, 31, drops down to the EPIHL's Manchester Phoenix. The Stockport native still lives in the area with his wife and family.

8th Nottingham Panthers' GB international forward **Jonathan Boxill** moves to Elite League rivals Belfast Giants. Boxill, 26, joined the Panthers in 2013 after eight years in the USA.

The Giants also tempt away Fife Flyers' hard man **Matt Nickerson**. Former Nottingham Panther **Matthew Myers** returns to his old team from Cardiff Devils.

11th Braehead Clan's power forward **Leigh Salters** also switches allegiance to the Devils. Devils' statement emphasises that 'of the six players in the Elite League last season who scored 32 goals or more, Salters is the only one who spent more 100 minutes in the cooler'.

Guildford's **David Longstaff**, who has over 100 caps for GB, returns to his home town club Whitley Warriors as their player-coach.

12th Dundee Stars neatly side-step the restrictive new rule for overseas netminders requiring a work permit (see box.). **Vlastimil Lakosil**, 36, is a native of the Czech Republic, which is a member of the EU, so he doesn't need a work permit.

15th Guildford's ex-GB defender **Neil Liddiard**, 36, returns to his home town side Swindon Wildcats after 12 seasons in the Spectrum.

21st Scandinavian goalie **Miika Wiikman**, 30, the newest Nottingham Panther, is the second Elite keeper to hold an EU passport.

23rd Basingstoke Bison's captain **Nick Chinn**

changes his mind about retiring. The 43-year-old firefighter and ex-GB forward accepts an invitation to play his 28th hockey season with the NIHL's Streatham Redskins.

Fife Flyers fans are upset when Glenrothes-born prospect **Craig Moore** opts for rival Elite League side Dundee Stars. The six-foot blueliner developed his game in Kirkcaldy before going to Canada and joining the Ontario Hockey Academy. Under Moore's captaincy, the under-20s won gold in Estonia last season.

24th Dundee Stars' GB defender **Paul Swindlehurst** is inked by Nottingham Panthers.

26th Guildford Flames' first new import is Slovenian winger **Matic Kralj**, 32, who played in the Elite League with Newcastle Vipers and Coventry Blaze a few years ago.

27th Canadian defenceman **Theo Peckham**, who played two full seasons in the NHL with Edmonton Oilers but spent a night in prison last

term after a bar-room brawl in Slovakia, agrees to line-up with Nottingham Panthers.

Top GB junior international forward **Ivan (Vanya) Antonov** moves from Bracknell Bees to EPIHL rivals Sheffield Steeldogs. The Russo-British forward, who has just turned 18, wants to study medicine at university in Sheffield.

JUNE

2nd **Corey McEwen**, son of former GB, Cardiff Devils and Peterborough forward **Doug McEwen**, becomes a Swindon Wildcat. Anglo-Canadian Corey, 22, was a junior at Peterborough before returning to Canada with his father in 2006.

8th Former GB defender **Kevin Phillips**, 29, leaves the Elite's Belfast Giants for the EPIHL's rebuilding Guildford Flames.

11th

Braehead Clan sign ex-NHLer **Ric Jackman**, a former Stanley Cup winning defenceman with Anaheim Ducks. The 36-year-old, who was in the Asian League with Nippon Paper Cranes last year, played almost 250 games for seven different NHL clubs during 1999-2007.

NEW RULES FOR IMPORT GOALIES IN 2015-16
'The people who administer the work permits [scheme] have tightened up the guidelines for import goalies. They have to have played in 75 per cent of games the previous year. [Up to now, this] rule was for games *dressed* in, not necessarily *played* in.

'It's almost impossible to find [an eligible] goalie [from] North America as so much of the goaltending is shared over there.

'So next year's goalies, not only in Sheffield but around the league, might be either those who played in the Elite League last season or a few EU passport holders, who could come from Europe or North America.'
Dave Simms, in his column in Sheffield's Star *newspaper*, 7 May 2015.

17th Sheffield Steelers find a third son of a famous name. Goalie **Tyler Plante**, 28, a 6ft 3ins American, is one of two sons of former (1992-96) Peterborough Pirates' defenceman **Cam Plante**.

24th In the first of two big off-season shockers (both on the same day), owner **Bobby McEwan** announces that he no longer has sufficient funds to run Hull Stingrays, partly due to the loss of Rapid Solicitors' sponsorship.

This reduces the Elite League to nine teams, a far-from-ideal number.

But wait! Within hours, the league declares it has a replacement team called Manchester Storm, which will be run out of Altrincham by the rink operators, Silverblades.

More on these blockbuster moves in our *Review of the Year.*

MK Lightning's Geordie netminder **Stephen Wall**, 33, comes close to completing a full deck of EPIHL clubs. The new-look Guildford Flames are his seventh team since he first played in the league for Peterborough in 2003-04.

25th The new Manchester Storm waste no time, bringing in ex-Hull Stingrays **David Phillips** and **Matty Davies**. Both are GB internationals.

EPIHL side Swindon Wildcats ink Slovakian forward **Miroslav Zálešák**, 35, who played a handful of games for the NHL's San Jose Sharks in 2002-04.

26th Telford Tigers snap up GB forward **Phil Hill**

from the Elite's Cardiff Devils, but the EPIHL club agree to release him to Sheffield Steelers for the pre-season Champions Hockey League contests.

27th The Elite's Braehead Clan make an intriguing goalie signing with **Chris Holt**, 30. His chequered career includes three seasons in the Russian KHL and a cup of coffee in the NHL. The Vancouver native replaces **Kyle Jones**.

JULY

1st **Neil Morris**, co-owner of Manchester Phoenix, completes a hat-trick of summer surprises with the announcement that his EPIHL team will play out of Deeside this coming season. See *Review of the Year.*

Swindon Wildcats appoint Canadian defenceman **Kenton Smith** as assistant/bench coach to head coach/netminder **Stevie Lyle.** The pair played together at Cardiff Devils.

2nd Belfast Giants sign forward **Kris Beech**, 34, a veteran of almost 100 NHL games.

3rd The Storm appoint **Omar Pacha**, 28, as player-coach. The Canadian led Hull Stingrays to the Elite League play-off semi-finals.

Make that a quartet of news-quakes - Sheffield Steeldogs' owner **Shane Smith** and American player-coach **Dominic Osman**, the ex-Stingrays forward, form a new EPIHL team in Hull, dubbed the Pirates.

Team captain **Tom Squires**, 28, *left,* takes over as coach of the Steeldogs. (See *Review of the Year.*)

And so it goes on - **Wayne Scholes'** company, Red Hockey Ltd (RHL), takes control of Deeside Dragons, the North Wales team currently playing in Div Two North of the National League, the sport's fourth division. The Dragons will share the Deeside ice with Manchester Phoenix, who are co-owned by RHL.

7th **Neil (Coach) Russell** is appointed general manager of Manchester Storm. Belfast native Russell, who has a background in business, has been a match-night assistant at the Odyssey. He is best known to fans as a colour commentator on the **Premier Sports** TV shows.

Guildford Flames keep ringing the changes with Slovak centreman **Erik Piatak**, 29, who played for Peterborough Phantoms in 2013-14 before moving to Kazakhstan.

9th Another out-of-work Hull Stingray finds a job - forward and assistant coach **Carl Lauzon** stays in the Elite League with Coventry Blaze.

10th The fourth ex-NHLer to come to the UK is Nottingham Panthers' Slovakian-Canadian winger **Juraj Kolnik**, 34, who chalked up 250 games with NY Islanders and Florida Panthers.

The Slovakian international played three seasons with **Chris McSorley**'s Geneva Eagles, including their 2011-12 A league winners.

13th Coventry Blaze also pick an ex-NHL Slovak international - giant 6ft 7in d-man **Boris Valábik**, 29, who spent a couple of seasons as an enforcer with Atlanta Thrashers.

Anglo-Finnish netminder **Jon Baston**, 21, is Hull Pirates' first import signing. He backstopped a Swedish Division One club last year.

21st Manchester Phoenix's coach **Tony Hand** hails his latest capture, 36-year-old Slovakian international

Stanislav Gron *left* "He's a big guy, but also very skilful on the puck." [If only our Tony was still playing, they'd have made a scarily productive duo - Ed.]

22nd Belfast Giants' Canadian netminder **Carsen Chubak** switches allegiance to Edinburgh Capitals.

23rd Champions Hockey League debutants Braehead Clan add a sixth NHLer to their roster - defenceman **Nathan (Nate) McIver**, 30, who turned out for Anaheim and Vancouver in 2006-09. His capture gives the Clan over 300 games of NHL experience, mostly from another new d-man, **Ric Jackman**.

25th Chris Lawrence, Nottingham Panthers' leading scorer and top import penalty taker, crosses the Irish Sea to become a Belfast Giant.

27th More ex-Hull Stingrays players find new Elite League teams - goalie **David Brown** joins Fife Flyers, **Zach Hervato** links up with Cardiff Devils and **Grant Toulmin** signs for Manchester Storm.

29th Tough guy **Erick Lizon** suddenly pulls out of his agreement with Nottingham Panthers for 'personal reasons'.

30th Belfast Giants appoint an experienced Canadian as player-coach. Offensive defenceman **Derrick Walser**, 37, has played on teams in the NHL, AHL, Germany and Switzerland. This enables **Steve Thornton** to concentrate on his managerial duties. Long-serving Giant **Rob Stewart** steps up as bench coach.

Forward **Brandon Benedict**, 33, returns to the Giants after four seasons in Nottingham.

31st Belfast's SSE Arena (formerly the Odyssey Arena) is keen to host the group of the 2017 World Championships in which GB plays, reports the *Belfast Telegraph*.

AUGUST

5th Glenn Billing, 18, GB's best player in the 2014 World Junior Championships, decides to try his hand with Milton Keynes Lightning of the EPIHL after two seasons in Swindon.

7th Ben Beeching, co-owner of Bracknell Bees, tells the fans in an email that the English IHA has insisted on all EPIHL games being video'd 'for discipline and coaching reasons'.

13th The English IHA's website lists 17 teams in their new, regionalised under-20 league. A national play-off weekend against their Scottish counterparts is scheduled for the end of the season... somewhere.

15th Nottingham Panthers' final, controversial signing for the 2015-16 season is ex-NHL enforcer **Cam Janssen** *above on left*. The American had 336 games in the world's biggest league, most recently with New Jersey Devils.

Photos on these pages by: Nottingham Post (Jordan Cownie), Peterborough Phantoms (Craig Scott), Simon Curtis (Nick Chinn), espn.com (Ric Jackman), Shropshire Star (Phil Hill), Arthur Foster (Tom Squires), eliteprospects.com (Stanislav Gron), Cam Janssen (New Jersey Devils).

PEOPLE IN THE NEWS

DAVID LONGSTAFF
GB legend returns to the Bay

DAVID LONGSTAFF (left) and SIMON LEACH in their younger days.　　Photo: Whitley Warriors

David Longstaff, holder of 101 GB senior caps and one of the sport's most popular players, stepped down from full-time pro hockey in May 2015 to coach and play for his home town team Whitley Warriors in the National League (NIHL).

The 41-year-old forward spent his last five seasons in the south of England where he won back-to-back league and cup doubles and the play-off crown with Guildford Flames of the English Premier League.

In 302 games with the Flames, 'Lobby' – as he's affectionately known - scored 124 goals and added 309 assists for 433 points. He led the club in points in his last three seasons.

The 6ft, 2in, 225lb forward arrived in the Surrey town in September 2010 after seven years with Newcastle Vipers following stops with Superleague's Sheffield Steelers, Swedish elite league side Djurgardens and Swiss club Sierre, as well as a short stint with Manchester Storm.

Internationally, he was the first player to reach 100 caps with the GB senior side; experience that included 11 consecutive World Championship appearances in 1994-2004.

"David has had a remarkable career, both in individual achievements and in terms of team success," said the Flames' head coach Paul Dixon. "He has been a valuable leader for this club and made a significant contribution."

Longstaff began his career with Whitley back in 1989 when he first appeared for the Warriors as a teenager in the (Heineken) British League. He went on to have a hugely successful spell with the Warriors, his best season coming in the 1994-95 campaign when he picked up a colossal 110 points in 44 games.

Warriors' new player-coach explained his decision: "I'd been with the Flames for five years and just felt it was time to move closer to home.

"I'm good friends with [Warriors' previous coach] Simon Leach and he mentioned to me that he was planning to step down. Things went on from there really.

"As far as coaching experience goes, I was involved with the GB national team when Tony Hand was head coach. I'm really looking forward to coaching on a day-to-day basis, and especially to working with the younger players. But I know it will be a learning curve for me."

SIMON KIRKHAM, UK's REF-IN-CHIEF
Simon Kirkham was re-appointed as the Referee-in-Chief of the governing body, Ice Hockey UK, in January 2015.

Kirkham, who was an official himself for 18 years, is also a supervisor with the world governing body, the IIHF.

His role as lead trainer and developer of British stripeys has been particularly successful, with many of our refs and linesmen being selected by the IIHF to officiate in various World Championships. The following were honoured this way in season 2014-15:
Men's World Championships: Division IA - *Lines:* Andrew Dalton; Division IIA - *Referee:* Liam Sewell; under-20, Division IA - *Referee:* Mike Hicks, *Lines:* James Kavanagh; under-18, Division IA - *Referee:* Tom Darnell; under-18, Division IB - *Supervisor:* Simon Kirkham; *Lines:* Ally Flockhart.
Women's World Championships: Division IIA (Dumfries) - *Lines:* Leigh Hetherington, Amy Lack; Qualifiers: *Referee:* Joy Johnston; under-18, Elite Division - *Referee:* Deana Cuglietta; under-18, Division I - *Referee:* Alice Stanley, *Lines:* Lorna Beresford.

SNAP SHOT
BOBBY ROBINS, one of the stars of Belfast Giants' Challenge Cup winning side of 2008-09, appeared in three NHL games with Boston Bruins last season.

The American forward made his debut on the Bruins' opening night - 8 October 2014 - days before his 33rd birthday, playing ten shifts and spending seven minutes in the bin.

BEN O'CONNOR

Back home

Not many young Brits could name-check as many clubs as **Ben O'Connor**.

By the time he turned 22 in 2010, the Durham-born defenceman had played for ten teams in Canada, England and Scotland as well as representing GB at 18, 20 and senior levels.

And that was only the start. He moved to France in 2010-11 and a year later to Kazakhstan, where he was the first Brit to play in the former Soviet republic.

The Kazakhs had spotted Ben when he was one of GB's stars on their silver medal winning team at the 2011 World Championships.

The Kazakh club, Sary-Arka Karaganda, gave him a contract that reportedly paid him more than double what most Elite League clubs could afford. But then the Kazakh league has a reputation for developing players for the top Russian circuit, the KHL.

"They play a Russian hockey style in Kazakhstan," O'Connor said at the time, "and we play for ten months instead of the usual eight. We also get to practice a lot more than they do in Britain, on and off the ice. For a young player, that's a great help."

He spent one season with Sary-Arka and two with Arlan Kokshetau, was twice voted the league's best defenceman and had one of his spectacular plays posted on YouTube.

Then, as suddenly as he left Britain he returned, in October 2014, to Sheffield, the city where he first played junior. The Elite League side is also the one where his Canada-born father **Mike O'Connor** used to patrol the blueline and is now their commercial manager.

Ben had to take a massive pay-cut, of course, but this didn't faze him. "It will be a dream come true to wear that shirt," he said. "I remember Dad wearing it when I was a kid and thinking that one day I wanted to play at the arena like he did for the Steelers."

He quickly established himself as a clever playmaker, counting 40 helpers among his 49 points over the season. He picked up a man of the match award in his first game and was selected as the league's player of the week when the Steelers won the title.

Topping off his domestic season, the journalists voted for O'Connor as their Best British Defenceman.

Internationals bring out his best game. He potted the winning goal against Poland in the 2011 World Championships, and this year in Eindhoven his spectacular penalty shot, which beat the Koreans, is already the stuff of legend.

The forthcoming season could be even better for the 26-year-old as he will be reunited at Sheffield with his old Coventry Blaze and GB coach **Paul Thompson**. 'Thommo' is a big O'Connor fan. "Ben can do things that many offensive defenceman in the NHL can't," he said.

■ There's more on Ben in *World Championships*.

PAUL SWINDLEHURST

Plays for NHL farm teams

Dundee Stars and GB defenceman **Paul Swindlehurst** enjoyed the hockey experience of a life-time in late 2014.

That September he played alongside some hot NHL prospects at Chicago Blackhawks' Rookie Tournament. This earned him a try-out with Chicago's top farm club, Rockford IceHogs of the American Hockey League.

The Best Young British Player of 2013-14 didn't quite make the team, instead signing a contract with Indy Fuel of the ECHL.

In two exhibition games for the Fuel he registered an assist in their two wins over Kelly Cup champs Alaska Aces, then turned out in their opening league game on 15 October. But the next day, the Fuel traded him to league rivals, Missouri Mavericks.

But instead, Paul returned to the Stars in November. At the end of the season he represented GB in the World Championships for the second time and scored his first goal.

RETIREMENT
Born to play

ALAN ARMOUR, who played most of his hockey in Swindon, retired at the end of the 2014-15 season after 24 years in the sport.

One of the game's characters, the Truro-born centreman came through the Swindon junior system in the late 1980s before breaking into the Wildcats at the age of 15.

During his time in Swindon, he won two league titles and a playoff championship, which marked the pinnacle of his long career.

When he hung up his equipment for the last time, he was in his second spell with the NIHL's Bristol Pitbulls, who signed him to provide experience and guidance to their young team.

Given the long commute that the homeless Pitbulls face every week, the life and enthusiasm that Armour brought to games and training sessions will be badly missed.

Armour said: "I could probably keep turning up every year until I'm 100. But I think now is the right time to start playing golf a bit more seriously. Golf is something that I actually can keep turning up to play until I'm 100!"

"When Bristol gets its new rink (hopefully, fingers crossed), I will no doubt be the first one calling people for training."

▲ See *New Rinks News* for the latest on Bristol's proposed new rink.

Photo credits: Sheffield Steelers (Ben O'Connor, Geoff Woolhouse); Dundee Stars (Paul Swindlehurst); Bristol Pitbulls (Alan Armour); Cardiff Devils (Jason Stone); Glasgow Daily Record (Tristan Harper).

RETIREMENT
Devils' legend

Cardiff Devils' legendary defenceman **JASON STONE** had his number 10 jersey officially retired by the club on 23 November 2014.

With over 1,000 games played and 21 seasons with the club, Stone was a fixture on the blueline for two decades and played on some of the best Devils' teams of all time.

He first dressed for the senior team as a 16-year-old in season 1988-89 and in his final season in the Elite League, 2009-10, he was honoured with a testimonial for his years of service to the club.

Jason, who turned 42 in December 2014, spent his last four seasons on the Devils' National League side.

His list of accolades includes four league championships, three play-off titles and two Challenge Cup trophies. In the inaugural season of the Superleague, he was picked as the Best British Defenceman on route to the league title.

He represented GB in six games in the 1998 World Championships.

SNAP SHOT

ROGER HUNT, who played for Murrayfield Royals in the late 1990s and coached Dundee Stars in the 2000s, won Canada's Memorial Cup in May 2015 as the general manager of Oshawa Generals. Roger was head coach of the GB under-20s in 2004 and 2005.

The Cup winner is rated the best junior team in Canada and Hunt is credited with assembling most of their line-up.

On the losing side in the Cup final was Kelowna Rockets' netminder **Jackson Whistle**, 19, son of British Hall of Famer **Dave Whistle**.

RETIREMENT
The ultimate team player

GEOFF WOOLHOUSE, 30, the long-time Sheffield Steelers and Nottingham Panthers back-up goalie, was forced into retirement at the end of 2014-15 by a chronic injury problem.

Though he rarely hit the headlines during his playing career, his departure from the game rates a very honourable mention. Steelers' PR man **David Simms** tells the story -

'In November with **Frank Doyle** and **Josh Unice** out, Woolhouse came to the party once more. He shouldn't have done, he was the most injured of our three goalies.

'He was a month away, said the doctors, from being able to skate, let alone play. Yet on the Saturday against Coventry he strapped the pads on and won the game. The bad news was that he ripped his groin once again and made it even worse.

'The Steelers were in Belfast the following day. Woolhouse arrived at the Arena car park and needed his team-mates to help him from the car and onto the bus, then onto the plane.

'Don't ask me how but 'House' not only played in Belfast but won in Belfast. He sacrificed his body for the team. He knew by playing that weekend that he was ending his season and probably his career.

'But his team needed him and he delivered.'

SNAP SHOT
DOUG CHRISTIANSEN, the former GB, Edinburgh Capitals, Belfast Giants and Sheffield Steelers coach, is now director of player development and recruitment for the United States (junior) Hockey League.

He has fond memories of his time in the UK but prefers to forget his first season in the Scottish capital when the Caps had six points by 1 December. "I remember a woman telling me that all her dad wanted for Christmas that year was my one-way flight home." he said.
                - from the Elite League Play-off Finals programme

MIKE BABCOCK
Ex-Warrior now a Maple Leaf

@brettperlini tweeted this photo when Babcock took on the Maple Leaf's coaching job -
'Good luck to Mike Babcock in Toronto, here's former leaf Freddy P [Perlini, Brett's father] walking around him in Fife.'

Older fans may remember the brief appearance in Britain of **Mike Babcock**, who was player-coach of Whitley Warriors in season 1987-88.

Since then, Canadian Babcock has gone on to become perhaps the most accomplished hockey coach in the world.

The 52-year-old was the first coach – and still the only one - to join the sport's elite Triple Gold Club by winning an Olympic Gold Medal (in 2010 and 2014), a World Championship title (2004), both with Canada, and a Stanley Cup with Detroit Redwings (2009).

The Redwings published a fascinating piece about Mike on their website when he was appointed boss of Toronto Maple Leafs in May 2015. Search Google for 'Babcock gained valuable experience in England'. Worth a read.

■ All NHL teams carry a large coaching staff. The Leafs has a markedly 'British' flavour.

Babcock's goalie mentor is ex-Fife Flyers' netminder **Steve Briere**. Canadian Briere, 38, padded up for the Flyers and later Basingstoke Bison and Bracknell Bees in 2002-06.

Their Skill Development Co-ordinator is **Mike Ellis**, 42, a GB forward who coached and skated alongside Briere in Bracknell in 2005-06. Ellis was also a player and coach with the Bison and Nottingham Panthers during his long stint here in 1995-2008.

TRISTAN HARPER
Vogue model

'Tristan Cameron-Harper has been modelling for around two years while he plays hockey for Braehead Clan and now he's poised for the international big time as a fashion model.

'His mum had modelled when she was younger and Harper soon followed suit. It was not an easy transition but he has grown increasingly comfortable with that scene. Now he hangs around at parties with Lewis Hamilton, Idris Elba and Samuel L Jackson, trying to blend in and not seem too star-struck.'

'A shot of him showing off his amazing muscles while chopping wood has now made it into fashion bible *Vogue*.

'The photograph was taken on a shoot with photographer Abbie Rodger and picked up and published online by *Vogue*'s Italian edition.

'[Dundee-born] Tristan [26] said: "This is tremendous news for Abbie and me. It's the biggest break I've ever had."

'Abbie, 26, is studying photography at West College Scotland's Paisley campus as well as running her business in Rothesay.

'She said: "I uploaded the picture to *Vogue*'s website as they have an area where you can create your own portfolio. They obviously liked it and decided to use it on their main site."'
- *Glasgow Daily Record, February 2015*

THE ICE HOCKEY ANNUAL
Published every year since 1976
Complete your collection of the sport's 'bible'
Go to www.icehockeyannual.co.uk/backissues

DOPING OFFENCES
Kyle Bochek

Former Coventry Blaze forward **Kyle Bochek** has been suspended for 18 months for taking a banned substance.

UK Anti-Doping said the Canadian, who was signed by the Blaze for the 2014-15 season, tested positive for the stimulant methylhexaneamine in an in-competition sample on 30 November 2014.

UKAD said Bochek admitted to the doping violation and that the banned substance came from a dietary supplement. Bochek provided evidence that it was not intended to enhance performance.

Bochek's ban, which was reduced from two years, keeps him out of the sport until 17 June 2016. He was released by the Blaze in December 2014 after playing in 28 games.
- *Coventry Telegraph, 31 March 2015*
Ed's note - This ban applies only in the UK. Bochek has returned to Tulsa Oilers of the ECHL.

Nicky Watt

The former English Premier League forward has been hit with an eight-year ban for two doping offences, reported the *Basingstoke Gazette*.

Watt, from Tadley, Hants, refused to provide a urine sample for an out-of-competition test on 27 May 2014. He then tested positive for the anabolic steroid stanozolol following another test on 17 June.

A National Anti-Doping Panel hearing held in November found Watt guilty of both offences, and banned him from all competition from 17 June 2014 to 16 June 2022.

Watt, 28, launched an appeal, but the decision and punishment was upheld.

Graham Arthur, director of legal at UKAD, said: "The length of the ban reflects the grave nature of his violations. Not only has he tested positive for a prohibited substance but he also made a deliberate decision not to comply with sample collection. If you are approached for testing, do not refuse or walk away as the consequences can be severe."

Watt, who was born in Irvine, Scotland, played over 500 games for seven teams spread over 12 campaigns. His last season, 2013-14, was spent with Peterborough Phantoms and Guildford Flames.

NEW RINKS NEWS

A sure sign that our economy is in good health is when finance becomes available to build ice rinks, sporting facilities that usually come at the far end of UK leisure's food chain.

Even so, we were a bit surprised when we went through our files and discovered there are nine rinks either under construction or on the drawing board. Only two – **Cardiff Bay** and **Leeds** – are definitely being built as we write this, but work at **Cambridge** may well have started by the time you are reading this.

One thing is certain. Only two permanent rinks suitable for serious ice hockey (**Streatham** and **Widnes**) have opened – and stayed open - in the last 12 years. The UK is lagging far behind most other north European nations in our provision of ice facilities.

Here's our latest list, alphabetically. A word of warning: from past bitter experience, it's likely that some will disappear without trace.

BRAEHEAD

Plans have been approved for a new indoor arena at the Braehead Shopping Centre.

The current arena at the Centre is the home of Braehead Clan of the Elite League, and Paisley Pirates of the Scottish National League.

The plans are part of a £200 million expansion of the Centre, which received planning permission in November 2014.

The new arena is expected to have a maximum seating capacity of 8,000 compared to around 3,500 (for ice hockey) of the existing building.

According to Glasgow's *Daily Record*, it was hoped that construction might start in 2015, though with a scheme of this size, this may be optimistic.

BRISTOL

After a couple of false starts, it seems odds-on that **Bristol Pitbulls** will get a new, full-size ice rink with up to 1,400 seats in a couple of years.

The NIHL team played only four seasons in the John Nike Leisuresport Centre in Frogmore Street before it was demolished in 2013 and replaced by flats.

There are several reasons for the Pitbulls to be cheerful. The developers, Baylis Estates, own the land at Cribbs Causeway where the new rink will be built as part of an indoor sports centre. They also have sufficient finance available.

Planet Ice, the UK's largest rink operators, have confirmed their willingness to run it, and the South Gloucestershire council are fully supportive of the project.

A planning application was expected to be submitted later this year (2015) and if all goes smoothly the rink could be open in time for the 2017-18 season.

■ According to **Martin Harris**'s rinks' bible, *Homes of British Ice Hockey* (Tempus Publishing, 2005) the Frogmore Street rink opened in 1966 and was home to several senior teams between 1971 and 1993.

The rink's design, with sloping boards and restricted seating, made it unsuitable for the game to be regularly played at a high level.

CAMBRIDGE

Canadian **David Gattiker** studied at Cambridge University and was captain of the ice hockey team in 1931.

A successful business life as a chemical engineer made him a wealthy man, and in 1993 he bequeathed £1 million to the university to help them bring 'a permanent ice hockey facility' to the city.

The university's Canadian ice hockey coach **Bill Harris** set up Cambridge Leisure & Ice Centre In 2000 to realise Mr Gattiker's dream. With the help of local people and groups and an injection of £2.5 million from the university in June 2015, the fight for ice was won.

The Cambridge Ice Arena will have a standard 56 by 26 metres ice pad, 500 seats and room for 600 spectators.

Catering for all ice sports as well as ice discos and public skating, it will be erected three miles from the city centre and a mile from the new Cambridge railway station, beside the Newmarket Road Park and Ride.

The land owner, Marshall Group Properties, is the developer.

According to the website www.cambridgeicearena.com: 'planning permission has been granted, the site is secured, negotiations with an operator are well advanced and the design has been developed. The project is being privately funded and welcomes additional support.'

The rink is a turnkey project, meaning that it is being supplied in a virtually ready-to-open condition. Consequently, it could be welcoming skaters in the second half of next year (2016).

■ Cambridge's Light Blues ice hockey team were formed in the early 1900s, but surprisingly this will be the first time they have had their own rink.

For over a century they have travelled hundreds of miles in most seasons, including regular trips to Switzerland, to play games. Their rivalry with Oxford University is legendary, though they only occasionally come out on the winning side. (See *Review of the Year*.)
www.cambridgeicearena.com.

CARDIFF BAY

The construction of the £16 million, two-storey Ice Arena of Wales (IAW) was delayed at the end of 2014 when developers Greenbank suffered a temporary shortfall in funding.

This forced a six months' postponement of the opening date of **Cardiff Devils'** new home until January 2016 at the earliest.

Steve King, one of the club's new owners, was "incredibly frustrated" by the delay. The Devils' mid-season move will be "extremely complicated in terms of budgeting and logistics," he said. The consortium that the Canadian heads even tried to buy the building from the developers in an effort to get it finished by the start of the 2015-16 campaign.

When the Devils' third venue in 30 years eventually does open, it should be the finest one the Elite League club have played in.

Located right next door to their current temporary home, the Big Blue Tent, the IAW's main pad will be Olympic size, 60 by 30 metres, seat 3,000 with first class sightlines, and have a four-sided video clock over centre-ice.

The new arena, which is the 'keystone' of the £400 million International Sports Village, will also boast a second ice surface, measuring 54 by 27 metres. The larger pad can stage other sports events and both surfaces can be made available for public skating.

Oh yes, did we mention? All ice-time for the hockey clubs will be free.
www.icearenawales.co.uk

LEEDS

We reported in the last *Annual* that a 1,500-seat rink with an Olympic-size ice pad is being erected close to Leeds Utd's Elland Road football ground and the M621 motorway.

The usual delays have occurred, but we understand that the builders are now on site and it is expected to open in spring 2016.

The rink will be the fourth full-size one under the Silverblades label after Widnes, Altrincham and Gillingham.

An ice hockey club will be formed and will probably enter a team in the National League (NIHL), subject to approval.
www.silver-blades.co.uk.

ROMFORD

London Raiders look like being homeless for a few more seasons before they can return to Romford.

According to a report in the *Romford Recorder* in January 2015, the site earmarked for the Raiders' new rink still had a building (Chaucer House) standing on it. Even when that has been demolished, two electrical sub-stations have to be installed before work on the rink can begin.

Meanwhile, though the Raiders' old home in Rom Valley Way has been demolished, supermarket chain Morrisons have admitted that they are 'unable to provide information on timescales at this time' on the building of their new store on the site.

Something to do with the current financial problems of supermarkets, perhaps.

The original plan, which was drawn up in 2012, was for the new leisure centre to be completely funded by the £25 million sale of the Rom Valley Way site to Morrisons. In December 2013, the council splashed out an extra £2 million for the project.

Apart from an ice rink, the new centre is to include a swimming pool and fitness suite.

■ There's more on this in our somewhat over-optimistic report in the last *Annual*.

■ Havering Council provided 'up to £7,500' in 2014-15 to ensure that ice skaters and ice hockey players from Havering would continue to have a future in their chosen sport. This enabled the Raiders to confirm their place in the NIHL, playing at the Lee Valley Ice Centre.

THANET

AN Olympic-sized ice rink and around 600 homes have been proposed for farmland at Haine Road in Thanet, Kent, the *Thanet Gazette* reported in May 2015.

Plans for the site also include four curling sheets, a water park and associated retail.

The development is the brainchild of Moirai Capital Investment and their local agent, former Margate FC chairman **Keith Piper**.

While a pre-planning application is being worked up, a local resident has set up a petition for the rink on Facebook at 'Real Olympic size ice rink in Thanet'.

WEST BROMWICH

Plans for a 1,500-seat ice rink in West Bromwich are "still very much alive", **Mike Petrouis**, chief executive of Planet Ice, told the *Express & Star* newspaper in March 2015.

He said the company will lodge plans with Sandwell Council once the multi-storey car park at the Queens Square Shopping Centre had been demolished. "The onus is on us to get the carp park bulldozed," he added.

If the plans are approved by councillors, he said work could start by the end of the year with the rink hopefully opening at the end of 2016.

A definite maybe, this one.

WEMBLEY

The Elite League, like their predecessors the Superleague, are dead keen on icing a team in London.

As we've reported in our last two editions, the league wants to ice a team in the famous *Wembley Arena* - now the SSE Arena - but they are not finding it easy to form the league's 'dream team'.

Various parties from the league have been to London to meet businessmen who have shown interest in the idea. And we recently learned that a fee had been paid to the league for the rights to its London franchise.

Neil Black, whose Aladdin Sports Management controls the league's Braehead Clan and Nottingham Panthers, is believed to be trying to form a consortium to run the franchise.

At the league's play-off weekend in April 2015 Mr Black told a meeting of the fans that there would "not be ice hockey in London for two years", that is in 2017-18. He volunteered no further information.

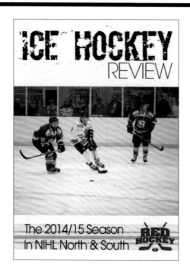

RINK ATTENDANCES

OVERALL PICTURE	2014-15	ATTENDANCES		2013-14	% change
	total	games	average	average	
ELITE LEAGUE					
League & Challenge Cup	791,885	302	2,622	2,334	12.3
*Play-offs, inc. finals	45,286	11	4,117	4,087	No diff.
Totals	**837,171**	**313**	**2,675**	2401	**11.4**
ENGLISH PREMIER LEAGUE (EPIHL)					
League	225,700	216	1,045	1000	4.5
Cup (semis and finals only)	6,500	6	1,083	1,021	6.1
Play-offs, inc. finals	16,500	11	1,500	1,606	-6.6
Totals	**248,700**	**233**	**1,067**	1023	**4.3**
Grand Totals	**1,085,871**	**546**	**1,989**	**1,743**	**14.1**

excludes third place play-off - attendance not recorded

THE TOP LEAGUE CROWD PULLERS	2014-15	ATTENDANCES		2013-14	% change
	league	total	average	average	
1 (1) Nottingham Panthers	Elite	141,077	5,426	5,239	3.6
2 (2) Belfast Giants	Elite	128,546	4,944	4,209	17.5
3 (3) Sheffield Steelers	Elite	101,840	3,917	3,644#	7.5
4 (4) Braehead Clan	Elite	80,608	3,100	2,582	20.0
5 (7) Fife Flyers	Elite	57,295	2,204	1,684	37.4
6 (5) Coventry Blaze	Elite	56,851	2,187	2,115	3.4
7 (10) Cardiff Devils	Elite	53,694	2,065	1,412	46.2
8 (6) Guildford Flames	EPIHL	41,299	1,721	1,865	-7.7
9 (8) Bracknell Bees	EPIHL	28,800	1,200	1,500	-25.0
10 (12) Dundee Stars	Elite	27,898	1,073	1,159	-7.4
11 (13) Basingstoke Bison	EPIHL	25,200	1,050	1,049	No diff.
12 (11) Manchester Phoenix	EPIHL	24,000	1,000	1,300	-23.1

List includes teams that averaged at least 1,000 fans at league games (excluding playoffs).
Elite teams played 26 home games, EPIHL teams played 24.
includes games at iceSheffield. Ave. crowds at Arena - 4,339 (4,827), ave. at iceSheffield - 1,328 (1,305).
Last season's position in brackets.
% change - based on the average crowd. No diff. = less than two per cent.
In the EPIHL, only Guildford Flames provided regular attendance figures. Other rinks' crowds are estimates.

Devils fans flock back to Cardiff Bay

Teams' fortunes differed widely during season 2014-15. *Cardiff Devils* proved that ownership is just as important, if not more so, than a team's roster when their crowds increased by almost half following the take-over by **Todd Kelman** and his Canadian business associates. But it's not quite so easy to explain why *Belfast Giants* drew more fans after the popular Mr Kelman left the Giants in the hands of **Steve Thornton** and the Odyssey Arena!

Scottish ice hockey is also a success story, well almost. *Fife Flyers* and *Braehead Clan* continued to build their crowds but *Dundee Stars* faltered and *Edinburgh Capitals* have yet to appear in our 1,000-fans-or-more list. *Guildford Flames* remain comfortably the biggest attraction outside the Elite League.

REVIEW OF THE YEAR

ALL CHANGE IN ALTRINCHAM

Storm rise again

(Did you see what we did there? – Ed.)

Fans used to getting their ice hockey fix at the Altrincham rink had a pretty miserable time in the summer of 2015.

They were caught in the cross-fire between Silverblades, the operators of the rink, and the owners of the EPIHL team, Manchester Phoenix.

Neil Morris, the owner of the Phoenix, was accused of falling behind with his rental payments to Silverblades.

There might have been more behind the row as it quickly degenerated into petty squabbling, ranging from holding rival meetings for the fans to – allegedly - hurling verbal insults at each other in public.

Though a mere skirmish compared to the Great Ice Wars of the early 2000s between the Superleague clubs and the rest, it was still upsetting for the club's 1,000-odd supporters.

Hull Stingrays' long-suffering followers also had a traumatic off-season (see below), but it wasn't quite in the same bracket.

Mr Morris, who had brought **Wayne Scholes** of Red Hockey on board as an investor, told the fans that any debts had been cleared.

He also insisted that the team would be playing at a new 3,000-seat, Olympic size arena in Manchester city centre.

By the time we went to press in late August, however, he and Mr Scholes had failed to supply any concrete details of this.

Instead, they were forced to adopt plan B, negotiating a deal for the Phoenix to play the 2015-16 season at the Deeside Leisure Centre.

Mark Johnson of Silverblades played his trump card on 24 June. The former player announced that his Ice Rink Co Ltd would be the new owners and operators of the senior ice hockey team in Altrincham.

The team would be called Manchester Storm, in honour of the former Superleague club, and – wait for it – play in the Elite League.

This left Altrincham's hockey fans with an agonising choice. To loyally follow the Phoenix 30 miles to North Wales or to stay at home and watch the new team in a higher league.

The *Annual* reckons Mark Johnson's trump card was an ace.

RED HOCKEY v PLANET ICE

● **Wayne Scholes**, boss of internet-based business Red Touch Media, bought Telford Tigers of the English Premier League (EPIHL) in October 2013 through another of his companies, Red Hockey Ltd.

In March 2015, the latter company purchased interests in two rival EPIHL clubs - 49 per cent of Precision Sports Marketing, owner of Bracknell Bees, and 34 per cent of Manchester Phoenix.

Four months later Red Hockey purchased 100 per cent of Deeside Dragons, who play in the National League.

► Red Touch Media sponsored the EPIHL's cup competition in 2014-15.

● **Silverblades** is one of the trade names of the businesses run by **Mike Petrouis**, whose companies operate several British ice rinks in this name or under the brand Planet Ice.

These include four of the ten EPIHL rinks at Altrincham, Basingstoke, Milton Keynes and Peterborough. (PI also run the Big Blue Tent in Cardiff Bay, home of the Elite's Devils.)

Planet Ice own and operate two of the league's clubs – Basingstoke Bison and Milton Keynes Lightning - and have a stake in the play-offs, which are held in the Planet Ice Arena in Coventry, aka the Skydome.

In the summer of 2015, The Ice Rink Co Ltd, another Petrouis business, entered Manchester Storm in the Elite League, playing out of Silverblades' Altrincham rink, which was previously the home of the EPIHL's Phoenix.

► Other rinks under the Silverblades umbrella, Gillingham, Widnes and a new one in Leeds, are possible future homes for EPIHL teams.

► Ice Media Productions (IMP-UK), which is associated with Planet Ice, controversially donated a prize of £5,000 to the 2014-15 runners-up in the EPIHL. (No prize is awarded to the league winner.)

► When IMP-UK produced a DVD of the EPIHL play-off weekend, Red Hockey refused permission for Telford Tigers' semi-final game to appear on it.

■ In another blast from the past, Altrincham's NIHL team will be named the Aces. The new team will take the place of Neil Morris's Manchester Minotaurs.

ALL CHANGE IN HULL

Pirates ahoy!

A few days after the collapse of **Bobby McEwan**'s Stingrays (see next story), ice hockey returned to the Hull Ice Arena, but in the lower English Premier League.

On 3 July 2015, **Shane Smith**, the owner of the EPIHL's Sheffield Steeldogs, received the go-ahead from EIHA chairman **Ken Taggart** to become part owner of a new team, the Pirates.

Smith's partner was former Stingrays' forward **Dominic Osman** who also took on the role of Pirates' player-coach.

Smith and Osman brought **Andy Daintith**, head coach of Hull's respected junior club, on board as development co-ordinator.

> Q - How are Hull Pirates going to keep fit?
> A - Arrrr, gym lad!
> *posted on www.thehockeyforum.co.uk*

On his controversial position as owner of two clubs (hardly unique in British ice hockey), Smith insisted: "Both sides will be run independently. I'm not the sort of person to order one of my coaches to let the other side win."

He added: "Hull has a really good fan-base and a good junior set-up. I think people will be surprised at the progress that's been made in the EPIHL since Hull [under **Mike** and **Sue Pack**] was in it a decade ago."

Stingrays run out of money

The thin ice on which our sport skates cracked again on 24 June 2015 when owner **Bobby McEwan** admitted that he no longer had the funds to continue running Hull Stingrays in the Elite League.

Saying this was "the hardest decision of my life", McEwan blamed "the loss of a major sponsor [see later], increased operational costs [the league's conference system], the introduction of ice-time charges [by the local authority] and the shortage of fans attending our matches".

What he didn't mention, though many fans did, was the off-putting state of Hull Ice Arena, which we have detailed later.

The Stingrays didn't post any attendance figures for last season but their crowds were believed to be around 500, the worst in the Elite and lower than many teams in the EPIHL.

McEwan, 55, said he felt "lower than low" and feared he might lose his house.

He apologised publically to coach **Omar Pacha,** his assistant **Carl Luzon,** and captain **Matty Davies**, but the message failed to get through to the players, according to defenceman **David Phillips**.

The Beverley native, who signed a two-year deal with the club in April, tweeted: 'Devastated about the news! A phone call would have been nice about what is happening instead of having to read it online, unbelievable...'

But he soon cheered up when he was one of the first players – along with Davies – to be picked by the new Manchester Storm.

The team's collapse was especially poignant as they were coming off one of the most successful spells in their recent history, reaching the play-off finals weekend.

McEwan took over the club in May 2012 when **Andy Buxton** and **Mike Cowley** of Coventry Blaze put it up for sale. They had run the team for two years after Stingrays' founders, **Mike** and **Sue Pack,** quit in August 2010 after seven seasons. Several teams called the Hull Ice Arena home before then.

(compiled from reports in the Hull Daily Mail)

■ In a press release on the same day, the Elite League announced that they had formed a new team, Manchester Storm, to take over the Stingrays' place. (See earlier article.)

■ Hull Stingrays' major backer was Rapid Solicitors, the law firm which used to be the title sponsor of the Elite League.

Rapid were bought out by rival Neil Hudgell Solicitors in October 2014 following Rapid's dispute with the NHS.

According to a report in the *Hull Daily Mail*, 'Rapid was accused of charging excessive legal fees to health authorities. The NHS Litigation Authority criticised the firm for charging over 80 times more in fees than patients received in litigation costs.'

ICE HOCKEY UK

Anderson is new chairman

Jim Anderson was appointed chairman of the sport's governing body for a three-year term in November 2014.

The 74-year-old Scot took the chairmanship on an interim basis after **Mohammed Ashraff** stood down earlier in the year.

Mr Anderson's first taste of the sport came in 1979 as a member of the board of the Kirkcaldy Ice Hockey Club and since then he has been an ever-present in Scottish ice hockey.

Among his more recent roles has been team leader of GB's under-20s for their World Championship games in Estonia.

Help sought from Sweden

Ice Hockey UK held a Strategy Workshop in York in February 2015, bringing together officials, management, coaches and players from all over the UK, along with officials from the regional governing bodies.

The workshop arose from the findings in Wharton Consulting's report in August 2014 (a 16-page PowerPoint presentation), which concluded that the governance of British ice hockey is 'dysfunctional' and 'fragmented'.

Among Wharton's recommendations for how the governing body could dig itself out of this deep hole was a comparison with the way Swedish ice hockey works.

This resulted in Swedish Ice Hockey Federation president, **Christer Englund**, giving a presentation at the workshop on the structure and strategy of the game in Sweden.

Commenting on the event, Mr Anderson said: "It went better than I expected". He accepted that "British ice hockey is not sustainable as presently structured" but he believed "we are now on the right road forward".

A new constitution for IHUK was to be drawn up, and be compliant with the guidelines laid down by the British Olympic Association, UK Sport and similar bodies. This will assist in obtaining funding for the sport. www.icehockeyuk.co.uk.

There is more information about the sport's governing bodies at the back of the Annual.

ENGLISH ICE HOCKEY ASSOCIATION

New four-year plan

The English Ice Hockey Association, which controls all English clubs outside the Elite League, has adopted a Development Strategy.

The four-year plan came about after the Association consulted experts in the field of sports governance, much as Ice Hockey UK did.

As if to emphasise Wharton's point that our game is dysfunctional, however, the regional body used a different consultancy - Minority and Disability Sports Consulting Ltd (MDSC).

The aims were similar to IHUK's – how to get some money and improve playing standards. The best way to do this, said MDSC, is for the EIHA and their clubs to follow the governance guidelines laid down by Sport England and similar bodies and organise themselves more efficiently.

A brief summary of the plan's main points:

Governance – a new EIHA Board of Directors, some appointed and some elected, to emerge over the next three years, i.e. by 2018.

Coaching – An EIHA coaching handbook to be produced by 2017.

Officiating – A national development programme for referees and off-ice officials to be created.

CLUBS -

■ Job descriptions to be drawn up for the main roles within a club: treasurer, chair, secretary, safeguarding officer and head coach.

■ Clubs to become limited companies, ideally by guarantee.

■ Minimum standards of governance to be implemented. If clubs fail to meet these standards they will be unable to vote. If they don't meet the standards for three consecutive years, they will be unable to play in competitive leagues.

■ An annual club conference to be introduced to support development and to engage with stakeholders.

SENIOR LEAGUE STRUCTURES

The drop-out of male players aged 16-18 is a concern. This is to be tackled by EPIHL teams employing a non-playing head coach by the start of the 2017-18 season. This person is to hold at least a UK level 3 coaching certificate (or equivalent) and to be in charge of all teams – senior and junior – in that rink.

►

EIHA - JUNIOR LEAGUE STRUCTURES
The problem of one-sided games is to be tackled by creating national play-offs for all age groups. To be implemented at the end of the 2017-18 season.

The *Annual* will endeavour to monitor the progress of this plan.

SHOOTOUT RECORD EQUALLED
Netminders **Brian Stewart** (Coventry) and **Mattias Modig** (Nottingham) each played a blinder in the Elite League game at the Skydome on 4 January 2015.

After 70 minutes of play, and a fairly evenly divided 70 shots, the Blaze were tied 1-1 with the visiting Panthers.

So into the dreaded penalty shootout. Dreaded by the players, that is. The 2,422 fans sat forward and tried to breathe normally as a stream of players tried to beat the keepers.

Chris Lawrence had five attempts for Nottingham but beat Stewart only once; Coventry's **Jereme Tendler** went for it four times and converted once; Modig blanked **Ryan O'Marra** three times. 23 shots and still even.

For Blaze's 12th try, **Jakub Sindel** went to the centre spot for his third effort to outwit Modig. He succeeded, Coventry were 2-1 winners, the crowd went wild and the teams equalled the all-time British record of 24 penalty shots.

The mark was set in April 1990 at Wembley Arena in the (Heineken) British Championship final. Cardiff Devils beat Murrayfield Racers 7-6 after Devil **Doug McEwen** bamboozled **Martin McKay**, and **Jeff Smith** memorably stopped Racer **Tony Hand**.

The milestone was reached again in March 2001 during a Superleague play-off quarter-final when **Stephane Roy** beat **Dave Trofimenkoff** to give Bracknell Bees a 4-3 victory over the Storm in the MEN Arena.

ISLE OF WIGHT
Ryde rink saved
Back with our friends, Planet Ice ....

Ice sports fans on the Isle of Wight spent an anxious couple of months early in 2015 after **Mike Petrouis** suddenly announced that Planet Ice Ryde Arena would close on 25 March.

Mr Petrouis said he had been funding the rink out of his own pocket as it had "not been financially viable for years".

The announcement took the Isle of Wight Council by surprise. Claiming that they had not been informed of the decision before it appeared in the local paper, a spokesman said:

"As owner of the freehold, we are seeking urgent clarification from [Planet Ice] as to how it intends to comply with the obligation in its 125-year lease to operate the facility as an ice rink for a minimum of 15 years, which started in February 2001."

The Council did not have the funds to run the rink themselves, though they offered practical assistance and said they would be raising the issue with Sport England.

Thousands of skaters hastily banded together, mainly via Facebook, to lobby for the rink to remain open.

> √ Planet Ice spent £4 million on an 18-month refit of the **MILTON KEYNES** rink, which has been greeted very favourably by the fans.
> √ At Planet Ice **COVENTRY** (the Skydome) proper ice hockey markings were painted clearly into the ice during the 2015 off-season.

Wightlink Raiders put on a Legends game on 4 March, featuring 35 players past and present. This attracted 452 fans and raised a decent sum towards saving the rink. A Fun Day by other rink users raised over £2,000.

A week later, the Ryde Arena Trust Ltd (RAT) was set up "as a properly constituted company, limited by guarantee" and opened negotiations with Mike Petrouis.

Just four days before the 25 March deadline, RAT announced that Planet Ice had agreed to keep the rink open until 11 April when the take-over could hopefully be completed. This would also enable the Raiders to see out their NIHL play-off campaign at home.

But the final agreement took another week. Only when the Raiders faced Invicta Dynamos on 18 April in front of 800 supporters for the play-off final, was Trust chairman **Ian Jenkins** able to confirm that the rink had been signed over to them at 10 o'clock that morning.

This really made the Raiders' day. **Jeremy Cornish**'s men went on to beat the Dynamos and win the southern play-offs.

BITISH ICE RINKS

In need of some TLC (tons of lovely cash)

All British ice rinks are showing their age, including those built in the 1980s with the benefit of substantial Sports Council grants.

The grants did not cover the heavy costs of maintenance and few local authorities can now afford this. Some rinks have closed already, and only half-a-dozen have had loving care lavished on them, which is not surprising when refurbishment costs several millions.

Here's an update on what went on in some rinks during 2014-15. The problems in Altrincham, Hull and Ryde help to explain why the teams have had their recent upheavals:

ALTRINCHAM – The 'temporary' rink has now been in existence for eight years. It looks like being around for considerably longer as plans for a new rink as part of a town centre redevelopment have fallen by the wayside.

The Ice Dome has room for 2,000 fans but the Phoenix have only been able to attract around half this number.

Many fans, not to mention the Phoenix's owners, would prefer to move into a site in the centre of Manchester.

Will this happen? And now the Ice Rink Co Ltd are running a pro team in the Silverblades rink, will they make major improvements to the Ice Dome? We'll have to wait and see.

BASINGSTOKE - Various improvements to the Bison's home were made during 2015, including painting and the installation of a steel staircase from rink-side to the windows of the bar, hopefully for an extra tier of seating there.

BELFAST - The home of the Elite League's Giants had a £3 million facelift in July 2015. The SSE Arena's 9,000 seats were to be replaced, as well as the decking and flooring areas.

GUILDFORD – The ice notoriously cracked in middle of a big Flames-Tigers EPIHL game in March, forcing its cancellation.

It's a clean, bright place but the roof leaks and the sightlines are awful. Food and drink facilities have deteriorated since a private leisure company took over running the rink two years ago. The Flames' owners have wanted a new building for years.

HULL – *This was posted on www.thehockeyforum.co.uk in February 2015:*
'Three games in a row have now been delayed due to the failings of the rink -

X Last week it was the **slow ticketing** facilities.

X A couple of weeks ago **broken Plexiglas** took ages to fix as they argued over whose responsibility it was.

X On Sunday the person who usually drives the **Zamboni** had to go home and other staff members appeared not to know how to drive it.

X The **lights go out** without warning with the danger of the game being called off.

X The **rink heating** has been off for a couple of months now.

X The **toilets** look like something out of 'Train Spotting'.

X Last month [a fan] tweeted a picture about the state of **the dressing room showers**.

'The fans have emailed the relevant councillors and there was a phone-in this morning (4 February) on BBC Radio Humberside about the state of the rink.

'The club have had a meeting with the local authority and they say the problems will be sorted for Sunday's game against Nottingham Panthers. Watch this space.'

RYDE – *From another post on The Hockey Forum in September 2014:*

X The **ice-making equipment** is faulty yet again and we have so far suffered two home games with wet ice.

X The *lights* were faulty again but with different ones not working from last week. This has been ongoing since the end of last season.

X Atmosphere is so *damp* that the plexi is dripping with condensation.

X *Seats, floors and walls* are filthy.

X *The ice markings* were poor last season and no *maintenance* has been done during the summer.

X As it hasn't rained for a while, I'll hold my comments on the *leaky roof and the mould on the walls* that were there last season.

X *-The away team changing room* is filthy, disgusting, freezing cold, exposed wiring, nails and screws poking out of the walls.

A couple of weeks later, however, the poster was able to report -

√ Last night the rink showed great improvement. ▶

'The lights were fixed and the ice looked a little more solid. Even the toilets stood to attention and it looked like someone had measured the distance between the disinfectant blocks and stood them up neatly on their ends. Still a way to go but a decent start.'

DISCIPLINE
The Dept of Player Safety

The Elite League introduced an entirely new form of disciplinary system in season 2014-15, after their discipline chief **Moray Hanson** resigned.

Hanson, a respected former international ref, quit in the summer of 2014 after only one year in the post. He was understood to be unhappy at being pestered with phone calls at all hours from clubs pleading for their players.

For a trial year, his duties were taken over by a Department of Player Safety (DOPS).

To avoid a repeat of the Hanson situation, no one knew exactly who was on DOPS. According to league chairman, **Tony Smith**, in an interview with Sheffield-based sports journalist **Seth Bennett**, it is "an independent group based in Europe and the UK."

Smith said the group's services have been used for several years by European leagues like Austria's and Germany's and have worked well.

"None of the owners or GMs know who the individuals are," he said, "and we don't think it makes any difference that the fans don't know, either."

The main aim of the Department was not to punish erring players but to look after their safety. To this end, DOPS and the league sent videos to help teams and players understand what calls they could expect when the players executed certain moves.

When a ban was deemed necessary, DOPS announced its length and explained how and why the decision was taken. This was accompanied by an explanatory video, showing the play at fault, why it was deemed illegal and detailing how and why the play went wrong.

The new system met with general approval and it was agreed to continue it into 2015-16.

OK, explanations over. Now for our regular sideways look at some of the major miscreants during season 2014-15.

Unfortunately, we have only been able to record incidents in the Elite League. The English IHA, which controls the EPIHL and NIHL, normally puts disciplinary decisions on its website at www.eiha.co.uk/discipline. But the pages were under reconstruction at press-time.

"Definitely the thinking in [the NHL] has changed. You don't see nearly as many heavyweights out there whose main job is to fight. Now you've got middleweights who fight, but who can also skate, kill penalties, and play a regular shift. That's how it should be." *Tanner Glass, New York Rangers' designated enforcer, after deliberately avoiding a fight with the opposition's hard man at the start of an NHL exhibition game at Madison Square Garden in September 2014. New York Post.*

ELITE LEAGUE
RILEY EMMERSON, Edinburgh Capitals
Messy start for DOPS

On 7 September 2014 ref **Neil Wilson** assessed Emmerson, a 6ft 8in Canadian winger, with a two-minute minor for boarding in the first minute of Edinburgh's 2-1 Challenge Cup defeat at home to Belfast Giants.

The play - a hit to the head - was later reviewed by DOPS as Belfast said their injured player, the 5ft 11in **Kevin Phillips**, had been 'diagnosed with concussion'.

DOPS duly upgraded the penalty to a match for boarding and handed down a draconian ten-game ban and a £1,000 fine.

But DOPS said the game video supplied by the Capitals missed the incident 'for technical reasons'. If further information could be supplied and/or the full game night footage seen, said the league, they were prepared to review the decision.

Caps duly appealed, and as Phillips was ruled fit to play the next weekend, the ban was reduced to three games, though the fine remained. Edinburgh boss **Scott Neil** undertook to ensure that full video footage would be supplied in future.

CHRIS FRANK, Braehead Clan

2 bans, 10 games, time to retire

The former NHL draft pick was banned on two separate occasions for a total of ten games.

This was his second season with the Clan and in each year, the 29-year-old American defenceman has been listed in the top four of the league's bad boys.

At the end of 2014-15 he retired 'for family reasons'.

Ban #1, 20 September 2014 at Cardiff Devils - four games for a check to the head. In their judgment DOPS said Frank's hit on Cardiff's hard man **Doug Clarkson** was 'recklessly targeted', he 'left his feet to make the hit', there was 'no intent to play the puck' and Clarkson suffered a concussion.

Frank was reported to have been given a talking-to by his coach **Ryan Finnerty**. But a month later in a rough game in Edinburgh where the teams shared 152 pims, he narrowly escaped another ban after hitting young Scot **Sean Beattie** in the head from behind.

Beattie was hospitalised with concussion the next day but, said the Clan, DOPS reviewed the incident and agreed that Frank's 10-minute misconduct was sufficient punishment.

Ban #2 - 14 February 2015 at Braehead v Cardiff Devils. No Valentine's Day sentiment from our Chris. He picked up four penalties in seven minutes in the last period (Devils were 3-0 up), the last two in a fight with **Tyson Marsh**.

When DOPS reviewed the game tape, however, they discovered that just before the fight, 'Frank rams his head upwards violently into the side of Marsh's head, who is unaware and unable to protect himself from this head-butting action, which knocks him to the ice'.

The Department added a match penalty for head-butting to Frank's game record and, as he was a repeat offender, suspended him for six games.

JOE GRIMALDI, Edinburgh Capitals

The Grim Reaper

We are reluctant to list, in a publication intended for family reading, all the offences committed by this American defenceman on a cold day in Nottingham on 3 January 2015.

But duty calls. According to DOPS, Grimaldi:

X 'speared **Max Parent** in the stomach area with intent and motioned to spear him again'.

X 'removed his helmet and threw it violently at Parent, which made contact in the head area of Parent.'

X 'violently punched the Panther while he was unaware and unable to protect himself.'

DOPS added, a trifle superfluously, that 'these are all reckless actions, with an attempt to injure', 'have no regard for the opposition player's safety' and 'his actions are not in any way a hockey play'.

The 28-year-old from New York State was suspended for 18 games and Edinburgh were reminded that under league rules, they have to play an import short for ten games.

The club sacked him immediately. (Panthers won 6-1.)

MATT NICKERSON, Fife Flyers

Nicked twice

This is our third American defenceman in trouble and the second two-time offender of 2014-15.

Nickerson was dismissed early in the third period of Fife's 4-2 home loss to fierce Scots rivals Braehead Clan on 2 January.

DOPS suspended the 6ft, 4in Flyer for three games, explaining: 'He violently punched Clan defenceman **Jeff Smith** from the team bench. Smith was unable to protect himself and became involved in altercations with numerous Fife players.'

His ban took into account that he had received a four-game fighting ban barely a month earlier in another home defeat, this time 4-1 to Sheffield Steelers.

According to newspaper reports, Nickerson steamed in from the blue line and blindsided ▶

Steeler **Cullen Eddy** by the left goal post, pushing him into the boards where he punched him in the head while he was on the ice. He then took on all the Steelers players on the ice at the time and continued to throw multiple punches while being restrained by the officials.

Flyers' coach **Todd Dutiaume** sailed close to the 'disrepute' wind when he complained publically about the way his player's latest case had been handled. "It seems they are just throwing at a dartboard and guessing how many games guys should get," he groused.

We don't think he meant the d-man deserved a longer spell on the sidelines.

DOPS stood firm, unlike in 2013-14 when Nickerson's 12-game ban was reduced, under pressure, to nine after an altercation with Chris Frank in another game against the Clan. (See *The Ice Hockey Annual 2014-15*.)

The Flyers released Nickerson in the off-season and he joined Belfast Giants.

SNAP SHOTS

SOLIHULL BARONS won 61 successive league games over two seasons, 2013-15, in the National League (NIHL).

The Barons, who compete in the league's Laidler Conference (formerly Division Two North), topped the group in season 2013-14 with a goal difference of +187 but declined promotion to the higher Moralee Conference.

After last season's even wider +248 they agreed to move up for the new term.

■ Cardiff Devils won 22 Elite League games on the trot between 30 October 2010 and 15 January 2011. *See page 111 of* The Ice Hockey Annual 2011-12 *for more details.*

THE UK ICE HOCKEY PLAYERS 100-YEAR REUNION DINNER took place at the end of July 2015 at the Ramside Hotel in Durham.

Organised by former players **Scott Plews** and **Frank Killen**, it was attended by around 250 players, coaches and officials. The proceeds were donated to cancer charities. *A full account of the successful event is at www.prohockeynews.com/columnist/david-carr. Click on 'Babcock, Heineken and 100 Years of British Hockey'.*

TELEVISION

Premier Sports, your home for hockey

In season 2014-15 for the first time, ice hockey fans could indulge their favourite sport on one TV channel, *Premier Sports*: -

√ 23 Champions Hockey League games, including the six played by Elite League side, Nottingham Panthers;

√ 17 Elite League games, including three play-off final contests from Nottingham;

√ 20 World Championship games, including all five of GB's matches in Eindhoven;

√ Over 500 NHL games (15 games a week), including all the play-off games for the Stanley Cup, and the outdoor Winter Classic and Stadium Series;

√ Around 40 Swedish Elite League games.

You can watch Premier Sports in HD on your TV or other screen via the following options - Sky channel 428, Virgin channel 551, TalkTalk channel 526. For details, visit www.premiersports.tv.

17 live Elite games

In their second season covering the Elite League, *Premier Sports* screened 17 games, much the same number as in 2013-14.

For the first time, however, the subscription channel was allowed to broadcast live all three play-off final contests from Nottingham.

The league got more exposure when *Premier Sports* showed Nottingham Panthers' six games in the new Champions Hockey League, which also went out live.

Despite the Elite's supposed reluctance to allow too much TV coverage for fear of scaring away fans, a Friday night TV game on 27 February at Braehead Arena drew a near-capacity crowd of 3,576 for the visit of the Clan's sister club, Nottingham Panthers.

The Nottingham finals attracted their usual close to sell-out crowds, too.

A total of 18 cameras were employed in the NIC. They had a big influence on the games as video reviews were used for several incidents.

All *Premier Sports'* games were hosted by **Aaron Murphy**, who was also the play-by-play commentator. The colour commentators were **Neil** (Coach) **Russell** and/or **Paul Adey**.

■ Thanks to a sell-out crowd in the NIC on 20 March, for the first time in their history Nottingham Panthers streamed their crucial Elite League Conference decider against Sheffield Steelers live on the internet for £10.

Commentators were veteran ice hockey broadcaster and Panthers' manager **Gary Moran**, and GB and Panthers' injured forward **David Clarke**.

SNAP SHOTS

Streatham's juniors were featured on *Game Changers*, Sky Sports' Saturday morning kids' programme on 20 December 2014. Canadian coach **Sean Scarbrough** demonstrated some of the skills needed to succeed at the game.

Owner **Wayne Scholes**, coach **Tom Watkins** and the Telford Tigers enjoyed a couple of minutes of national fame on the same day when BBC1's **Ben Smith** fronted a report on the team and their dramatically improved fortunes for *Saturday Sportsday*.

Two EPIHL games on big screen

The EPIHL's play-off final from Coventry on 5 April between Manchester Phoenix and Peterborough Phantoms was shown on *Premier Sports* the next day with commentary from **Graham Bell** and **Lee Jones**.

The second leg of the English Challenge Cup final was streamed live on www.247.tv, the production company for *Premier Sports*, and shown over May Bank Holiday (3 May) on *Premier Sports*' TV channel.

With only three cameras in use at Telford, the Cup final coverage was limited.

The internet commentary was by **Paul Shuttleworth** and **Mark Elliott** of BBC Radio Shropshire. On TV, the show's producer **Adrian Battersby** was joined by **Paul Wheeler.**

NATIONAL LEAGUE ON RADIO

Fans enjoyed a rare chance to hear an NIHL game on 21 March 2015 when BBC Radio Oxford broadcast live, on DAB and online, from the Big Blue Tent in Cardiff Bay.

The occasion was the crucial league relegation battle between Oxford City Stars and Cardiff NIHL Devils.

Andrew Self was the host and play-by-play man, with ex-Stars player **James Schall** providing the colour.

95th VARSITY MATCH

Dark Blues are whitewashed

Cambridge University beat Oxford University 10-0 on 7 March 2015 in an historic match at Planet Ice Peterborough.

French netminder **Romain Tourenne** (Downing College) rewrote the Varsity records with the Light Blues' first shutout since 1939. Back then the game was staged in London's now defunct Empress Hall in Earl's Court.

Cambridge's scorers were led by **Christopher Finch** with four goals and **Martin (Dr Marty) Smoragiewicz** with four points.

The margin of victory was Cambridge's largest for over half-a-century, and their 11-1 triumph at the old Richmond rink in 1962.

This means the Light Blues have now won half of the last six encounters between these ancient seats of learning. But the tide of history is still on the side of their rivals. Oxford's all-time tally of 63 wins is more than double Cambridge's 30. Two games have been drawn.

Cambridge will be hoping to narrow this gap when their new rink opens in the city. See *New Rinks News*.

■ The annual Varsity Match between Oxford and Cambridge universities has been played since the turn of the 20th century.

The ancient contest has been recognised by the IIHF and the Hockey Hall of Fame as the world's longest running rivalry.

The teams battle for the right to hoist the Patton Cup, named after **Major B.M. 'Peter' Patton,** the founder and first President of the British Ice Hockey Association.

■ In Nottingham's inter-varsity game on 29 April 2015, the University of Nottingham beat Nottingham Trent University 4-3 at the NIC. We understand the arena sold out their 6,500 seats within 10 minutes of the tickets going on sale.

Published every year since 1976
Complete your collection of the sport's 'bible'
Go to *www.icehockeyannual.co.uk/backissues*

PRE-SEASON GAMES 2014
Panthers in France

29/31 August 2014, Napoleon Cup, Amiens
Amiens-**Panthers** 3-4 so (*NOT goal scorers* Boxill, Lee, Hook, wps: Lawrence).
Rouen-**Panthers** 1-3 (Graham, Parent, Jacina).
Three Rivers Un. Patriots (Quebec)-**Panthers** 6-5 so. (Graham 2, Farmer, Lachowicz, Benedict).
Panthers won Napoleon Cup. (Point for draw in regulation against Canadians was sufficient.)

17/18 August 2014, Ljubljana, Slovenia
Olympia Ljubljana-**Panthers** 3-1. Mosey (Jacina).
Ljubljana-**Panthers** 4-3. *NOT* goal *scorers*: Graham, Parent, Cohen.

Danes and 'Thommo' in Fife
30/31 August 2014, The Bay Hotel Challenge Cup, Kirkcaldy, Fife
Fife Flyers-Aalborg 4-2
Fife Flyers-Aalborg 3-8.
Aalborg win cup 10-7 on aggregate
No other details available. The Danish Al-Bank Ligaen side was coached by **Paul Thompson.**

Italians in Scotland
29 August 2014, Challenge match, Dundee
Dundee Stars-Asiago 4-3.
30/31 August 2014, Aladdin Cup, Braehead
Braehead Clan-Asiago 1-3.
Braehead Clan -Asiago 4-2.
*5-5 after second game. **Braehead win Aladdin Cup** in shootout after **Derek Roehl** scores*
Asiago Hockey 1935 were twice Italian Serie-A champions and four times Playoff champions. They have also won three Italian Cups and two Italian Supercups. They were Serie-A runners-up in 2013-14 and reached the play-off semi-finals.

SNAP SHOTS

THE WORLD'S OLDEST KNOWN ICE HOCKEY STICK will be unveiled at the Canadian Museum of History on Canada Day 2017.

The publicly funded Museum paid $300,000 Canadian for the artefact, though it would have fetched a great deal more on the open market.

The stick, fashioned from a single branch of a Nova Scotia sugar maple, is believed to date back to the mid to late 1830s.

The stick was purchased for $1,000 by **Mark Presley** *above* who discovered it hanging in a barber's shop in Nova Scotia.
www.sportsnet.ca/magazine/worlds-oldest-hockey-stick/

BRIAN BURKE, President of Hockey Operations for the NHL's Calgary Flames, visited Belfast in August 2015.

At the charity event, organised by Belfast Giants and the Irish Ice Hockey Association, the American of Irish descent shared stories and insights into his illustrious career at the top of NHL ice hockey.

His CV includes spells as general manager with Toronto Maple Leafs, Vancouver Canucks and Anaheim Ducks, where he won the Stanley Cup in the 2006-07 season.

All proceeds from the occasion were devoted to the development of junior ice hockey throughout the island of Ireland.
www.kingdomofthegiants.com/podcast
YouTube - IIHA An Evening with Brian Burke.

premier sports HD

OVER
600
GAMES THIS SEASON

SUBSCRIBE NOW
WWW.PREMIERSPORTS.TV   0871 663 9000

AND MORE QUOTES

Tweets of the Year

We interrupt this **marriage** to bring you **HOCKEY SEASON**

A heartfelt pre-season tweet from a fan.

Headlines of the Year

'Jeff plays for Sheffield Underdogs!' *From story in Sheffield's* Star *about ex-Steeler* **Jeff Legue** *lacing 'em up for the English Premier League's Steeldogs against the more favoured Telford Tigers.*

'Sheffield Steelers, Cardiff City, Cardiff Devils ... and doing the Ayatollah!' *Yes, this is a headline, not a crossword clue. According to the story in Sheffield's* Star, *it refers to Welshman* **Phil Hill**'s *favourite sports teams, and his favourite goal celebration.*

'GB win but Mafia threat curbed Alex's celebrations'. *Eye-catching headline on a story in* The Northern Scot *which said GB under-20 player* **Alex Forbes** *had revealed to the paper 'how the reputation of local Mafia figures meant the GB under-20 squad couldn't celebrate their gold medal success in Tallinn'. But the article never quite explained what the threat was.*

'Ice hockey player asks Queen for city rink'. *From the Brighton & Hove* Argus *on 11-year-old* **Sonny Keywood**'s *enterprising letter to Her Majesty. (Brighton-based Sonny plays for Guildford's juniors.)*

'Capitals coach: Screw the nut and make the play-offs'. *According to the Edinburgh Evening News, this is what Edinburgh's* **Richard Hartmann** *told his men before the latest dust-up with their deadly rivals, Fife Flyers. Whatever it means, it didn't work as the Caps lost 2-0 at home.*

'Vlad the Impaler'. *We've cheated here because we never actually saw this headline. But when Guildford Flames' Slovakian,* **Vladimir Kutny**, *got a spearing penalty at Sheffield Steeldogs in only his second game, what else could you write?*

'Ryde rink RATs aim to save sinking ship'. *Nice one over a report on the Ryde Arena Trust (RAT)'s effort to raise funds to save the Planet Ice rink from closure.*

'Welsh team goes down against Scots at Murrayfield two days before* **Warren Gatland**'s *men arrive, but Cardiff Devils earn Elite League ice hockey point in close fought battle.' Snappy headline (not) on* Wales Online's *report of the Devils losing at Edinburgh Capitals. [Mr Gatland is apparently the captain of the Wales rugby team].*

'Big Ben strikes again'. *On the IIHF's report of* **Ben O'Connor** *scoring twice for GB in a World Championship game against Korea.*

'All aboard the good ship Sheffield Steelers as Nelson signs up'. *A 'groaner' from the Sheffield* Star *when* **Levi Nelson** *joined the Steelers' 2015-16 roster.*

'Capitals Add Size With Bigos'. *Keep groaning. This from an Edinburgh Capitals' email in June 2015 referring to new defenceman* **Kyle Bigos**. *But he's unquestionably on the large side – 6ft, 5ins and 18 stone. Crumbs!*

Murphism

"There's a pizza lying right there in the crease but he couldn't get a bite of it." **Aaron Murphy**, **Premier Sports** *commentator, describing a missed shooting opportunity in front of goal.*

Hard-working and happy-go-lucky Brits

"The GB players have come in and brought a happy-go-lucky atmosphere to the team. They've worked incredibly hard on and off the ice, but they bring more to the locker room. They have the rare ability to lighten the load. When things get rough, they naturally lift everyone up and have great personalities." **Jake Laime**, *coach of Ogden (Utah) Mustangs of the Western (United) States Hockey League where seven British players have appeared in the last four seasons.*

Hand speaks up – ice hockey is a mess

"Ice hockey across the whole of the country is too fragmented. Nobody knows who is running what. Here in the EPIHL, we know the EIHA run the league but other teams are just doing it for themselves.

"There isn't a nationwide Great Britain set-up and I don't feel we are developing youngsters as well as we should be.

"Of course, it isn't perfect here in the EPIHL, but it's crazy in the Elite League. To have teams with 13 or 14 imports isn't good for the young British guys.

"This should have been addressed ten years ago, but the numbers have kept going up and up. All we hear is that the British players want too much money, but it's the clubs that have the power. They don't have to pay that much.

"At the moment [the Elite League] is saturated [with imports] and it's the only one in Europe like that.

"It's very easy to get focused on your own organisation but at some point all of us need to come together for the betterment of British ice hockey."

Tony Hand MBE, coach of Manchester Phoenix.

Like an NHLer

"**Ben** [O'Connor] changes a game. And he helps us win more games than cost us mistakes.

"If we're winning 3-2 with two minutes to go, I'd put him out there and tell him: 'Shut it down Ben, be mature, make the smart play, don't make the Hollywood play.'

"He's one hell of a player. And I'm so happy he's on our team. I've been coaching in Sweden and Denmark with NHL talent and Ben can do things that many offensive defencemen in the NHL couldn't."

Paul Thompson, looking forward to coaching the GB defenceman at Sheffield Steelers in season 2015-16.

'A bums-on-seats industry'

"I don't think TV is the essential thing to keep growing the league. I've said it before and I'll say it again, ice hockey is a bums-on-seats industry."
Gary Moran, *general manager of Nottingham Panthers.*

Heck of a league but .....

"For the most part [the Elite League] is a heck of a league but it has a reputation for being massively physical that it doesn't deserve.

"When I was there, there were times when it was dangerous playing. Some players – a very small number – would go after your knees. Once you get rid of those players you'll have a great league." **Nathan Robinson** *(above) of Nottingham Panthers, one of the league's best imports in 2014-15, speaking after the* **Joe Grimaldi** *affair (see Review of the Year).*

"I think the Elite League doesn't have maybe the best reputation because a lot of players view it as a league that has too much fighting in it. But there is some good hockey played in the league and this proves it." **Paul Adey**, *a former Panther and one of the best GB players of his era; coach of Elite League's 2013-14 winners Belfast Giants; and diplomat; commentating on* **Premier Sports** *during the Panthers' first game in the Champions Hockey League.*

With grateful acknowledgements to BBC Sport Online, Coventry Telegraph, Nottingham Post, Sheffield Star, Shropshire Star, South Wales Echo, Swindon Advertiser, Yorkshire Post, www.thehockeyforum.co.uk, www.rinkreport.wordpress and various club websites.

Major Teams 2014-15

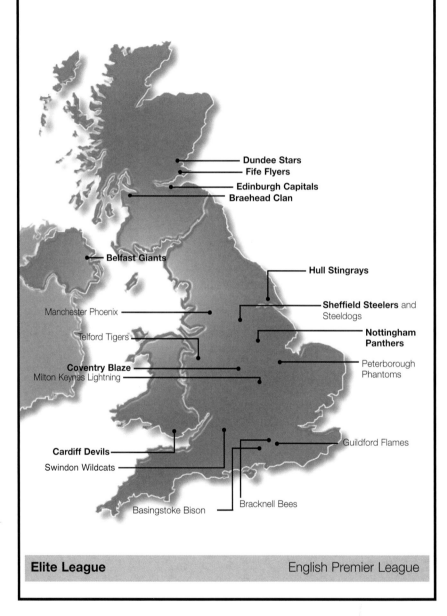

Dundee Stars
Fife Flyers
Edinburgh Capitals
Braehead Clan

Belfast Giants

Hull Stingrays

Manchester Phoenix

Sheffield Steelers and Steeldogs

Telford Tigers

Nottingham Panthers

Coventry Blaze
Milton Keynes Lightning

Peterborough Phantoms

Cardiff Devils
Swindon Wildcats

Guildford Flames

Basingstoke Bison

Bracknell Bees

Elite League	English Premier League

BASINGSTOKE BISON

PLAYER	*ALL COMPETITIONS					ENGLISH PREMIER LEAGUE					PLAY-OFFS				
Scorers	GP	G	A	Pts	Pim	GP	G	A	Pts	Pim	GP	G	A	Pts	Pim
Ciaran Long	47	35	33	68	94	45	33	31	64	94	2	2	2	4	0
Joe Greener	48	29	33	62	134	46	28	31	59	134	2	1	2	3	0
Doug Sheppard (I)	50	15	33	48	10	48	14	31	45	10	2	1	2	3	0
Tomas Karpov (I)	42	20	27	47	16	40	19	27	46	14	2	1	0	1	2
Miroslav Mantroba (I)	50	9	32	41	132	48	9	31	40	132	2	0	1	1	0
Joe Rand (I)	50	18	21	39	32	48	16	21	37	32	2	2	0	2	0
Aaron Connolly	45	20	13	33	36	43	20	11	31	36	2	0	2	2	0
Andrew Melachrino	42	7	15	22	26	40	7	15	22	26	2	0	0	0	0
Nicky Chinn	42	4	14	18	83	44	4	14	18	71	2	0	0	0	12
Kurt Reynolds	50	1	16	17	79	48	1	15	16	77	2	0	1	1	2
Michael Wales	44	5	8	13	62	42	5	8	13	58	2	0	0	0	4
Joe Baird	45	1	8	9	64	43	1	7	8	64	2	0	1	1	0
Grant Rounding	33	3	5	8	14	31	3	5	8	14	2	0	0	0	0
Cameron Wynn	47	4	3	7	4	45	4	3	7	4	2	0	0	0	0
Stuart Mogg	50	2	3	5	6	48	2	3	5	6	2	0	0	0	0
Ryan Watt 1	18	0	5	5	20	16	0	5	5	18	2	0	0	0	2
Declan Balmer	41	0	5	5	91	39	0	5	5	66	2	0	0	0	25
Brendan Baird	34	0	1	1	6	32	0	1	1	6	2	0	0	0	0
Rick Skene	5	0	0	0	22	5	0	0	0	22					
Matt Selby	9	0	0	0	41	9	0	0	0	41					
Dean Skinns (N)	50	0	0	0	2	48	0	0	0	2	2	0	0	0	0
Winning shots		4		4			4		4			0		0	
Bench penalties					6					6					0
TEAM TOTALS	50	177	275	452	980	48	170	264	434	933	2	7	11	18	47
Netminders	GP	Mins	SOG	GA	Sv%	GP	Mins	SOG	GA	Sv%	GP	Mins	SOG	GA	Sv%
Dean Skinns	50	3035	1563	157	90.0	48	2916	1444	149	89.7	2	119	55	8	85.5
Winning shots				3					3					0	
Empty net goals			3	3				3	3				0	0	
TEAM TOTALS	50	3035	1566	163	89.6	48	2916	1447	155	89.3	2	119	55	8	85.5

Also appeared: Dan Weller-Evans (N).

Also played for: 1 Bracknell Bees.

Shutouts: Skinns – league: 21 Sep at Peterborough Phantoms (39 saves), 31 Jan v Bracknell Bees (20).

*All competitions = league and play-offs only. EIHA did not record player statistics for the English Challenge Cup.

(I) ITC holder

Beaten back by the Flames

GRAHAM MERRY *Basingstoke Gazette*

After the Bison's double-winning season, player-coach **Doug Sheppard** kept faith with the players that had served him so well.

The only major loss was Elite League-bound British defenceman **Zach Sullivan**, while the additions were another young GB junior international, defender **Declan Balmer**, along with local forward **Grant Rounding** and netminder **Dan Weller-Evans**.

The Herd opened their English Premier League campaign with five straight wins and their first loss - at home to Guildford Flames – only came after a shoot-out.

But the Surrey side went on to beat the Bison in four out of their six meetings. These defeats eventually proved vital, as Guildford took second place in the league while the Bison had to settle for third.

There were other factors. A pivotal contest was the Bison's first visit to their arch-rivals, Bracknell Bees, who were having a poor season.

BEES STING

But that evening the Bees had a sting in their tail with **Lukas Smital** netting the game-winner ten seconds from time.

The defeat was also costly as the Bison missed out by a single point from booking a semi-final place in the English Challenge Cup.

Then after they lost young British defenceman **Matt Selby** to a season-ending injury, further members of the blueline brigade were sidelined. At one point, they were down to three defencemen.

The Herd's hopes of taking second spot were dashed again when import forward **Tomas Karpov** broke his wrist. But he was back in time for the play-offs with the Bison eager to defend their crown against Manchester Phoenix.

When Sheppard's flock won the first leg of their quarter-final in Altrincham 5-4 and led the second leg 2-1, visions of a return to Coventry rose into view.

But the Phoenix hit back to win the game and the tie, leaving the Bison to look back on a campaign where they must have felt they deserved a lot more.

PLAYER AWARDS

Players' Player (Mark Scotchmer Award)

	Ciaran Long
Player of the Year	Aaron Connolly
British Player of the Year	Kurt Reynolds
Coach's Player	Joe Greener
Most Improved Player	Stuart Mogg

LEADING PLAYERS

Aaron Connolly *born 1 June 1993, Northfleet, Kent*
A physical, hard-working forward with grit and determination, who made things happen. A leader on and off the ice.

Ciaran Long *born 9 February 1991, Birmingham*
The sharp-shooter, who became the team's first Brit to score four goals in an EPIHL game, was a lethal finisher from close range or distance.

MOST PROMISING PLAYER

Stuart Mogg *born 1 August 1994, Basingstoke*
Started his second full senior season as a forward but ended it looking at home on the blue line. Should only get better as a defenceman.

FACT FILE 2014-15

English Premier League	Third
Play-offs	Quarter-finalists
English Challenge Cup	Fourth in first round

HISTORY

Founded 1988 as Beavers. Name changed to Bison in May 1995.

Leagues English (Premier) League 2009-15, 1988-90; Elite League 2003-09; British National League 1998-2003; Superleague 1996-98; British League, Premier Div 1993-96; British League, Div One 1990-93;

Honours: English Premier League play-offs 2013-14; English Premier Cup 2013-14; British League, Div One & play-offs 1992-93; English League (promotion) play-offs 1989-90; *Benson and Hedges Plate* 1999-2000 & 2000-01.

BASINGSTOKE BISON *left to right, back row: :* Tony Skinns (equipment), Alan Parrott (staff), Glen Wells (medic), Stuart Mogg, Joe Greener, Michael Wales, Miroslav Vantroba, Joe Rand, Ciaran Long, Declan Balmer, Cameron Wynn, Ryan Watt, Brendan Baird, Matthew Plested (physio), Darren Pierman (staff), Drew Poulson (equipment), Ade Worship (staff); *front row:* Dan Weller-Evans, Grant Rounding, Andy Melachrino, Doug Sheppard, Joe Baird, Nicky Chinn, Aaron Connolly, Kurt Reynolds, Thomas Karpov, Dean Skinns.

photo: Grant King

BELFAST GIANTS

PLAYER	ALL COMPETITIONS					ELITE LEAGUE					PLAY-OFFS				
Scorers	GP	G	A	Pts	Pim	GP	G	A	Pts	Pim	GP	G	A	Pts	Pim
Raymond Sawada	62	24	43	67	93	52	21	38	59	89	4	2	2	4	2
Mike Kompon	55	23	39	62	65	45	19	34	53	61	4	1	3	4	2
Evan Cheverie	61	14	43	57	54	51	13	34	47	48	4	0	4	4	0
Colin Shields	61	18	35	53	20	51	13	26	39	14	4	1	4	5	0
Robby Sandrock	62	6	39	45	46	52	5	36	41	46	4	0	1	1	0
Darryl Lloyd	61	19	25	44	83	51	17	19	36	73	4	2	2	4	0
Craig Peacock	60	24	19	43	40	50	23	18	41	24	4	1	1	2	0
Adam Keefe	60	13	23	36	132	50	10	18	28	126	4	3	2	5	2
Jeff Mason	59	8	23	31	18	51	6	19	25	12	4	1	2	3	0
Calvin Elfring	60	6	23	29	47	50	4	19	23	45	4	0	1	1	0
Mark McCutcheon	36	6	19	25	10	32	4	18	22	8	1	1	1	2	0
David Phillips	59	4	18	22	101	49	4	17	21	101	4	0	0	0	0
Kevin Westgarth	43	13	7	20	95	36	13	7	20	87	4	0	0	0	4
Cody Brookwell	56	6	13	19	43	48	5	10	15	37	4	1	1	2	0
Mark Garside	40	10	6	16	22	34	8	6	14	18	4	2	0	2	4
Kevin Saurette	21	6	7	13	10	18	4	7	11	8					0
Nathan Robinson 1	14	6	6	12	4	10	3	3	6	4	4	3	3	6	0
Kevin Phillips	62	3	8	11	14	52	3	6	9	10	4	0	2	2	0
Stephen Murphy (N)	22	0	2	2	0	15	0	2	2	0	4	0	0	0	0
Andrew Dickson (N)	58	0	1	1	2	51	0	0	0	2	1	0	1	1	0
Carsen Chubak (N)	43	0	0	0	6	37	0	0	0	2	3	0	0	0	4
Winning shots		2		2			2		2			0		0	
Bench penalties					14					10					2
TEAM TOTALS	62	211	399	610	919	52	177	337	514	825	4	18	30	48	20
Netminders	GPI	Mins	SOG	GA	Sv%	GPI	Mins	SOG	GA	Sv%	GPI	Mins	SOG	GA	Sv%
Stephen Murphy	18	1010	528	45	91.48	15	1	441	37	91.6					
Carsen Chubak	42	2526	1147	110	90.41	36	2160	979	95	90.3	3	190	73	5	93.2
Andrew Dickson	5	217	108	15	86.1	4	157	76	9	88.2	1	60	32	6	81.3
Winning shots				6					4					1	
Empty net goals			3	3				3	3				0	0	
TEAM TOTALS	62	3753	1786	179	90.0	52	2318	1499	148	90.1	4	250	105	12	88.6

Also appeared: Curtis Huppe 2, Rory Sempey (N).

Also played for: 1 Nottingham Panthers; 2 Guildford Flames, Milton Keynes Lightning.

Shutouts: Chubak - league: 17 Jan at Sheffield Steelers (38 saves), 20 Mar v Coventry Blaze (24);
play-offs: 27 Mar v Cardiff Devils (19).

All Competitions = league, play-offs and cup.

Four games were played for league and cup points

BELFAST GIANTS *left to right, back row:* Jason Ellery, Mark Garside, Mike Kompon, Kevin Phillips, Curtis Huppe, Evan Cheverie, David Phillips, Kevin Westgarth, Cody Brookwell, Ray Sawada, Mark McKutcheon, Robbie Sandrock, Darryl Lloyd, Jeff Mason; *front row:* Stephen Murphy, Carson Chubak, Calvin Elfring, Colin Shields, Steve Thornton (head coach), Adam Keefe, Rob Stewart (asst. coach), Kevin Saurette, Craig Peacock, Andrew Dickson.

photo: Michael Cooper.

Euro games take a toll

WAYNE HARDMAN

Giants, the defending Elite League title-holders, faced a difficult recruiting task in the summer of 2014 after their winning coach **Paul Adey** left and their respected general manager **Todd Kelman** switched to Cardiff Devils.

Before departing, Kelman recruited a new coach **Steve Thornton**, who had guided the Giants to the play-off title and a league runners-up place in season 2009-10.

Though the ex-GB and Superleague forward had been out of hockey for four years, when Kelman left Thornton was given the title of director of hockey operations, making him the club's general manager as well as coach.

Fortunately, **Colin Shields** and **Evan Cheverie**, Thornton's top two scorers when he was last in the Odyssey, were still on the payroll, and the entire blueline corps returned, including **Calvin Efring**, the Best Defenceman of 2013-14.

The Brit contingent of sniper **Craig Peacock**, defender **Kevin Phillips** and netminder **Stephen Murphy** were also still around from the coach's last spell on the bench.

Murphy's groin injury in early November, plus an extended series of European games in the Continental Cup, were perhaps the biggest causes of the Giants' disappointing campaign.

New Canadian goalie **Carsen Chubak** played well enough but never gave his team-mates quite the same confidence that 'Murph' did.

The emotional high and lows of the games in Germany and France carried over into their domestic contests, and clearly tired a team that was probably the oldest in the league.

Even the February addition of ex-Nottingham Panthers winger **Nathan Robinson** ("the most dangerous player on the ice when we played them," said Thornton) failed to lift the squad.

The Giants' best effort came in the play-off quarter-finals with convincing double defeats of Kelman's favoured Cardiff Devils.

A close-fought semi in Nottingham against the late blossoming Coventry Blaze ended in a draw, and none of the Giants' three penalty shooters beat the impressive Blaze keeper.

PLAYER AWARDS

Players' Player	Adam Keefe
Most Valuable Player	Darryl Lloyd
Coach's Player	Ray Sawada
Best Forward	Darryl Lloyd
Best Defenceman	Jeff Mason
Fans' Favourite	Adam Keefe
Unsung Hero	Mark Garside
Community Service	Calvin Elfring

LEADING PLAYERS

Adam Keefe born 26 April 1984, Brampton, Ontario.
In his third season as skipper, the rugged winger – nicknamed AK47 - toned down his punishing style, turned up his points production and earned the respect of his team-mates.

Darryl Lloyd born 10 February 1984, Pickering, Ontario
Like Keefe - the pair are known as the Bruise Brothers for obvious reasons - he impressed this season by almost doubling his output and keeping his cooler-time down.

Ray Sawada born 19 February 1985, Richmond, BC, Canada
Joining from the Finnish elite league, his strength, skill and mean streak ensured that he rose to the top of the team's scoring chart.

FACT FILE 2014-15

Elite League	Fifth
Conference	Fourth in Erhardt
Play-offs	Semi-finalists
Challenge Cup	Quarter-finalists

HISTORY

Founded: 2000.
Leagues: Elite League 2003-15, Superleague 2000-03.
Honours: Elite League, Erhardt Conference 2013-14, 2012-13; Elite League 2013-14, 2011-12, 2005-06; Elite League Play-off Champions 2009-10; Challenge Cup, Knockout Cup 2008-09; Crossover Games 2004-05; Superleague Playoffs 2002-03; Superleague 2001-02.

Northern Ireland's Canadian Sports Bar
One of Europes top Ice Hockey Bars
Over 200 jerseys on display from around the world
Six Screens for live sports events

www.rockiessportsbar.com

ODYSSEY PAVILLION   028 9046 7020

BRACKNELL BEES

PLAYER	*ALL COMPETITIONS					ENGLISH PREMIER LEAGUE				
Scorers	GP	G	A	Pts	Pim	GP	G	A	Pts	Pim
Lukas Smital (I)	40	27	21	48	102	40	27	21	48	102
Ivan (Vanya) Antonov	43	19	22	41	8	43	19	22	41	8
Radek Hubacek (I)	40	17	17	34	36	40	17	17	34	36
Jan Bendik (I)	43	6	15	21	73	43	6	15	21	73
Matt Foord	48	8	10	18	36	48	8	10	18	36
Matt Towalski	48	8	9	17	62	48	8	9	17	62
James Galazzi	46	7	5	12	166	46	7	5	12	166
Pavel Strycek (I)	48	2	10	12	77	48	2	10	12	77
Scott Spearing	44	1	8	9	185	44	1	8	9	185
Jake Pitchley	13	2	5	7	8	13	2	5	7	8
Ryan Watt 2	21	0	7	7	89	21	0	7	7	89
Samuel Waller	48	2	4	6	79	48	2	4	6	79
Harvey Stead	46	0	6	6	24	46	0	6	6	24
Danny Ingoldsby	25	4	1	5	12	25	4	1	5	12
Lewis Turner 1	47	0	4	4	62	47	0	4	4	62
Thomas Beesley	6	2	1	3	0	6	2	1	3	0
Rio Grinell-Parke	2	1	1	2	0	2	1	1	2	0
Chris Wiggins 3	8	1	1	2	104	8	1	1	2	104
Joshua Smith	22	1	1	2	12	22	1	1	2	12
Harvey Pitcher	8	0	1	1	10	8	0	1	1	10
Ben Paynter	6	0	0	0	4	6	0	0	0	4
Joshua Tetlow	13	0	0	0	4	13	0	0	0	4
Ilya Antonov	24	0	0	0	2	24	0	0	0	2
Jordan Gregory	34	0	0	0	6	34	0	0	0	6
Tom Annetts (N)	48	0	0	0	2	48	0	0	0	2
Alex Mettam (N)	48	0	0	0	6	48	0	0	0	6
Winning shots		0		0			0		0	
Bench penalties					26					26
TEAM TOTALS	48	108	149	257	1195	48	108	149	257	1195
Netminders	GP	Mins	SOG	GA	Sv%	GP	Mins	SOG	GA	Sv%
Alex Mettam	48	1990	1252	137	89.1	48	1990	1252	137	89.1
Tom Annetts	48	905	517	73	85.9	48	905	517	73	85.9
Winning shots				3					3	
Empty net goals			3	3				3	3	
TEAM TOTALS	48	2895	1772	216	87.8	48	2895	1772	216	87.8

Also appeared: Tom Relf, Daniel Rose.

Also played for: 1 Cardiff Devils, 2 Basingstoke Bison, 3 MK Lightning.

*All competitions = league only. EIHA did not record Cup statistics

(I) ITC holder

BRACKNELL BEES *left to right*, *back row (standing)*: unidentified, Brian Miller (equipment), Ivan (Vanya) Antonov, Josh Smith, Lewis Turner, Pavel Strycek, Jordan Gregory, Sharon Brogden (physio), Danny Ingoldsby, Sam Waller, Ryan Watt, Simon Lazarczuk (equipment), Harvey Stead, Mitch Stead (asst. coach); *front row, left to right*: Tom Annetts, Jan Bendik, Scott Spearing, Radek Hubacek, Matt Foord, Lukas Smital, James Galazzi, Matt Towalski, Alex Mettam.

photo: Chris Callaghan/Blueline Photography

Good crowds, bad finish

RICHARD ASHTON *Bracknell News*

Bracknell Bees endured a chastening season in the English Premier League as they were cut adrift at the bottom, disastrously losing their last 20 games of the campaign.

Back in the off-season of 2014, budget restrictions were a key factor in player-coach **Lukas Smital** losing some of his best forwards.

Shaun Thompson left for Manchester Phoenix and **Ollie Bronnimann** for Guildford Flames, while veterans **Rob Lamey** and **Tony Redmond** hung 'em up. Luckily, **Matt Towalski** was free to join after the collapse of Slough Jets.

Import forward **Kamil Tvrdek** was replaced by another Czech **Radek Hubacek.**

Smital targeted a play-off spot but a quintet of defeats to start the season set an unfortunate precedent. A rare triumph came in the sixth game with a 7-3 win over Sheffield Steeldogs when player of the season **Vanya Antonov** scored a hat-trick.

While results continued to go up and down, off the ice the club's marketing team was playing a blinder. Bees set a new league record in October when a crowd of more than 2,800 watched them beat Guildford Flames 4-1 in the first local derby of the year between the rivals.

A brace of home wins against the Phoenix and the Steeldogs again arrived in November, but there was little joy on the road.

The only success in a miserable December came in the English Challenge Cup against the lower league Wightlink Raiders.

A sense of optimism returned at the start of 2015 with league victories over Milton Keynes Lightning (4-3) and Swindon Wildcats (3-1), allied to another cup triumph against the Raiders (7-4), but they proved to be a false dawn.

An horrific losing run ended the campaign - the nadir was a 10-1 trouncing at Swindon on 7 February – and the Bees ended 19 points adrift of the eighth-placed Steeldogs.

They won just one game away from home all season, and just seven of 48 in total.

The team's general manager **Ben Beeching** said sadly: "I totally accept that the right blend of youth and experience wasn't there. Simply, that was our downfall."

PLAYER AWARDS

Players' Player	James Galazzi
Player of the Year	Ivan (Vanya) Antonov
Best Forward	Matt Towalski
Best Defenceman	Lewis Turner
Best British Player (Colin White Memorial Award)	Ivan (Vanya) Antonov
Most Improved Player	Danny Ingoldsby
Unsung Hero (Keith Robinson Memorial Trophy)	Matt Foord

LEADING PLAYERS

Ivan (Vanya) Antonov *born 12 May 1997, Moscow, Russia*
In his second senior season, the slight (5ft 9ins, 163lbs) forward continued to astonish with his agility, speed and stick-handling skills. Represented GB at under-18s and under-20s.

James Galazzi *born 25 November 1983, Oakville, Ontario, Canada*
In his sixth season with the Bees after coming up through the ranks, the gritty and hard-working forward is an agitator, with an ability to irritate the opposition.

Lewis Turner *born 27 February 1993, Woking, Surrey*
A cornerstone of the defence and a real warrior, the former GB under-20 was briefly called up to the Elite League by Cardiff Devils.

FACT FILE 2014-15

English Premier League	Ninth
Play-offs	Did not qualify
English Challenge Cup	Fifth in qualifying group

HISTORY

Founded: 1987.

Leagues: English Premier League (EPL) 2005-15; British National League (BNL) 2003-05; Superleague 1996-2003; British League, Premier Div. 1991-95; British League, Div. One 1995-96, 1990-91; English League 1987-90.

Honours: English Premier League and Playoff Championship 2006-07; EPL Cup 2007-08 & 2005-06; BNL and Winter Cup 2004-05; Superleague 1999-2000; Promotion play-offs 1990-91; English League 1989-90.

BRAEHEAD CLAN

PLAYER	ALL COMPETITIONS					ELITE LEAGUE					PLAY-OFFS				
Scorers	GP	G	A	Pts	Pim	GP	G	A	Pts	Pim	GP	G	A	Pts	Pim
Stefan Meyer	61	36	38	74	22	51	31	35	66	20	2	0	0	0	2
Neil Trimm	62	29	45	74	34	52	26	41	67	28	2	1	1	2	2
Matt Keith	61	20	50	70	94	51	18	44	62	59	2	0	0	0	2
Leigh Salters	60	32	35	67	112	50	30	33	63	106	2	0	0	0	0
Scott Pitt	62	32	29	61	41	52	28	25	53	35	2	0	0	0	4
Derek Roehl	62	21	24	45	147	52	15	23	38	126	2	2	0	2	2
Scott Aarssen	62	2	40	42	40	52	1	31	32	36	2	0	2	2	2
Ben Davies	62	9	22	31	14	52	7	16	23	14	2	0	1	1	0
Jamie Fritsch	62	3	28	31	52	52	3	23	26	44	2	0	1	1	4
Matt Haywood	48	10	14	24	14	40	9	11	20	14	2	1	0	1	0
Ryan Kavanagh	37	6	15	21	12	27	6	12	18	6	2	0	1	1	0
Lee Esders	49	8	9	17	54	42	6	8	14	46					
Zack Fitzgerald	52	2	12	14	371	44	2	12	14	304	2	0	0	0	8
Chris Frank	49	3	9	12	255	42	3	7	10	229	2	0	1	1	2
Tristan Harper	57	3	5	8	70	47	3	5	8	62	2	0	0	0	2
Zach Sullivan	62	1	7	8	2	52	1	7	8	2	2	0	0	0	0
Kyle Jones (N)	62	0	2	2	0	52	0	2	2	0	2	0	0	0	0
Jeff Smith	24	0	2	2	75	23	0	2	2	75					
Winning shots		2		2			1		1			0			
Bench penalties					10					6					0
TEAM TOTALS	62	219	386	605	1419	52	190	337	527	1212	2	4	7	11	30
Netminders	GPI	Mins	SOG	GA	Sv%	GPI	Mins	SOG	GA	Sv%	GPI	Mins	SOG	GA	Sv%
Kyle Jones	62	3703	1853	155	91.6	52	3093	1530	132	91.4	2	124	72	5	93.1
Joe Myers	3	34	16	2	87.5	3	34	16	2	87.5					
Winning shots				1					1					0	
Empty net goals			1	1				1	1				0	0	
TEAM TOTALS	62	3737	1870	159	91.5	52	3127	1547	136	91.2	2	124	72	5	93.1

Shutouts: Kyle Jones (9) – cup: 14 Sept at Edinburgh Capitals (22 saves), 28 Sept at Hull Stingrays (30), 1 Nov v Dundee Stars (32), 21 Feb v Dundee Stars (39), 22 Feb at Dundee Stars (18); league: 11 Oct at Edinburgh Capitals (15), 12 Oct at Dundee Stars (24), 4 Jan at Edinburgh Capitals (15), 7 Feb v Belfast Giants (36).

All Competitions = league, play-offs and cup.

Two games were played for league and cup points.

Clanti-climax

RONNIE NICHOL

The Clan came within a whisker of the Elite League's main prize, losing out on the regular season title to Sheffield Steelers in a race that went to the final weekend.

In his second year behind the bench, **Ryan Finnerty** hired AHL tough guy **Zack Fitzgerald** on defence, and ex-Nottingham Panther **Leigh Salters** and former Steeler **Stefan Meyer** up front. Meyer was hailed as the marquee signing.

The core of the side returned, including goalie **Kyle Jones**, defenders **Chris Frank** and **Scott Aarssen**, and skilful forward **Neil Trimm**.

Clan's British line-up was bolstered by **Ben Davies** from Cardiff Devils and youngster **Zach Sullivan** from the English Premier League.

After a brilliant start when they won their first four games, the Clan went top of the league on 18 October. From that point on they were never out of the top three.

A potent partnership was struck up between Trimm and new signing **Scott Pitt**, with both men hanging around the top of the scoring charts up to the turn of the year.

With Jones in great form - he led the league in shutouts early on - and the crowds increasing, there was a real buzz around the place.

Then in late January the team were shocked by Coventry Blaze in the quarter-finals of the Challenge Cup. Clan's 3-1 lead in the first leg at the Skydome was blown in their own barn, and they went on to lose in the shootout.

Things were never quite the same after that.

Moreover, the Clan's sometimes overly physical play (Frank and Fitzgerald were among the league's top three bad boys) resulted in several bans, and with some players nursing niggling injuries, depth became a problem.

League losses in Sheffield (2-0) and Nottingham (6-0) and a shock 2-1 reverse in Edinburgh doomed them to the runners-up spot.

The consolation prize was Champions Hockey League qualification.

In the play-off quarters, seventh place Hull Stingrays eliminated the Clan, whose top five league scorers tallied only one goal between them. But overall, this was the Clan's best season to date.

PLAYER AWARDS

Player of the Year	Leigh Salters
Supporters' Player	Leigh Salters
Best Forward	Leigh Salters
Best Defenceman	Jamie Fritsch
Coach's Player	Kyle Jones
Best Young Player	Zach Sullivan
Unsung Hero	Scott Aarssen

LEADING PLAYERS

Kyle Jones born *22 August 1983, North Delta, BC, Canada*
The goalie was the coach's go-to guy. Icy calm under pressure, he led the league with nine shutouts and was the main reason for the team's fine season.

Leigh Salters born *27 March 1989, London, Ontario, Canada*
One of the league's best power forwards, he could hit, score and scrap with the best of them.

MOST PROMISING PLAYER

Zach Sullivan born *14 July 1994, Redhill, Surrey, England*
Defenceman earned his soubriquet as the team's Young Player of the Year by being composed, never flustered, and playing a simple game. Previously with Basingstoke Bison.

FACT FILE 2014-15

Elite League	Runners-up
Conference:	First in Gardiner
Play-offs	Quarter-finalists
Challenge Cup	Quarter-finalists

HISTORY

Founded: March 2010 by a consortium headed by **Neil Black**, whose Aladdin Sports Management owns Nottingham Panthers.

Leagues: Elite League 2010-15.

Honours: Elite League, Gardiner Conference 2014-15, 2012-13.

BRAEHEAD CLAN *left to right,* *back row, standing:* Rachel Calderwood (physio), Zach Sullivan, Tristan Harper, Neil Trimm, Leigh Salters, Scott Pitt, Jamie Fritsch, Matt Haywood, Ben Davies, Ross Gaughan (equipment); *front row:* Joe Myers, Lee Esders, Zack Fitzgerald, Stefan Meyer, Matt Keith, Ryan Finnerty (head coach), Chris Frank, Scott Aarssen, Derek Roehl, Ryan Kavanagh, Kyle Jones.

photo: Al Goold

CARDIFF DEVILS

PLAYER	ALL COMPETITIONS					ELITE LEAGUE					PLAY-OFFS				
Scorers	GP	G	A	Pts	Pim	GP	G	A	Pts	Pim	GP	G	A	Pts	Pim
Joey Martin	64	27	57	84	49	50	21	46	67	45	2	1	0	1	0
Brent Walton	65	29	48	77	40	51	21	38	59	32	2	1	0	1	0
Jake Morissette	66	27	46	73	16	52	23	38	61	12	2	0	0	0	0
Joey Haddad	66	27	36	63	98	52	22	28	50	78	2	0	2	2	2
Andrew Lord	64	23	40	63	67	50	18	31	49	53	2	0	2	2	0
Andrew Hotham	66	21	39	60	149	52	18	33	51	137	2	1	0	1	0
Doug Clarkson	61	20	23	43	184	49	17	21	38	144	2	0	0	0	0
Chris Culligan	64	15	28	43	27	51	11	25	36	20	2	0	0	0	0
Carl Hudson	58	14	29	43	71	45	11	23	34	59	2	0	0	0	0
Matthew Myers	46	18	17	35	71	37	14	14	28	40	2	0	1	1	2
Tyson Marsh	63	8	25	33	88	51	8	21	29	82	2	0	0	0	0
Jesse Mychan	45	10	16	26	157	37	9	12	21	132	1	0	1	1	0
Mark Richardson	66	6	19	25	10	52	5	10	15	8	2	0	0	0	0
Trevor Hendrikx	58	5	13	18	182	45	4	10	14	145	2	0	0	0	0
Josh Batch	66	3	15	18	92	52	3	11	14	86	2	0	0	0	0
Chris Jones	66	2	9	11	22	52	2	8	10	16	2	0	0	0	0
Markku Tahtinen	20	3	4	7	16	15	2	4	6	12	2	0	0	0	2
Ben Bowns (N)	66	0	1	1	0	52	0	1	1	0	2	0	0	0	0
Luke Piggott	66	0	1	1	10	52	0	0	0	6	2	0	0	0	0
Winning shots		2		2			1		1			0		0	
Bench penalties					8					6					0
TEAM TOTALS	66	260	466	726	1357	52	210	374	584	1113	2	3	6	9	6
Netminders	GPI	Mins	SOG	GA	Sv%	GPI	Mins	SOG	GA	Sv%	GPI	Mins	SOG	GA	Sv%
Ben Bowns	64	3681	1728	158	90.9	51	2897	1326	130	90.2	2	120	53	6	887.0
Mike Will	9	299	160	16	90.0	8	239	115	14	87.8					
Winning shots			2					2					0		
Empty net goals		7	7				5	5					2	2	
TEAM TOTALS	66	3980	1895	183	90.3	52	3136	1446	151	89.6	2	120	55	8	85.5

Also appeared: Adam Harding; Lewis Turner 1.

Also played for: 1 Bracknell Bees.

Shutouts: Bowns (8) - cup: 26 Oct at Coventry Blaze (38 saves); league: 23 Nov v Edinburgh Capitals (22), 19 Dec at Fife Flyers (19), 30 Dec v Hull Stingrays (24), 18 Jan at Coventry Blaze (33), 8 Feb v Sheffield Steelers (24), 14 Feb at , Braehead Clan (23), *7 March v Dundee Stars (12).

Will - league: *7 March v Dundee Stars (14).   * shared

. All Competitions = league, play-offs and cup.   One game played for league and cup points.

CARDIFF DEVILS *left to right, back row:* Adam Harding, Luke Piggott, Chris Jones, Chris Culligan, Andrew Hotham, Josh Batch, Doug Clarkson, Jesse Mychan, Callum Buglass, Joey Haddad, Carl Hudson, Mark Richardson, David Owen (equipment); *front row:* Mike Will, Brent Walton, Jake Morrissette, Trevor Hendrikx, Todd Kelman (managing director), Tyson Marsh, Andrew Lord, Neil Francis (bench coach), Matthew Myers, Joey Martin, Ben Bowns.

Photo: Kris Agland

Happy days are here again!

ROB STUART

The Devils won their first silverware for nine years, gave the Elite League's front-runners the fright of their lives, qualified for the play-offs, and the fans flocked back.

What a difference good ownership makes.

When a 'consortium of Canadian businessmen' – completely unknown in the UK – took over the Devils in the off-season, the fans could be forgiven for being sceptical after the string of disastrous owners they had been saddled with for years.

The appointment of **Andrew Lord** as head coach didn't inspire them much, either, as the Canadian forward had only limited coaching experience. But he ended up as the journalists' choice for the league's Coach of the Year.

New general manager **Todd Kelman** earned immediate respect as he had a formidable CV from his multi-trophy-winning Belfast Giants and years of playing in the UK.

The club's recruiting proved fruitful, with a rugged core – the Devils were the league's second most penalised team – and three forwards, new boys **Joey Martin** and **Jake Morissette** and the returning **Brent Walton**, who finished in the top ten scorers,

Kelman took a chance on GB stopper **Ben Bowns**, an outstanding home-grown prospect, who was only 23. The gamble paid off as the Englishman racked up eight shutouts.

The key month was March. On the 8th, Lord and **Chris Culligan** scored in under two minutes and the Devils held on for a 2-1 win at Sheffield's Motorpoint Arena for the their first Challenge Cup in the Elite League era.

Then came the bigger challenge of finishing on top of the league table. After a difficult run-in, they needed to beat the Steelers in their own barn again. It wasn't to be.

On 21 March Sheffield avenged their Cup loss with a 2-1 victory. But the Devils ended only two points out of first place.

At the end of the month their attempt to reach the play-off weekend was halted when they were knocked out by a Coventry Blaze side which had been re-energised under their new, American coach.

PLAYER AWARDS

Players' Player	Joey Martin
Player of the Year	Ben Bowns
Most Valuable Player	Ben Bowns
Best Forward	Joey Martin
Best Defenceman	Andrew Hotham
Coach's Player	Tyson Marsh
Fans' Favourite	Trevor Hendrikx
Unsung Hero	Mark Richardson

LEADING PLAYERS

Andrew Hotham *born 29 August 1986, Barrie, Ontario, Canada*
The 6ft 2ins blueliner won the respect of the league with the honour as their Best Defenceman, and the respect of his opponents as one of the Devils' enforcers.

Joey Martin *born 29 July 1988, Thorold, Ontario, Canada*
Of the team's top points scorer, coach Lord said: "He's the complete package – skill, heart and determination – and plays his best in the most pressure-filled games. He's a good person, too."

MOST PROMISING PLAYER

Chris Jones *born 4 January 1991, Cardiff*
A tenacious forward who played in all situations, often against the opposition's top lines, he was always working to improve himself.

FACT FILE 2014-15

Elite League	Third
Conference	Third in Erhardt
Play-offs	Quarter-finalists
Challenge Cup	Winners

HISTORY

Founded 1986. Purchased from **Paul Ragan** in June 2014 by Canadian businessmen **Steve King**, **Craig Shostak**, **Brian Parker** and **Kelly Hughes**.

Leagues: Elite League 2003-15; British National League 2001-03; Superleague 1996-2001; British League, Premier Div. 1989-96; British League, Div. One 1987-89; British League, Div. Two 1986-87.

Honours: Challenge Cup 2014-15, 2005-06; Elite League Knockout Cup 2006-07.
See *The Ice Hockey Annual 2010-11* for earlier Honours.

COVENTRY BLAZE

PLAYER	ALL COMPETITIONS					ELITE LEAGUE					PLAY-OFFS				
Scorers	GP	G	A	Pts	Pim	GP	G	A	Pts	Pim	GP	G	A	Pts	Pim
Ryan O'Marra	62	19	37	56	80	47	15	23	38	68	4	1	4	5	2
Steven Goertzen	59	16	30	46	33	44	13	26	39	27	4	1	2	3	2
Ashley Tait	60	8	30	38	20	44	3	23	26	16	4	2	2	4	2
Ben Arnt	68	17	18	35	18	52	15	16	31	14	4	1	0	1	2
Jereme Tendler	59	18	12	30	20	45	13	11	24	18	3	2	0	2	0
Cale Tanaka	66	12	16	28	48	52	12	10	22	32	2	0	0	0	2
Derek Lee	44	9	16	25	10	31	7	12	19	4	4	1	1	2	0
Russell Cowley	67	7	17	24	33	52	5	12	17	31	4	0	4	4	0
Ross Venus	68	6	15	21	20	52	3	14	17	18	4	1	0	1	0
Jakub Sindel	44	12	8	20	47	35	9	7	16	45	3	0	0	0	0
Rory Rawlyk	34	6	14	20	36	27	5	9	14	24					
Craig Cescon	68	6	14	20	185	52	3	13	16	129	4	1	0	1	6
Justin DaCosta	44	2	17	19	31	36	1	16	17	25	4	1	1	2	0
Jim Jorgensen	24	2	12	14	44	17	2	9	11	38	4	0	2	2	2
Kyle Bochek	28	4	8	12	75	20	3	6	9	45					
James Griffin	52	6	4	10	22	38	4	4	8	12	4	0	0	0	0
Mike Egener	45	2	7	9	93	33	2	5	7	64	4	0	1	1	4
Mark Smith	56	2	4	6	32	40	2	2	4	26	4	0	0	0	0
Steven Chalmers	51	3	2	5	30	38	3	2	5	26	4	0	0	0	2
Vladimir Nikiforov	7	1	3	4	0	6	1	1	2	0					
Trevor Frischmon	3	1	1	2	0	3	1	1	2	0					
Gareth O'Flaherty	40	0	1	1	0	34	0	1	1	0	4	0	0	0	0
Brian Stewart (N)	68	0	0	0	28	52	0	0	0	24	4	0	0	0	0
Winning shots		7		7			5		5			1		1	
Bench penalties					20					16					0
TEAM TOTALS	68	166	286	452	925	52	127	223	350	702	4	12	17	29	24
Netminders	GPI	Mins	SOG	GA	Sv%	GPI	Mins	SOG	GA	Sv%	GPI	Mins	SOG	GA	Sv%
Brian Stewart	68	4088	2389	185	92.3	52	3115	1774	139	92.2	4	250	163	8	95.1
Connor Ranby	2	30	19	3	84.2	2	30	19	3	84.2					
Winning shots			2					1					0		
Empty net goals			2	2				2	2				0	0	
TEAM TOTALS	68	4118	2410	192	92.0	52	3145	1795	145	91.9	4	250	163	8	95.1

Also appeared: Sam Ellis (N), Niklas Ottoson, Dale White.

Shutouts: Stewart (4) – league: 6 Sept at Fife Flyers (31 saves), 13 Sept v Dundee Stars (33), 7 March v Edinburgh Capitals (29), 18 March at Hull Stingrays (38).

All Competitions = league, play-offs and cup

Chuck'd a trophy

ANTONY HOPKER

It was truly a season of two halves for the Blaze. What looked like being their worst campaign ever instead finished with them being crowned the Elite League's play-off champions.

The season started optimistically under returning coach **Marc LeFebvre**, with his self-styled 'blue collar' side. Unfortunately, they were short on creativity and structure.

Had it not been for the regular heroics of netminder **Brian Stewart**, the Blaze might have been further down the table than sixth when LeFebvre was released in November.

Injuries were also a factor, but the side lacked natural goal scorers. **Jereme Tendler** (from Hull Stingrays) and **Rory Rawlyk** (Dundee Stars) never looked comfortable.

After a brief period with ex-Sheffield Steelers forward **Steven Goertzen** and returning defenceman **Mike Egener** in charge, in came **Chuck Weber** from the Russian KHL.

With a glittering North American career behind him, he quickly put in place strict systems, intensive training and extra practices.

Some of the newcomers responded well – American university grad **Ben Arnt** started scoring, and ex-NHLer **Ryan O'Marra** became the warrior leader on the first line.

In the Challenge Cup, the Blaze completed an unlikely comeback to knock high-flying Braehead Clan out of the quarter-finals, before succumbing to a superior Cardiff Devils side.

Meanwhile, they had sunk to ninth in the league, their lowest ever position, setting several unwanted club records on the way. But they eventually levered themselves back to sixth.

It all came together at the perfect time. In the play-off quarter-finals they up-ended and out-coached the favoured Nottingham Panthers.

At the finals weekend Coventry saw off Belfast Giants in the semis – thanks in no small part to Stewart's heroics in the penalty shoot-out.

Weber's charges completed their extraordinary turn-around with a superlative first two periods in an enthralling final that knocked out league champs Steelers, almost ten years to the day after the Blaze last took the title.

PLAYER AWARDS

Players' Player	Brian Stewart
Player of the Year	Brian Stewart
Coach's Player	Brian Stewart
Best Forward	Ryan O'Marra
Best Defenceman	Brian Stewart
Best Plus/minus	James Griffin
Clubman of the Year	Mark Smith
Best British Player	Russell Cowley
Most Improved Player	Ross Venus

LEADING PLAYERS

Ryan O'Marra born 9 June 1987, Tokyo, Japan
The former Edmonton and Anaheim NHL forward signed off his career with a trophy and his team's scoring title, mostly down to his high work rate.

Brian Stewart born 19 February 1985, Burnaby, BC, Canada
Joint top goalie in the league, facing more shots (2,389) than any of his rivals, he was the engine behind his team's success, standing tall under attack and keeping them in games many times.

MOST PROMISING PLAYER

Ross Venus born 28 April 1994, Solihull, England
Though he started the year as the tenth forward, he spent most of it on the top lines. Didn't score as much as he promised but his game-winner in the play-off final was a highlight-reel moment.

FACT FILE 2014-15

Elite League	Sixth
Conference	Fifth in Erhardt
Play-offs	Champions
Challenge Cup	Semi-finalists

HISTORY

Founded: 2000, after the club moved from Solihull where they played as the Barons.
Leagues: Elite League 2003-15; British National League 2000-03.
Honours: Elite League 2009-10, 2006-08, 2004-05; Elite League Play-off Championship 2014-15, 2004-05; Challenge Cup 2006-07, 2004-05; Elite Knockout Cup 2007-08; British National League & Playoff Championship 2002-03.

COVENTRY BLAZE *left to right, back row:* Stephen Goertzen, Jim Jorgensen, Ashley Tait, Russell Cowley, Craig Cescon, James Griffin, Mark Smith; *middle row:* Vladimir Nikiforov, Ryan O'Marra, Jakub Sindel, Derek Lee, Justin DaCosta; *front row:* Ross Venus, Brian Stewart (lying on ice), Ben Arnt, Steven Chalmers, Cale Tanaka, Connor Ranby, Mike Egener, Jereme Tendler.

photo: Scott Wiggins.

DUNDEE STARS

PLAYER	ALL COMPETITIONS					ELITE LEAGUE				
Scorers	GP	G	A	Pts	Pim	GP	G	A	Pts	Pim
Chris Blight	47	11	31	42	45	40	9	23	32	30
Shane Lust	48	17	19	36	64	43	14	19	33	54
John Dolan	57	14	17	31	22	51	13	17	30	20
Igor Gongalsky	57	14	15	29	172	49	13	14	27	164
Kevin Quick	60	4	23	27	34	52	3	21	24	32
John Mitchell	25	11	15	26	32	19	8	8	16	26
Jeff Hutchins	56	5	20	25	119	49	5	19	24	76
Sean Ringrose	34	9	14	23	10	32	9	14	23	10
Ryan Grimshaw	50	7	13	20	55	47	6	13	19	55
Sam McCluskey	54	3	17	20	97	46	3	14	17	79
Martin Cingel	51	7	9	16	50	45	6	6	12	46
Matt Ryan	24	6	10	16	24	18	3	7	10	14
James Issacs	44	3	11	14	74	41	3	10	13	72
Bari McKenzie	58	7	6	13	54	50	7	6	13	34
Rob Ricci	15	6	4	10	8	10	5	2	7	2
Brad Plumton	58	3	7	10	366	50	2	5	7	313
Kyle Gibbons	14	4	4	8	12	14	4	4	8	12
Paul Swindlehurst	39	3	2	5	32	37	3	2	5	30
Timo Kuuluvainen	6	1	0	1	2	6	1	0	1	2
Lewis McIntosh	3	0	0	0	2	2	0	0	0	2
Joonas Liimatainen	11	0	0	0	4	6	0	0	0	0
Marc Cheverie (N)	60	0	0	0	2	52	0	0	0	2
Craig Holland (N)	60	0	0	0	2	52	0	0	0	2
Winning shots		6		6			6		6	
Bench penalties					8					8
TEAM TOTALS	60	141	237	378	1290	52	123	204	327	1085
Netminders	GPI	Mins	SOG	GA	Sv%	GPI	Mins	SOG	GA	Sv%
Marc Cheverie	59	3425	1868	206	89.0	51	2969	1626	178	89.1
Craig Holland	7	219	134	23	82.8	6	191	116	17	85.3
Winning shots				3					3	
Empty net goals			6	6				5	5	
TEAM TOTALS	60	3644	2008	238	88.1	52	3160	1747	203	88.4

Also appeared: Robbie Hill, Ziga Svete.

Shutouts: Cheverie – league: 8 Feb v Fife Flyers (29 saves).

All Competitions = league and cup.

Two games were played for league and cup points.

DUNDEE STARS *left to right, back row:* Andy Bell (physio), Sean Ringrose, Bari McKenzie, James Isaacs, Shane Lust, Paul Swindlehurst, Kyle Gibbons, Ryan Grimshaw, John Dolan, Sam McCluskey, Jack Inglis (equipment) Kevin Ward (equipment); *front row:* Marc Cheverie, Kevin Quick, Chris Blight, Jeff Hutchins, Martin Cingel, Igor Gongalsky, Brad Plumton, Craig Holland.

photo: Derek Black

Hutch's last stand

ALAN JOHNSTON

For the Stars' loyal fans, this was a season best forgotten, especially after the successes of 2013-14.

Over the summer of 2014 the club lost its way, despite the directors' significantly enhancing coach **Jeff Hutchins'** spending power.

Hutchins opted to rebuild with established veterans rather than reload with young, hungry players which had historically been club policy.

His job wasn't made any easier when netminder **Dan Bakala**, the Elite League's player of the year, and their top scorer, **Nico Sacchetti**, moved away. Former Sheffield Steelers' and Cardiff Devils' Anglo-Canadian forward **Chris Blight** turned out to be the Stars' highest scorer, but his output was a pale shadow of Sacchetti's.

Bakala's replacement, **Marc Cheverie**, was handicapped by persistent injury, though he showed flashes of brilliance late in the season.

On the blueline, **Ryan Grimshaw** and **James Isaacs** were unselfish and uncompromising, **Brad Plumton** brought personality, while the smooth skating **Kevin Quick** sparkled in his role as the team's puck moving defenceman.

Up front, the gritty and tenacious Kiev-born Canadian forward **Igor Gongalsky** fought for 60 minutes every night, and Scotsmen **Bari McKenzie** and John Dolan selflessly battled with their hearts on their sleeves.

The defeats began to accumulate from the first days of the season. By November the cracks were obvious to all. Despite upset victories over the Steelers and Nottingham Panthers, the Stars remained nailed to the cellar floor.

The coach stuck to his guns, however, firmly believing that the full-scale makeover of the club would eventually bring results. It didn't.

In a last desperate throw of the dice he opted for the 1-3-1 trap. It was painful to the eye and unsuited to the roster. When the dust settled the Stars could boast only six regulation wins, a mighty 14 points out of a play-off spot.

As this was the second time in Hutchins' three years behind the bench that the Stars had missed the play-offs, he was released at the end of the season.

PLAYER AWARDS

Player of the Year	John Dolan
Coach's Player	James Isaacs
Supporters' Player	Brad Plumton
Writers' Player	Kevin Quick
Most Improved Player	Craig Holland

LEADING PLAYERS

John Dolan born 8 January 1981, Dundee.
In his 13th season, the veteran forward lost little of his speed and agility. Combined with a good hockey brain, he was effective in all three zones.

Kevin Quick born 29 March 1988, Buffalo, New York
The hard working ex-NHL blueliner with Tampa Bay was the team's best playmaker, while adding leadership to the room and some razzle-dazzle to the arena.

MOST PROMISING PLAYER

Robbie Hill born 23 May 1994, Dundee
The defender played only a handful of senior games in his second season but he has the hunger and skill which will soon bring him more opportunities.

FACT FILE 2014-15

Elite League	Tenth
Conference:	Fifth
Play-offs	Did not qualify
Challenge Cup	Fourth in group

HISTORY

Founded: 2001 by the **Ward** brothers, **Charlie, Mike** and **Stephen**.
Leagues: Elite League 2010-15; Celtic League 2008-10; Scottish National League 2005-08; Northern League 2005-10; British National League 2001-05.
Honours: British National League Play-off Champions 2004-05 & 2001-02; British National League 2001-02; Caledonian Cup 2002.

EDINBURGH CAPITALS

PLAYER	ALL COMPETITIONS					ELITE LEAGUE				
Scorers	GP	G	A	Pts	Pim	GP	G	A	Pts	Pim
Rene Jarolin	53	30	26	56	10	47	29	22	51	8
Dennis Rix	58	17	28	45	24	52	17	27	44	20
Daniel Naslund	54	10	33	43	12	50	10	32	42	12
Greg Collins	53	17	25	42	68	48	16	23	39	62
Jade Portwood	53	19	19	38	63	47	18	18	36	59
Riley Emmerson	50	14	18	32	165	45	12	17	29	134
Richard Hartmann	40	13	17	30	24	34	12	15	27	20
Marcel Petran	53	3	24	27	78	47	3	22	25	64
Loren Barron	37	2	25	27	59	37	2	25	27	59
Lukas Bohunicky	36	1	13	14	31	33	1	13	14	29
Joe Grimaldi	18	3	6	9	165	14	2	6	8	102
Kyle Flemington	54	2	6	8	130	48	2	6	8	99
Jay King	58	3	4	7	36	53	1	3	4	28
Callum Boyd	46	1	5	6	32	40	1	4	5	30
Jordan Steel	53	3	1	4	6	47	3	0	3	6
Michal Benedik	11	0	2	2	16	11	0	2	2	16
Tomas Hiadlovsky (N)	58	0	2	2	75	52	0	2	2	73
Ashley Calvert	2	0	0	0	2	2	0	0	0	2
David Beatson	34	0	0	0	8	31	0	0	0	6
Sean Beattie	41	0	0	0	16	35	0	0	0	12
Winning shots		6		6			6		6	
Bench penalties					16					12
TEAM TOTALS	58	144	254	398	1036	52	135	237	372	853
Netminders	GPI	Mins	SOG	GA	Sv%	GPI	Mins	SOG	GA	Sv%
Kevin Forshall	1	51	39	3	92.3	1	51	39	3	92.3
Tomas Hiadlovsky	58	3474	2072	221	89.3	52	3111	1863	202	89.2
Craig Mallinson	1	8	10	2	80.0	1	8	10	2	80.0
Winning shots				6					5	
Empty net goals				4	4				3	3
TEAM TOTALS	58	3533	2125	236	88.9	52	3170	1915	215	88.8

Also appeared: Cam Brownley 1, Sean Donaldson, Graham Rodger (N), James Wallace.

Also played for: 1 Sheffield Steeldogs.

All Competitions = league and cup

Two games were played for league and cup points.

Runs and bans

ROB STUART

Another difficult season for the small budget Capitals ended with **Richard Hartmann**'s team in ninth place in the Elite League, just one point out of the play-offs.

A 6-3 defeat at high-flying Cardiff Devils in mid-March doomed them to miss out on the post-season fun for the second straight year.

Canadian defender **Kyle Flemington** explained: "We should have been a play-off team but we were hit pretty hard when guys were hurt or suspended. When we had a full bench we played pretty well and went on runs where we didn't lose for a month."

After returning for his fourth season as player-coach, Slovakian Hartmann was quick to snap up his fellow countryman, **René Jarolin**, who had twice top-scored for the club in 2011-13 but was not re-signed in 2013-14.

He also brought in three Slovakian defenders, **Michal Benadik**, **Lukas Bohunicky** and **Marcel Petran**, and goalie **Tomas Hiadlovsky**. "We are first and foremost a team with an attractive brand of European-rooted hockey," he said.

But, as insurance, he added some "grit and a bit of nastiness" in three North Americans - 6ft 7ins Flemington, **Riley Emmerson** 6ft 8in, and ex-Nottingham Panther **Joe Grimaldi**.

This was not a success. Emmerson was banned for 10 games in September (later reduced to three), and Grimaldi was fired in January after receiving an 18-game ban for some high jinks at his old team's arena.

As Flemington said, the Caps were streaky. Early on they endured a stretch of 13 games without a win, hitting rock bottom in November when they were demolished 10-0 in Cardiff.

Ironically, that triggered a seven-game unbeaten run when they picked up 13 from a possible 14 league points.

Another purple patch came in February with six wins out of seven, and Jarolin scoring four goals in one weekend on the way to his third club scoring title.

But overall Edinburgh lost almost half their games at Murrayfield and won only seven on the road. Hartmann duly paid the price with his job.

PLAYER AWARDS

Players' Player	Rene Jarolin
Player of the Year	Rene Jarolin

LEADING PLAYERS

René Jarolin born 16 September 1981, Skalica, Slovakia
After a season back in his home country, the slick winger returned and topped the scoring again, though with slightly fewer points.

Jade Portwood born 9 November 1988
Tenacious on the boards and never giving up on a play, the quietly spoken centreman was admired by fans and teammates alike.

MOST PROMISING PLAYER

Jay King born 1 February 1996, Edinburgh
The teenaged defenceman, who has represented his native Scotland four times at junior level, continued to improve in his first full senior season, with his forceful, intelligent play producing seven points.

FACT FILE 2014–15

Elite League	Ninth
Conference	Fourth in Gardiner
Play-offs	Did not qualify
Challenge Cup	Fifth in qualifying group

HISTORY

Founded: 1998. Previous teams in the Murrayfield rink were: *Murrayfield Royals* 1995-98, 1962-66, 1957-58; *Murrayfield Racers* 1966-94; *Edinburgh Racers* 1994-95; *Edinburgh Royals* 1958-61, 1952-56.

Leagues: *Capitals* - Elite League 2005-15; British National League 1998-2005; *Other teams* - see *The Ice Hockey Annual 2005-06*.

Past Honours: *Murrayfield Racers* - see *The Ice Hockey Annual 1998-99*.

EDINBURGH CAPITALS *left to right, back row:* Jordan Steel, James Wallace, Loren Barron, Jay King, Richard Hartmann; *middle row:* Jock Hay, Sean Beattie, Marcel Petran, Daniel Naslund, Riley Emmerson, Kyle Flemington, David Beatson, Michal Benadik, David Beatson snr. (equipment); *front row:* Kevin Forshall, Dennis Rix, Jade Portwood, Greg Collins, Rene Jarolin, Tomas Hiadlovsky.

photo: Jan Orkisz

FIFE FLYERS

PLAYER	ALL COMPETITIONS					ELITE LEAGUE					PLAY-OFFS				
Scorers	GP	G	A	Pts	Pim	GP	G	A	Pts	Pim	GP	G	A	Pts	Pim
Ned Lukacevic	62	28	38	66	70	52	25	32	57	34	2	1	0	1	0
Bobby Chaumont	62	27	37	64	20	52	18	30	48	18	2	0	0	0	0
Jordan Fulton	59	24	39	63	174	49	19	31	50	162	2	1	1	2	4
Matt Reber	55	22	39	61	40	50	20	37	57	24	2	0	1	1	12
Scott Fleming	62	26	33	59	100	52	22	30	52	67	2	0	0	0	0
Chris Auger	50	17	30	47	16	41	16	26	42	14	2	0	1	1	0
Jamie Milam	62	12	28	40	70	52	11	25	36	66	2	1	0	1	0
Kyle Haines	53	10	22	32	46	44	10	19	29	34	2	0	0	0	0
Danny Stewart	62	10	12	22	80	52	9	10	19	74	2	1	1	2	0
Matt Nickerson	54	3	18	21	231	46	2	15	17	192	2	0	0	0	4
Niko Suoraniemi	34	2	15	17	26	31	2	13	15	26	2	0	0	0	0
Stephen Gunn	62	6	2	8	12	52	5	2	7	8	2	1	0	1	0
Josh Scoon	61	3	4	7	20	51	2	2	4	16	2	0	0	0	0
Thomas Muir	59	0	7	7	104	49	0	5	5	89	2	0	1	1	2
Chris Wands	54	3	2	5	14	49	2	0	2	14	2	0	0	0	0
Jamie Wilson	62	2	3	5	12	52	2	3	5	8	2	0	0	0	0
Todd Dutiaume	3	1	2	3	4	2	1	1	2	4					
Kyle Horne	32	0	3	3	52	29	0	3	3	52					
Euan Forsyth	60	0	2	2	28	51	0	2	2	18	2	0	0	0	0
Allan Anderson	60	0	0	0	2	51	0	0	0	2	2	0	0	0	0
Winning penalty shots		5		5			4		4			0		0	
Bench penalties					16					12					0
TEAM TOTALS	62	201	336	537	1137	52	170	286	456	934	2	5	5	10	22
Netminders	GPI	Mins	SOG	GA	Sv%	GPI	Mins	SOG	GA	Sv%	GPI	Mins	SOG	GA	Sv%
Kevin Regan	60	3537	1831	181	90.1	51	3014	1570	160	89.8	2	119	51	6	88.2
Jack Asted	2	86	42	5	88.1										
Blair Daly	5	67	43	6	86.0	5	67	43	6	86.0					
Greg Blais	1	59	28	5	82.1	1	59	28	5	82.1					
Winning shots				2					2					0	
Empty net goals			7	7				7	7				0	0	
TEAM TOTALS	62	3749	1951	206	89.4	52	3140	1648	180	89.1	2	119	51	6	88.2

Also appeared: Renny Marr (N).

Shutouts: Regan (4) – league: 25 Oct v Dundee Stars (20 saves), 31 Dec at Edinburgh Capitals (29), 21 Feb v Hull Stingrays (24); cup: 27 Sept v Braehead Clan (23).

All Competitions = league, play-offs and cup

Two games were played for league and cup points

FIFE FLYERS *left to right, back row:* Chris Auger, Danny Stewart, Allan Anderson, Josh Scoon, Matt Reber, Euan Forsyth, Thomas Muir; *middle row:* Colin McAlpine (equipment), Matt Nickerson, Kyle Horne, Jamie Wilson, Stephen Gunn, Ned Lukacevic, Todd Dutiaume, Jamie Milam, Chris Wands, Scott Fleming, Jim Watson (trainer), Stewart Brown (equipment); *front row:* Kevin Regan, Jordan Fulton, Jack Wishart (club director), Kyle Haines, Tom Muir (club director), Bobby Chaumont, Blair Daly.

photo: Martin Watterston

Coming up short

ALLAN CROW *Fife Free Press*

Fife Flyers' season summed up in three words: coming up short.

The new players, who were unveiled as an upgrade on those who moved on, instead came up short.

The team came up one goal short in a thrilling play-off quarter-final comeback against league champions Sheffield Steelers.

The Challenge Cup quarter-finals were reached, only for the five-goal first leg loss to Nottingham Panthers to give them too much do to reach the semis. Short again.

The season began amid talk of a challenge for silverware, building on the momentum of their first Elite League play-off finals weekend.

At the heart of the team **Jordan Fulton, Scott Fleming** and **Kyle Haines** grafted every night, and netminder **Kevin Regan** was as reliable as ever.

Matt Nickerson brought intensity and physical dominance to the defence, but Fife were too reliant on the big man for protection. **Ned Lukacevic** dazzled and infuriated in equal measure.

There were highs - a stonking 6-1 win in Belfast, and three victories in Nottingham - but they lived in the shadow of Braehead Clan, and made heavy weather of putting clear blue water between themselves and Hull Stingrays and Edinburgh Capitals in the play-off race.

Each game night left the fans wondering if they'd see the real Flyers - gutsy, inspired and playing with a bit of swagger - or a group of players who seemed to conjure new ways to make the easiest of plays.

Too often the rink groaned in despair at yet another turnover.

The season ended on three straight losses. As the Flyers crawled into the play-offs in eighth and last spot you could feel the frustration in the dressing room.

The season came up short for Canadian centreman **Chris Auger**, too, when he was checked into the boards at the Cardiff bench. The door hadn't been secured, he crashed to the concrete and was out for weeks.

The freak accident somehow summed up the season.

PLAYER AWARDS

Fife Free Press *Mirror of Merit*	Kevin Regan
Players' Player	Kevin Regan
Player of the Year	Kevin Regan
Best Forward	Scott Fleming
Best Defenceman	Kyle Haines
Best British Player	Chris Wands
Most Improved Player	Chris Wands
Goal of the Year	Chris Wands

LEADING PLAYERS

Kyle Haines *born 26 September 1987, Weyburn, Saskatchewan, Canada.*
The heart of the team's defence, he was a respected figure on and off the ice, soaking up the ice time and laying it on the line every game.

Kevin Regan *born 25 July 1984, South Boston, Massachusetts, USA.*
The match-winning goalie set the highest standards for himself and was an integral part of the team every single night.

BEST YOUNG PLAYER

Chris Wands *born 23 March 1988, Kirkcaldy*
Local man became local hero in January with his tying marker against Cardiff Devils, which earned him the Goal of the Year award. After a mazy solo run, he chipped the puck off the back boards and netted his own rebound. Not bad for a stay-at-home defenceman.

FACT FILE 2014-15

Elite League	Eighth
Conference	Second in Gardiner
Play-offs	Quarter-finalists
Challenge Cup	Quarter-finalists

HISTORY

Founded: 1938.
Leagues: Elite League 2011-15; Northern League 2005-11, 1966-82; Scottish National League 2005-07, 1981-82, 1946-54, 1938-40; (*Findus*) British National League (BNL) 1997-2005; Northern Premier League (NPL) 1996-97; British League 1982-96, 1954-55.
Major Honours: See *The Ice Hockey Annual 2006-07.*

GUILDFORD FLAMES

PLAYER	*ALL COMPETITIONS					ENGLISH PREMIER LEAGUE					PLAY-OFFS				
Scorers	GP	G	A	Pts	Pim	GP	G	A	Pts	Pim	GP	G	A	Pts	Pim
David Longstaff	50	15	47	62	20	48	15	47	62	18	2	0	0	0	2
Matt Towe	50	13	46	59	62	48	13	45	58	62	2	0	1	1	0
Marcus Kristofferson (I)	45	24	29	53	26	43	22	28	50	22	2	2	1	3	4
Ben Campbell	49	11	27	38	20	47	11	27	38	20	2	0	0	0	0
Tom Duggan	33	9	24	33	24	31	9	22	31	24	2	0	2	2	0
Roman Tvrdon (I)	27	15	14	29	55	25	14	12	26	53	2	1	2	3	2
Danny Meyers	43	9	19	28	30	41	9	18	27	30	2	0	1	1	0
Branislav Kvetan (I)	47	13	13	26	137	45	12	13	25	137	2	1	0	1	0
Andrew McKinney	50	11	14	25	81	48	10	14	24	81	2	1	0	1	0
David Savage	46	11	13	24	24	44	11	13	24	24	2	0	0	0	0
Jez Lundin	50	10	12	22	48	48	10	11	21	48	2	0	1	1	0
Jozef Kohut (I)	25	10	11	21	38	25	10	11	21	38					
Vladimir Kutny (I)	27	11	9	20	37	25	11	9	20	37	2	0	0	0	0
Owen Fussey	19	10	5	15	8	19	10	5	15	8					
Paul Dixon	36	1	13	14	24	36	1	13	14	24					
Andrew Hemmings	43	2	7	9	18	43	2	7	9	18					
Curtis Huppe (I) 1	5	4	1	5	6	5	4	1	5	6					
Sam Godfrey	50	0	4	4	64	48	0	3	3	64	2	0	1	1	0
Neil Liddiard	49	0	3	3	73	47	0	3	3	73	2	0	0	0	0
Oliver Bronnimann	11	0	2	2	8	11	0	2	2	8					
Stuart Potts	6	0	1	1	4	6	0	1	1	4					
James Hadfield (N)	49	0	1	1	0	47	0	1	1	0	2	0	0	0	0
Gregg Rockman (N)	36	0	0	0	12	34	0	0	0	12	2	0	0	0	0
Winning shots		3		3			3		3			0		0	
Bench penalties					18					14					4
TEAM TOTALS	50	182	315	497	837	48	177	306	483	825	2	5	9	14	12
Netminders	GP	Mins	SOG	GA	Sv%	GP	Mins	SOG	GA	Sv%	GP	Mins	SOG	GA	Sv%
James Hadfield	49	1850	985	85	91.4	47	1730	936	79	91.6	2	120	49	6	87.8
Gregg Rockman	34	1151	643	61	90.5	34	1151	643	61	90.5					
Sam Calder	15	4	6	1	83.3	15	4	6	1	83.3					
Winning shots			2					2					0		
Empty net goals			2	2				1	1				1	1	
TEAM TOTALS	50	3005	1636	151	90.8	48	2885	1586	144	90.9	2	120	49	7	85.7

Also appeared: Milos Melicherik.

Also played for: 1 Belfast Giants, Milton Keynes Lightning.

Shutouts: Hadfield – cup: 28 Sept v Wightlink Raiders (25 saves).

*All competitions = league and play-offs only. EIHA did not record player statistics for English Challenge Cup.

(I) ITC holder

Tigers on their backs

ANDY SMITH

With the English Premier League (EPIHL) being shaken up by Red Hockey's takeover of Telford Tigers, the Flames had to settle for second place and the runners-up prize of £5,000 from UK media company IMP-UK.

After a rare trophy-less season in 2013-14, coach **Paul Dixon** released **Andrew Sharp, Nicky Watt, Mark Lee, Dean Holland** and **Martin Opatovsky**. Experience was brought in with the GB and Elite League trio of defenceman **Danny Meyers** (Sheffield) and forwards **Matt Towe** (Braehead) and **Owen Fussey**.

Returnee **Ollie Bronnimann**, GB junior blueliner **Sam Godfrey** and gritty Canadian forward **Andrew McKinney** completed his signings.

After the Flames' inconsistent form in the first months of the season, Dixon released Fussey, Bronnimann and Canadian **Curtis Huppe** and signed two Slovaks, **Roman Tvrdon** and Vladimir **Kutny**. The changes brought immediate results.

The season was dominated by the rivalry with the newly rich Tigers, who won all eight of the teams' head-to-heads.

After their first defeat – 7-1 at the Spectrum - Dixon admitted: "You'd have to go back many years to find a game where we failed to that degree." The following night he dropped a number of players for the narrow 4-3 Cup win at the National League's (NIHL) Chelmsford Chieftains.

The real Cup challenges came from the EPIHL teams. But even with Telford seeded into the other division the Flames only reached the runners-up spot again, this time in a three-way tie with Swindon Wildcats and Milton Keynes Lightning.

They met the Tigers in the semi when their early 3-0 lead was overturned for a 4-3 loss, and then followed by a 5-2 defeat in Shropshire.

Aside from the top spot, the league race was one of the closest for years. In the play-off quarter-finals the difference in league placing between Guildford and the Lightning was never going to be reflected on the ice.

The two sides duly battled to a 5-5 aggregate in the second leg in front of a sold-out Spectrum, only for **Lewis Hook** to give the Lightning a late winner. So for the first time the Flames failed to make the play-off finals weekend.

PLAYER AWARDS

Players' Player	Marcus Kristofferson
Player of the Year	Marcus Kristofferson
Players' British Player	Matt Towe
Fans' British Player	James Hadfield
Sportsmanship Award	Andrew Hemmings

LEADING PLAYERS

James Hadfield *born 4 October 1992, Sheffield*
In his third season with the club, he started all their games from December and proved himself a genuine first choice netminder in this league.

Marcus Kristoffesen *born 22 January 1979, Osterunds, Sweden*
The team's leading marksman for the second year in a row, he was good under pressure, being their only top six scorer to pot goals in the play-offs. Fan favourite and potential legend.

MOST PROMISING PLAYER

Sam Godfrey *born 2 February 1994, Swindon*
After signing from Swindon, the former GB under-18 and under-20 defenceman was paired with experienced d-men to help his development. Coach showed confidence in him.

FACT FILE 2014-15

English Premier League	Runners-up
Play-offs	Quarter-finalists
English Challenge Cup	Semi-finalists

HISTORY

Founded: 1992.

Leagues: English Premier League (EPL) 2005-15; British National League (BNL) 1997-2005; (Southern) Premier League (PL) 1996-98; British League, Div. One 1993-96; English League 1992-93.

Honours: EPL Play-off Champions 2010-11; EPL 2012-13, 2011-12, 2007-08, 2005-06; English Premier Cup 2012-13, 2011-12, 2009-10, 2006-07; BNL Championship 2003-04, 2000-01, 1997-98; BNL 2000-01, 1997-98; Southern Premier League 1997-98; *ntl* Cup 2000-01; *Benson and Hedges* Plate 1998-99.

GUILDFORD FLAMES *left to right, back row:* Andrew Hemmings, Andy McKinney, Ben Campbell, Sam Godfrey, Jozef Kohut, Marcus Kristoffersson, Vladimir Kutny, Danny Meyers, Branislav Kvetan, Roman Tvrdon, David Savage, Tom Duggan; *front row:* Gregg Rockman, Stuart Potts (asst. coach), Jez Lundin, David Longstaff, Paul Dixon (head coach), Neil Liddiard, Milos Melicherik (asst. coach), Matt Towe, James Hadfield.

photo: Alan Bone

HULL STINGRAYS

PLAYER	ALL COMPETITIONS					ELITE LEAGUE					PLAY-OFFS				
Scorers	GP	G	A	Pts	Pim	GP	G	A	Pts	Pim	GP	G	A	Pts	Pim
Carl Lauzon	63	32	38	70	96	52	28	33	61	78	4	1	3	4	10
Cory Tanaka	60	28	36	64	28	51	26	25	51	22	2	2	2	4	2
Jordan Mayer	59	28	27	55	20	48	23	20	43	14	4	0	2	2	0
Eric Galbraith	63	24	27	51	77	52	17	26	43	64	4	5	0	5	4
Zach Hervato	49	16	24	40	74	41	12	22	34	66	4	2	2	4	6
Matty Davies	40	10	27	37	20	33	8	24	32	12					
Dominic Osman	63	12	24	36	32	52	10	22	32	22	4	2	0	2	4
Will Frederick	44	11	23	34	23	37	10	18	28	19	4	0	4	4	2
Brendan Jamison	58	1	20	21	26	47	0	17	17	24	4	1	2	3	0
Jordan Knox	34	7	13	20	6	31	7	13	20	4	2	0	0	0	2
Omar Pacha	50	4	15	19	98	43	4	14	18	92	4	0	0	0	4
Sam Towner	59	5	6	11	16	48	5	5	10	14	4	0	0	0	0
Yan Turcotte	57	1	10	11	229	46	1	10	11	164	4	0	0	0	8
C.J. Chartrain	15	1	7	8	8	11	0	5	5	4					
Jamie Chilcott	63	0	6	6	32	52	0	5	5	26	4	0	1	1	4
Matt Larke	11	1	3	4	2	7	0	1	1	2					
Pavel Gomeniuk	3	0	0	0	6	3	0	0	0	6					
Thomas Ralph	57	0	0	0	2	49	0	0	0	2	4	0	0	0	0
David Brown	63	0	0	0	18	52	0	0	0	12	4	0	0	0	2
Winning shots		4		4			3		3			0		0	
Bench penalties					16					14					0
TEAM TOTALS	63	185	306	491	829	52	154	260	414	661	4	13	16	29	48
Netminders	GPI	Mins	SOG	GA	Sv%	GPI	Mins	SOG	GA	Sv%	GPI	Mins	SOG	GA	Sv%
David Good	1	4	3	0	100.0	1	4	3	0	100.0					
David Brown	63	3790	2213	218	90.1	52	3150	1775	179	89.9	4	214	163	10	93.9
Jeff Lill	1	30	20	5	75.0						1	30	20	5	75.0
Winning shots				6					6					0	
Empty net goals			7	7				7	7				0	0	
TEAM TOTALS	63	3824	2243	236	89.5	52	3154	1785	192	89.2	4	244	183	15	91.8

Also appeared: Scott Robson, Tom Stubley.

Shutouts: Brown – league: 18 Oct v Edinburgh Capitals (21 saves), 18 March v Coventry Blaze (30).

All Competitions = league and cup.

One game was played for league and cup points.

HULL STINGRAYS *left to right, back row:* Jordan Knox, Jordan Mayer, Cory Tanaka, Dominic Osman, Eric Galbraith, Will Frederick, Tom Ralph, Jamie Chilcott, Tom Stubley, Sam Towner, Ben Neves (physio); *front row:* David Brown, Brendan Jamison, Carl Lauzon, Matty Davies, Omar Pacha, Bobby McEwan (club owner), Zach Hervato, Yan Turcotte, David Good, Jeff Lill.

photo: Arthur Foster

'Rays find sting

CATHY WIGHAM *Hull Daily Mail*

Bobby McEwan didn't so much throw the baby out with the bathwater, as demolish the entire bathroom in his summer Stingrays team revamp.

The club's owner retained just two of 2013-14's 11 imports - rookie coach **Omar Pacha** and his side-kick **Carl Lauzon**, who replaced reluctant departee **Sylvain Cloutier**.

Only four of the club's British contingent survived the cull.

In came a raft of new signings, most of whom had never played in Britain and few fans had actually heard of.

If McEwan had been running a popularity contest, he would not have been among the front-runners.

But nine months later, few were complaining as the Stingrays made the Elite League's play-off semi-finals.

Only a last-minute, controversial goal against league champs Sheffield Steelers put paid to Stingrays' final hopes.

HULL CAN COMPETE WITH THE BEST

At Nottingham, neutral fans were woken up to the fact that the Stingrays could compete with the best the league had to offer – a fact the Hull fans had grasped before Christmas.

True, they only finished seventh in the league, but Pacha's bunch of largely unknown imports like forwards **Jordan Mayer** and Eric Galbraith did the business, as did the likes of **Brendan Jamison** and **Yan Turcotte** on defence and **David Brown** in goal.

Arguably, only a run of injuries and the early-season departures for "personal reasons" of players like **Kurtis Dulle**, **Matt Larke** and **CJ Chartrain** prevented the club from grabbing sixth.

"When we recruited last summer we picked a lot of guys straight out of university," said McEwan. "A lot of people doubted us and said we would finish bottom of the table with kids, but the thing with kids is they're ambitious."

"We gave them a platform to play in a good league in Europe and put themselves in the shop window, and there's no better shop window than going to the [Elite's] final four."

PLAYER AWARDS

Players' Player	David Brown
Supporters' Player of the Year	David Brown
Coach's Player	Eric Galbraith
Best Forward	Carl Lauzon
Best Defenceman	Brendan Jamison
Rookie of the Year	Jordan Mayer

LEADING PLAYERS

David Brown *born 1 February 1985, Stoney Creek, Ontario, Canada*
Netminder signed on a two-year deal to incorporate his Executive MBA programme at the local university. A consistent performer, a reliable team-mate and a favourite of the fans.

Eric Galbraith *born 8 April 1988, Quesnel, BC, Canada*
At 6ft 4ins, he cut an imposing figure. Very speedy, good fore-checker and racked up the points.

MOST PROMISING PLAYER

Tom Stubley *born 30 November 1998, York*
The locally-trained defenceman has great vision, makes good passes and skates well. Good all-round game. Arrived on the big stage with an MOM performance at the NIC in the third/fourth place play-off.

FACT FILE 2014-15

Elite League	Seventh
Conference	Third in Gardiner
Play-offs	Semi-finalists
Challenge Cup	Fifth in qualifying group

HISTORY

Founded: 2003. Bought by former player **Bobby McEwan** in June 2012. Previous Hull teams were *Thunder* 1999-2003, *Kingston Hawks* 1996-99, *Humberside (Sea) Hawks* 1988-96.
Leagues: Elite League 2006-15; English Premier League 2005-06; British National League 2003-05.
Honours: None. *Humberside Hawks* – British League, Div One 1990-91; English League 1988-89.

MANCHESTER PHOENIX

PLAYER	ALL COMPETITIONS					ENGLISH PREMIER LEAGUE					PLAY-OFFS				
Scorers	GP	G	A	Pts	Pim	GP	G	A	Pts	Pim	GP	G	A	Pts	Pim
Frantisek Bakrlik (I)	49	41	47	88	136	45	37	44	81	132	4	4	3	7	4
Robin Kovar (I)	52	33	49	82	93	48	29	45	74	89	4	4	4	8	4
Tony Hand	48	11	49	60	36	44	11	45	56	36	4	0	4	4	0
Michal Psurny (I)	42	19	33	52	6	41	19	33	52	6	1	0	0	0	0
Shaun Thompson	52	22	28	50	26	48	20	27	47	24	4	2	1	3	2
Adam Walker	46	14	25	39	8	42	13	23	36	6	4	1	2	3	2
James Archer	44	13	22	35	32	40	11	17	28	28	4	2	5	7	4
Bobby Chamberlain	50	13	14	27	54	46	12	14	26	54	4	1	0	1	0
Johan Burlin (I)	52	6	13	19	56	48	5	10	15	52	4	1	3	4	4
Joe Graham	43	3	14	17	81	39	3	12	15	77	4	0	2	2	4
Ben Wood	50	4	11	15	32	46	3	11	14	28	4	1	0	1	4
James Neil	50	2	10	12	18	46	2	10	12	18	4	0	0	0	0
Jacob Corson-Heron	39	3	4	7	20	35	2	3	5	20	4	1	1	2	0
Jack Watkins	39	4	2	6	8	35	4	2	6	6	4	0	0	0	2
Luke Boothroyd	26	2	4	6	22	26	2	4	6	22					
Jared Dickinson	47	2	3	5	4	43	2	3	5	4	4	0	0	0	0
Stephen Fone (N)	48	0	1	1	0	44	0	1	1	0	4	0	0	0	0
Declan Ryan (N)	51	0	1	1	2	47	0	1	1	2	4	0	0	0	0
Winning shots		4		4			4		4			0		0	
Bench penalties					16					14					2
TEAM TOTALS	52	196	330	526	650	48	179	305	484	618	4	17	25	42	32
Netminders	GP	Mins	SOG	GA	Sv%	GP	Mins	SOG	GA	Sv%	GP	Mins	SOG	GA	Sv%
Stephen Fone	52	1848	1176	102	91.3	44	1608	1021	86	91.6	4	240	155	16	89.7
Declan Ryan	47	1313	734	72	90.2	47	1313	734	72	90.2					
Winning shots				4					4					0	
Empty net goals			3	3				3	3				0	0	
TEAM TOTALS	52	3161	1913	181	90.5	48	2921	1758	165	90.6	4	240	155	16	89.7

Also appeared: Cade King, Gareth O'Flaherty.

Shutouts: Ryan (3) – cup: *25 Oct at Solway Sharks (10), 2 Nov at Blackburn Hawks (21),

7 Dec v Bracknell Bees (26). * shared with Harry Greaves

All competitions = league and play-offs only. EIHA did not record player statistics for the English Challenge Cup.

(I) ITC holder

A big Hand for Tony

MIKE APPLETON

It was always going to be a tough ask, backing up the successes of the 2013-14 season in an increasingly competitive English Premier League, but the Phoenix never expected it to be as difficult as it turned out.

Player-coach **Tony Hand MBE** retained the top scorers from his title-winning side - **Michal Psurny, Robin Kovář** and **Frantisek Bakrlik** - and added Swede **Johan Burlin** to replace **Robert Schnabel,** their 'irreplaceable' rock in defence.

He recruited three forwards - ex-Phoenix **Adam Walker** from Telford Tigers, **Bobby Chamberlain** (Hull Stingrays) and **Shaun Thompson** (Bracknell Bees). Hand himself iced alongside returnee **James Archer.**

The coach's insistence that he would limit his ice-time "to allow youth to come through" was tested early on due to long-term injuries.

49 ASSISTS FOR 47-YEAR-OLD

Defenceman **Luke Boothroyd,** the 2013-14 player of the year, missed almost half the league campaign and all the play-offs, while Archer and Psurny were also sidelined.

Consequently, the coach dressed for 48 league and play-off games, and notched 60 points, mostly assists, of course.

The Phoenix's failure to win close games cost them dear. The keys to the previous season's trophies – scoring prowess and the ability to grind out results – were missing.

A case in point was Telford Tigers, one of their greatest challengers. The Phoenix lost seven of the sides' eight meetings, including the two-legged Cup final.

They finished the league campaign in a disappointing sixth place, but eased past Swindon Wildcats and Milton Keynes Lightning in the play-offs.

That brought a match-up with Peterborough Phantoms in the showpiece final, but Manchester couldn't outwit their opponent's energetic style. This wasn't surprising, perhaps, after such an injury-riddled season.

It was a sad way to end Hand's illustrious career, but he left the ice to a standing ovation from the huge crowd in Coventry.

PLAYER AWARDS

Players' Player	Stephen Fone
Player of the Year	Frantisek Bakrlik
Coach's Player	James Neil
Best Forward	Frantisek Bakrlik
Best Defenceman	Ben Wood
Best Utility Player	Jack Watkins
Fans' Favourite	Robin Kovář
Unsung Hero	Jacob Corson-Heron

LEADING PLAYERS

Frantisek Bakrlik born 2 June 1983, Litvinov, Czech Republic
Club's top scorer in his second season, he was their 'go to' forward, whose speed and strength intimidated the opposition.

Shaun Thompson born 13 July 1987, Slough, England
The former Bracknell Bee was clean, efficient and workmanlike, a vital component of the team's second and - when needed - third line.

MOST PROMISING PLAYER

Jared Dickinson born 30 November 1994, Salford, England
Energetic, pacey and tough, the forward from the second team Minotaurs had limited ice time but was important in the run to the Cup final.

FACT FILE 2014-15

English Premier League	Sixth
Play-offs	Finalists
English Challenge Cup	Finalists

HISTORY

Founded: 2003 by **Neil Morris.** Played at Manchester's MEN Arena in season 2003-04, moved to the Altrincham Ice Dome in February 2007. Did not play in seasons 2004-06.
Leagues: English Premier League 2009-15, Elite League 2006-09, 2003-04.
Honours: English Premier League 2013-14, 2010-11; English Premier League play-offs 2012-13.

MANCHESTER PHOENIX *left to right, back row:* Dale Gibbon (equipment), Craig Cooke (equipment), Shaun Thompson, Jared Dickinson, Johan Burlin, Adam Walker, Frantisek Bakrlik, Robin Kovar, Joe Graham, Michal Psurny, Jack Watkins, Bobby Chamberlain, Paul Turner (equipment); *front row:* Declan Ryan, James Neil, Ben Wood, Luke Boothroyd, Neil Morris (club owner), Tony Hand MBE, James Archer, Jacob Corson-Heron, Stephen Fone.

photo: Richard A Allan.

MILTON KEYNES LIGHTNING

PLAYER	*ALL COMPETITIONS					ENGLISH PREMIER LEAGUE					PLAY-OFFS				
Scorers	GP	G	A	Pts	Pim	GP	G	A	Pts	Pim	GP	G	A	Pts	Pim
Milan Kostourek (I)	51	39	32	71	124	48	38	31	69	122	3	1	1	2	2
Blaz Emersic (I)	51	21	28	49	14	48	19	27	46	12	3	2	1	3	2
Lewis Hook	49	23	22	45	14	46	21	20	41	14	3	2	2	4	0
Petr Horava (I)	46	8	29	37	106	43	8	29	37	104	3	0	0	0	2
Jordan Cownie	44	11	25	36	18	41	10	22	32	18	3	1	3	4	0
Adam Carr	51	12	23	35	20	48	12	20	32	18	3	0	3	3	2
Leigh Jamieson	50	11	20	31	84	47	11	19	30	84	3	0	1	1	0
Michael Farn	39	2	20	22	57	36	2	20	22	55	3	0	0	0	2
Stanislav Lascek (I) 3	20	9	9	18	14	20	9	9	18	14					
Curtis Huppe (I) 1	19	7	6	13	0	16	4	6	10	0	3	3	0	3	0
Grant McPherson	47	3	10	13	171	44	3	9	12	171	3	0	1	1	0
Ross Bowers	49	3	10	13	42	46	3	9	12	42	3	0	1	1	0
Marek Curilla (I)	12	4	8	12	8	12	4	8	12	8					
Ben Russell	44	1	8	9	10	41	1	8	9	8	3	0	0	0	2
Ross Green	37	1	6	7	26	37	1	6	7	26					
Tom Carlon	10	3	3	6	18	10	3	3	6	18					
John Connolly	25	1	5	6	33	22	0	4	4	33	3	1	1	2	0
Chris Wiggins 2	35	2	2	4	91	32	1	2	3	87	3	1	0	1	4
Lewis Christie	47	0	4	4	67	44	0	4	4	67	3	0	0	0	0
Connor Goode	15	0	2	2	0	15	0	2	2	0					
Nick Poole (I)	1	0	1	1	4	1	0	1	1	4					
Nidal Phillips	27	0	1	1	14	24	0	1	1	14	3	0	0	0	0
Stephen Wall (N)	48	0	1	1	0	45	0	1	1	0	3	0	0	0	0
Winning shots		2		2			2		2			0		0	
Bench penalties					18					18					0
TEAM TOTALS	51	163	275	438	953	48	152	261	413	937	3	11	14	25	16
Netminders	GP	Mins	SOG	GA	Sv%	GP	Mins	SOG	GA	Sv%	GP	Mins	SOG	GA	Sv%
Stephen Wall	48	2003	1281	117	90.9	45	1824	1159	107	90.8	3	179	122	10	91.8
Jordan Hedley	46	1052	612	70	88.6	46	1052	612	70	88.6					
Damien King	2	31	14	4	71.4	2	31	14	4	71.4					
Winning shots			2					2					0		
Empty net goals			5	5				3	3				2	2	
TEAM TOTALS	51	3086	1912	198	89.6	48	2907	1788	186	89.6	3	179	124	12	90.3

Also appeared: Aidan Archer (N), Edward Knaggs, Jamie Line, Ryan Lubbock (N), Josh Nicklin, Alex Whyte.

Also played for: 1 Belfast Giants, Guildford Flames; 2 Bracknell Bees; 3 Sheffield Steeldogs.

Shutouts: Hedley – league: 11 Oct v Bracknell Bees (29 saves).

*All competitions = league and play-offs only. EIHA did not record player statistics for the English Challenge Cup.

(I) ITC holder

MILTON KEYNES LIGHTNING *left to right, back row:* Milan Kostourek, John Connolly, Edward Knaggs, Lewis Christie, Lewis Hook, Ben Russell, Jordan Cownie, Ross Green; *middle row:* Bob Marshall (match night co-ordinator), Daniel Watkins (stick boy), Andy Watkins (mascot), Dave Bunyan (supporters club chairman), Alex Whyte, Petr Horava, Blaz Emersic, Curtis Huppe, Chris Wiggins, Nidal Phillips, Ross Bowers, Michael Farn, Andy Richardson (equipment), Digory Little (match night co-ordinator), Ashley Page (physio); *front row:* Jordan Hedley, Lewis Clifford (asst. coach), Grant McPherson, Harry Howton (club chairman), Adam Carr, Vito Rausa (manager), Leigh Jamieson, Nick Poole (coach), Stephen Wall.

Photo: Tony Sargent.

Home but not Huppe

PAUL BROOKMAN

The Lightning endured the worst season in their 13-year history, finishing seventh in the English Premier League, their lowest ever position.

The campaign was saved only by their qualification for the play-off finals weekend.

The Lightning had played their home games in Coventry's Skydome during 2013-14 while their home rink was refurbished. When the Leisure Plaza wasn't ready for the new term, they had to stay in Coventry until late October.

Coach **Nick Poole** said: "Looking back, we all thought coming back into the old place would kick-start our season and life would be easy. Unfortunately it wasn't, and losing a key player like **Tom Carlon** was a tough blow, too."

The crowds packed the Plaza for the first home game only for Sheffield Steeldogs to spoil the party with a 2-1 win.

Popular ex-MK forward **Chris Wiggins** returned in Carlon's place but when results didn't improve, import **Stan Lascek** - the previous season's top scorer - was axed in late November.

In came Czech, **Marek Curilla**, but he failed to impress and was released in favour of Guildford Flames stalwart, **Curtis Huppe**. But the veteran Canadian was clearly unfit.

Poole's one successful overseas recruit was Czech forward **Milan Kostourek** who ended the year as the team's top points scorer. Indeed, without him the Lightning might have struggled to qualify for the play-offs.

The capture of 18-year-old **Lewis Hook** from Peterborough Phantoms was also a shrewd move as he finished among the leading scorers.

In the play-offs, the Lightning managed to avoid league winners Telford Tigers by moving up to seventh place in the last month. Instead, they stunned runners-up Guildford to qualify for the finals.

In Coventry, however, their hopes were ended in the semi-final by Manchester Phoenix. In a close fought game, they conceded two late, empty-net goals and went down 7-4.

Despite the poor campaign, the fans were still shocked when Poole was 'kicked upstairs' to be general manager and his place was taken by GB's head coach **Pete Russell**.

PLAYER AWARDS

Players' Player	Lewis Hook
Most Valuable Player	Milan Kostourek
Top Scorer	Milan Kostourek
Best Defenceman	Ross Green
Coach's Award	Grant McPherson
Most Improved Player	Lewis Hook

LEADING PLAYERS

Blaz Emersic born 10 October, 1980, *Ljubljana, Slovenia*
Returned to his best form in his fifth full season and formed a fruitful alliance with Cownie and Hook.

Milan Kostourek born 9 January 1983, *Czech Republic*
A fan favourite as he dazzled defences with his silky skills, ending as the team's top scorer and sixth best in the league.

MOST PROMISING PLAYER

Lewis Hook born 18 August 1996, *Peterborough, Cambridgeshire*
Showed maturity far beyond his years, ripping apart defences on numerous occasions. A key part of GB's under-20 silver medal world championship team.

FACT FILE 2014-15

English Premier League	Seventh
Play-offs	Semi-finalists
English Challenge Cup	Third in qualifying group

HISTORY

Founded: 2002 by **Harry Howton**. Run by rink operators Planet Ice since summer 2013.

The original club in Milton Keynes was formed in 1990 as *Kings*. Rink closed 1996-98 and 2013-14. Team played in Coventry's Skydome in 2013-14.

Leagues: *Lightning* English Premier League (EPL) 2002-15; *Kings* British National League 1999-2002; English League (Premier Div) 1998-99, 1990-91; British League, Premier Div 1994-96; British League, Div One 1991-94.

Honours: *Lightning* EPL 2009-10, 2003-05; EPL Play-offs 2002-06.

NOTTINGHAM PANTHERS

PLAYER	ALL COMPETITIONS					ELITE LEAGUE					PLAY-OFFS				
Scorers	GP	G	A	Pts	Pim	GP	G	A	Pts	Pim	GP	G	A	Pts	Pim
Chris Lawrence	61	25	38	63	135	51	18	34	52	113					
Robert Farmer	55	16	28	44	176	48	12	24	36	170	2	0	0	0	0
Robert Lachowicz	64	14	29	43	16	52	14	25	39	14	2	0	0	0	0
Cody Wild	48	11	29	40	16	38	7	26	33	6	2	1	2	3	4
Bruce Graham	49	16	23	39	62	37	14	17	31	48	2	0	1	1	2
Greg Jacina	58	14	23	37	121	47	13	17	30	107	2	0	0	0	4
Brandon Benedict	56	10	24	34	36	47	6	20	26	34	2	1	1	2	0
Chris Higgins	36	11	22	33	30	31	11	19	30	26	2	0	1	1	0
Jonathan Boxill	64	7	26	33	70	52	6	20	26	62	2	0	1	1	2
Guillaume Doucet	27	19	10	29	34	23	16	9	25	30	2	2	0	2	2
Evan Mosey	62	12	16	28	34	52	10	13	23	32	2	0	0	0	0
David Clarke	24	11	14	25	16	20	9	10	19	14					
Max Parent	45	11	12	23	77	36	9	9	18	67	2	0	0	0	2
Charles Landry	60	6	11	17	56	48	6	10	16	48	2	0	0	0	0
Stephen Lee	41	3	14	17	31	31	2	8	10	27	2	0	0	0	2
Nathan Robinson 1	18	5	11	16	40	13	3	11	14	11					
Mike Berube	61	2	14	16	34	51	2	12	14	30	2	0	0	0	0
Bryan Schmidt	64	2	8	10	61	52	2	7	9	46	2	0	0	0	0
Sam Oakford	54	2	5	7	14	44	1	5	6	8	2	0	0	0	0
Colby Cohen	14	2	4	6	33	12	2	3	5	31					
Jordan Cownie	2	1	0	1	2	1	1	0	1	0					
Lewis Hook	1	0	0	0	2										
Ollie Betteridge	7	0	0	0	2	5	0	0	0	2					
Craig Kowalski (N)	31	0	0	0	10	22	0	0	0	10					
Mattias Modig (N)	38	0	0	0	14	34	0	0	0	14	2	0	0	0	0
Winning shots		2		2			2		2						
Bench penalties					26					24					
TEAM TOTALS	64	202	361	563	1148	52	166	299	465	974	2	4	6	10	18

Netminders	GPI	Mins	SOG	GA	Sv%	GPI	Mins	SOG	GA	Sv%	GPI	Mins	SOG	GA	Sv%
Craig Kowalski	29	1638	778	65	91.6	21	1199	562	44	92.2					
Mattias Modig	34	1897	962	86	91.1	30	1697	863	76	91.2	2	120	56	5	91.1
Dan Green	11	342	137	17	87.6	9	260	97	12	87.6					
Winning shots				5					4					0	
Empty net goals			6	6				5	5				0	0	
TEAM TOTALS	64	3877	1883	179	90.5	52	3156	1527	141	90.8	2	120	56	5	91.1

Also appeared: Sam Gospel, Tom Hovell.

Also played for: 1 Belfast Giants.

Shutouts: Kowalski (4) - league: 16 Jan v Coventry Blaze (29 saves), 23 Jan at Belfast Giants (33), 1 Feb v Belfast Giants (30), 7 March v Braehead Clan (27).

Modig (2) – league: 29 Nov at Hull Stingrays (23 saves), 26 Dec at Sheffield Steelers (23).

All Competitions = league, play-offs and cup   *Two games were played for league and cup points.*

High price for Euro entry

MATT DAVIES *Nottingham Post*

Corey Neilson has only once failed to win major silverware since being appointed the Panthers' coach in 2008 – in his first season.

After the cupboard was left bare in 2014-15, bar the Erhardt Conference, the most successful coach in the club's history was relieved to be allowed to fight another day.

The season began with a roster that was high on speed, blessed with skill and heart, but lacking a heavyweight enforcer.

Panthers packed their bags for Europe, brimming with optimism as they took part in the first ever Champions Hockey League.

They were the tournament's rank outsiders, but they held their own against Finnish side Lukko Rauma and sprang a huge surprise by beating German DEL club Hamburg Freezers on their own ice.

Swedish team Luleå, who eventually won the title, were a cut above and Panthers went out at the first stage, but with their heads held high.

The experience took its toll. In the Elite League they lost, sometimes heavily, to the less regarded Edinburgh Capitals, Dundee Stars, Hull Stingrays and Fife Flyers.

With the pressure on, the players came out fighting during the festive season, beating eventual champions Sheffield Steelers twice, before winning nine of the next 12 games.

But that was as good as it got. They lost eight of the next nine with the only win coming against Sheffield in the first leg of the Challenge Cup semi-finals.

They were eventually knocked out of the Cup after crumbling in the second leg, ending their five-year grip on the trophy.

Having a huge hand in the defeat was a goaltender, briefly called up from the EPIHL, who had played in Nottingham as a boy and used to watch the Panthers. **Sam Gospel**'s shootout heroics for the Steelers inflicted the lowest point of a disappointing season on the Panthers' fans.

There was mitigation for falling short, most notably a horrendous run of injuries for the second year in a row, but the Erhardt Conference title was scant reward for a team that could have achieved more.

PLAYER AWARDS

Players' Player	Brandon Benedict
Player of the Year	Robert Farmer
Supporters' Player	Evan Mosey
Most Valuable Player	Chris Lawrence
British Player of the Year	Robert Farmer
Most Consistent Player	Charles Landry
Most Entertaining Player	Robert Farmer
The Gary Rippingale Trophy (Team Spirit)	
	Jonathan Boxill

LEADING PLAYERS

Robert Farmer *born 21 March 1991, Nottingham*
Stepped up to the plate, often taking on fights he couldn't win. Coupled with his runners-up spot in the club's scoring, it's easy to see why he was his team's talisman.

Chris Lawrence *born 5 February 1987, Toronto, Canada.*
The big (6ft, 2ins) centreman, blessed with a powerful shot and great skill, was the team's leading points scorer. But he divided opinion as some perceived his relaxed style as laziness.

MOST PROMISING PLAYER

Jordan Cownie *born 1 August 1995, Dundee*
The GB junior international was called up from the EPIHL for only a couple of Elite games, but he scored a goal and also showed promise in his two outings in the Champions Hockey League.

FACT FILE 2014-15

Elite League	Fourth
Conference	First in Erhardt
Play-offs	Quarter-finalists
Challenge Cup	Semi-finalists

HISTORY

Founded: 1946. Purchased by Aladdin Sports Management in 1997. Moved to National Ice Centre in 2000. Did not operate in 1960-80. **Leagues:** Elite League 2003-15; Superleague 1996-2003; British League (Premier Div) 1982-96 and 1954-60; English National League 1981-82 and 1946-54; Inter-City Lge 1980-82. **Honours:** Elite League 2012-13; Elite League Play-offs 2010-13, 2006-07; Challenge Cup 2009-14, 2007-08, 2003-04. Previous years in *The Ice Hockey Annual 2004-05.*

NOTTINGHAM PANTHERS

Robert Farmer

Greg Jacina

Robert Lachowicz

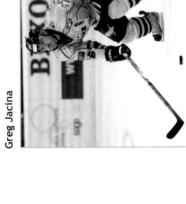

Brandon Benedict

Evan Mosey

Jonathan Boxill

photos: Nottingham Panthers & Nottingham Post.

PETERBOROUGH PHANTOMS

PLAYER	ALL COMPETITIONS					ENGLISH PREMIER LEAGUE					PLAY-OFFS				
Scorers	GP	G	A	Pts	Pim	GP	G	A	Pts	Pim	GP	G	A	Pts	Pim
Milan Baranyk (I)	50	27	35	62	55	46	24	35	59	53	4	3	0	3	2
Edgars Bebris (I)	49	24	35	59	55	45	23	29	52	28	4	1	6	7	27
Darius Pliskauskas (I)	44	28	24	52	20	40	25	21	46	18	4	3	3	6	2
Luke Ferrara	44	26	23	49	20	40	24	20	44	18	4	2	3	5	2
James Ferrara	51	9	34	43	52	47	8	33	41	46	4	1	1	2	6
Slava Koulikov (I)	45	9	31	40	12	41	8	29	37	12	4	1	2	3	0
Marc Levers	48	14	21	35	84	44	13	19	32	80	4	1	2	3	4
Tom Norton	52	6	22	28	48	48	5	21	26	48	4	1	1	2	0
Donatas Kumeliauskas (I)	21	10	12	22	16	17	9	10	19	6	4	1	2	3	10
Will Weldon	52	6	13	19	108	48	6	12	18	81	4	0	1	1	27
Edgars Apelis (I)	28	5	10	15	59	28	5	10	15	59					
Alan Lack	28	6	8	14	66	28	6	8	14	66					
James Hutchinson	28	1	9	10	30	28	1	9	10	30					
Cameron McGiffin	47	1	9	10	26	43	1	8	9	26	4	0	1	1	0
Scott Robson	45	4	3	7	28	41	3	3	6	26	4	1	0	1	2
Greg Pick	38	0	6	6	138	34	0	5	5	136	4	0	1	1	2
Jason Buckman	52	2	1	3	18	48	2	1	3	18	4	0	0	0	0
Robert Ferrara	20	0	3	3	8	16	0	2	2	8	4	0	1	1	0
Janis Auzins (I) (N)	50	0	3	3	47	46	0	3	3	47	4	0	0	0	0
Bradley Moore	21	1	1	2	4	19	1	1	2	4	2	0	0	0	0
Greg Blais (N)	4	0	1	1	0	4	0	1	1	0					
Connor Stokes	13	0	1	1	4	13	0	1	1	4					
James White	9	0	0	0	2	9	0	0	0	2					
Martins Susters (I)	20	0	0	0	4	16	0	0	0	4	4	0	0	0	0
Mason Webster	21	0	0	0	32	17	0	0	0	32	4	0	0	0	0
Nathan Pollard	18	0	0	0	2	18	0	0	0	2					
Winning shots		3		3			3		3			0		0	
Bench penalties					16					14					2
TEAM TOTALS	54	182	305	487	954	48	167	281	448	868	4	15	24	39	86
Netminders	GP	Mins	SOG	GA	Sv%	GP	Mins	SOG	GA	Sv%	GP	Mins	SOG	GA	Sv%
Janis Auzins (I)	50	3008	1854	154	91.7	46	2768	1716	146	91.5	4	240	138	8	94.2
Sam James	6	69	28	3	89.3	6	69	28	3	89.3					
Greg Blais	4	62	21	3	85.7	4	62	21	3	85.7					
Winning shots				2					2						
Empty net goals		9	9				9	9							
TEAM TOTALS						48	2899	1774	163	90.8	4	240	138	8	94.2

Also appeared: Ryan Fraley, Adam Long (N), Conor Pollard, Simon Price (N), Josh Wicks (N).

Shutouts: Auzins (2) – league: 16 Nov at Bracknell Bees (38 saves), 3 Jan v Bracknell Bees (27).

*All competitions = league and play-offs only. EIHA did not record player statistics for English Challenge Cup.

PETERBOROUGH PHANTOMS *left to right, back row:* Scott Glenwright (equipment), Connor Stokes, Brad Moore, Cam McGiffin, Scott Robson, Greg Pick, Mason Webster, Edgars Bebris, Martins Susters, Milan Baranyk, Donatas Kumeliauskas, Darius Pliskauskas, Jason Buckman, James White, Robert Ferrara, Will Weldon, Callum Owen (equipment), Rochelle Owen (physio); *front row:* Janis Auzins, Luke Ferrara, James Hutchinson, Lee Elias (development co-ordinator), James Ferrara, Slava Koulikov, Oleksandr Koulikov (coach), Marc Levers, Tom Norton, Adam Long.

photo: Tom Scott

Koulikov pulls off play-offs

ROB STUART

In his full season behind the Phantoms' bench, **Slava Koulikov** guided his men to their highest finish in the English Premier League for six years.

But that wasn't the best bit. They went on to capture the play-off trophy, beating league winners Telford Tigers and **Tony Hand**'s Manchester Phoenix in two enthralling games.

"This moment will stay in my life forever. I will not forget my first trophy as a coach."

Slava Koulikov. *Peterborough Telegraph*

The Russia-born Koulikov used his network of contacts to pick up some talented East Europeans during the off-season.

His key signings were Latvian forward **Edgars Bebris**, from league rivals Sheffield Steeldogs, his fellow countryman, netminder **Janis Auzins**, and Czech forward **Milan Baranyk**. Nottingham-born defenceman **Tom Norton** was welcomed back after a year tuning up his game in the Elite League with the Panthers.

Peterborough were never out of the top five all season, reached a high of third, and came within touching distance of contenders Guildford Flames and Basingstoke Bison.

Some of their most memorable games came against league favourites, Telford Tigers. January produced two wins - 5-4 in Telford at the start of the month and 3-2 at home at the end.

Auzins made 48 stops in the first game, which was only the second time the Tigers had been beaten on their own patch in 60 minutes.

The season will always be most warmly recalled for their play-off successes. Reaching Coventry by knocking out their great rivals Swindon Wildcats was satisfying in itself.

Facing the Tigers in the semi-final was a challenge the whole team were up for. Auzins was on top form, **Darius Pliskauskas** and **Luke Ferrara** each tallied three points and the Tigers were the unlikely losers.

In the final, the Phantoms built a 3-0 lead after only 13 minutes (Baranyk two goals, Bebris three assists) against the Phoenix and held on for their first silverware since their treble year of 2008-09.

PLAYER AWARDS

Players' Player	Edgars Bebris
Player of the Year	Janis Auzins
Most Valuable Player	Milan Baranyk
Coach's Player	James Ferrara
Best Forward	Milan Baranyk
Best Defenceman	Tom Norton
Most Improved Player	Greg Pick
Young Player of the Year	
	Cam McGiffin/Scott Robson
Unsung Hero	Dan Breen

LEADING PLAYERS

Janis Auzins born 8 May 1991, Riga, Latvia. A graduate of Russia's under-21 league, the six-foot goalie was the key to his team's fine season, winning games and performing minor miracles in their play-off triumph.

Milan Baranyk born 6 February 1980, Nove Mesto na Morave, Czech Republic Veteran adjusted quickly to the British game and ended as the club's top scorer. A former Czech junior international and Polish champion.

MOST PROMISING PLAYER

Cameron McGiffin born 26 July 1996, Bath, Somerset
The GB under-18 international from Swindon's youth system continued to improve his defensive skills in his second year in the league.

'Blood, Sweat & Tears – Ice Hockey in Peterborough' by **Stuart Latham** is now on sale.

FACT FILE 2014-15

English Premier League	Fourth
Play-offs	Champions
English Challenge Cup	Fourth in
	qualifying round

HISTORY

Founded: 2002 by **Phil Wing** and **Rob Housden**. In April 2015 the club was taken over by **Dave** and **Jo Lane**, directors of team sponsor *Dalrod*. The previous team in Peterborough was the *Pirates* 1982-2002.
League: English Premier League 2002-15.
Honours: League winners 2008-09, 2002-03; Play-offs 2014-15, 2008-09; Premier Cup 2008-09, 2003-04, 2002-03.
Pirates - see *The Ice Hockey Annual 2010-11*.

SHEFFIELD STEELERS

PLAYER	ALL COMPETITIONS					ELITE LEAGUE					PLAY-OFFS				
Scorers	GP	G	A	Pts	Pim	GP	G	A	Pts	Pim	GP	G	A	Pts	Pim
Mathieu Roy	68	46	55	101	50	52	36	43	79	42	4	4	2	6	0
Michael Forney	69	43	44	87	81	52	33	34	67	63	4	1	2	3	0
Colton Fretter	65	29	40	69	71	48	24	30	54	40	4	2	0	2	0
Tyler Mosienko	64	26	40	66	44	49	21	30	51	38	4	0	3	3	2
Ben O'Connor	57	9	40	49	42	48	8	39	47	32	4	0	0	0	4
Robert Dowd	60	25	19	44	84	47	19	16	35	70	4	3	1	4	2
Cullen Eddy	66	8	30	38	171	50	6	24	30	111	4	0	3	3	2
Jonathan Phillips	68	5	32	37	57	52	4	28	32	49	4	0	1	1	2
Gord Baldwin	55	9	18	27	37	43	4	14	18	25					
Darrell Hay	69	7	20	27	32	52	3	16	19	30	4	1	1	2	0
Dustin Kohn	44	1	21	22	35	30	1	16	17	19	4	0	2	2	4
Jason Hewitt	56	7	12	19	66	39	4	9	13	46	4	0	0	0	6
Jay Latulippe	29	6	10	16	26	22	6	7	13	18					
Tomas Petruska	17	5	11	16	14	13	5	10	15	12					
Jeff Legue 1	34	10	5	15	16	25	9	4	13	12	4	0	0	0	0
Phil Hill	69	4	11	15	36	52	3	6	9	30	4	0	0	0	0
Rod Sarich	64	3	7	10	39	51	3	5	8	31	4	0	0	0	0
Mark Thomas	68	2	7	9	82	51	0	4	4	67	4	0	0	0	0
Danny Bois	15	2	5	7	22	13	2	3	5	18					
Luke Ferrara	22	2	1	3	0	18	0	0	0	0					
Devin Didiomete	5	1	1	2	12	3	1	0	1	2					
Frank Doyle (N)	43	0	2	2	0	33	0	1	1	0					
Sam Gospel (N)	1	0	1	1	0										
Pascal Morency	2	0	0	0	9	1	0	0	0	0					
Winning shots		2		2			1		1			0		0	
Bench penalties					10					6					0
TEAM TOTALS	69	252	432	684	1036	52	193	339	532	761	4	11	15	26	22
Netminders	GPI	Mins	SOG	GA	Sv%	GPI	Mins	SOG	GA	Sv%	GPI	Mins	SOG	GA	Sv%
Andrew Jaszczyk	1	12	9	0	100.0										
Geoff Woolhouse	4	152	74	6	91.9	3	133	65	6	90.8					
Josh Unice	23	1363	601	50	91.7	17	1026	450	34	92.4	4	237	109	11	89.9
Frank Doyle	43	2583	1224	104	91.5	33	1985	932	87	90.7					
Sam Gospel	1	60	30	4	86.7										
Winning shots				4					3					0	
Empty net goals		4	4				4	4				0	0		
TEAM TOTALS	69	4170	1942	172	91.1	52	3144	1451	134	90.80	4	237	109	11	89.9

Also appeared: Jack Dransfield.

Also played for: 1 Sheffield Steeldogs

Shutouts: Unice (5) – league: 25 Jan at Cardiff Devils (36 saves), 31 Jan v Dundee Stars (27),
#4 March v Braehead Clan (21), 11 Mar v Cardiff Devils (26), 14 Mar v Coventry Blaze (24).
Doyle (3) – league: 21 Nov at Braehead Clan (30 saves); cup: 8 Jan at Dundee Stars (20),
17 Jan v Belfast Giants (31).

 # at iceSheffield.

All Competitions = league, play-offs and cup

Fourth league trophy

SCOTT ANTCLIFFE

Despite an injury-plagued season Sheffield Steelers lifted the Elite League title, narrowly beating Braehead Clan by a single point. But the team didn't fare as well in the Challenge Cup and play-offs, losing in the final both times.

Injuries struck early with Montreal winger **Pascal Morency** sustaining a concussion during his league debut away in Cardiff.

In a freak coincidence, his replacement, former NHLer **Danny Bois**, was concussed on his debut away in Braehead.

Further players came and went during the season, including **Devin DiDiomete, Jay Latulippe**, and a return for fan favourite **Jeff Legue**, who rejoined from Steelers' EPIHL neighbours, the Steeldogs.

Despite the disruption, the Steelers won the first 12 of their 15 league games, with much of their success being attributed to the formidable forward line of **Mathieu Roy, Mike Forney** and **Colton Fretter.**

The injury jinx next struck pivotal netminder **Frank Doyle**, whose old hand ailment recurred.

Coach **Gerad Adams** moved swiftly. Less than 24 hours later a relative unknown, **Josh Unice**, arrived at the House of Steel.

The 25-year-old one-time USA junior international made an instant impact, helping the club to win seven of their next nine games, including three shutouts.

But he couldn't prevent the Devils from lifting the Challenge Cup, even though Sheffield had home advantage in the first one-off final.

The league race came to a thrilling climax. On 20 March in the Great Satan's NIC home, Roy netted a double, including the OT winner.

This gave the Steelers a two-point lead with a game in hand, and only the Devils between them and the title.

Back at home 24 hours later they captured their fourth Elite League trophy in front of the *Premier Sports* cameras, beating the Devils 2-1, this time with Legue netting the decisive goal.

Despite carrying this momentum into the play-off weekend with a good win over a resilient Fife Flyers, in the final Adams was out-coached by Coventry Blaze's experienced **Chuck Weber.**

PLAYER AWARDS

Players' Player	Mathieu Roy
Kidz of Steel Award	Mathieu Roy
Player of the Year (away)	Tyler Mosienko
Coach's Player	Phil Hill
Best British Player	Ben O'Connor

LEADING PLAYERS

Tyler Mosienko born 21 March 1984, West St Paul, Manitoba, Canada
Feisty forward endeared himself to the fans with his skating ability, smooth hands, great shot and a relentless work ethic.

Mathieu Roy born 14 November 1986, Amos, Quebec, Canada
A resilient leader on the ice and a fan favourite, the former ECHL Kelly Cup winner was the club's and the Elite's top points scorer.

BEST YOUNG PLAYER

Luke Ferrara born 7 June 1993, Peterborough, England
The former GB under-20 international joined on a two-way contract and showed tremendous speed and a strong work rate.

FACT FILE 2014-15

Elite League	Winners
Conference	Runners-up in Erhardt
Play-offs	Finalists
Challenge Cup	Finalists

HISTORY

Founded: 1991. **Tony Smith** of Rhino Sports took control of the club in July 2011.

Leagues: Elite League 2003-15; Superleague 1996-2003; British League, Premier Div 1993-96; British Lge, Div 1 1992-93; English Lge 1991-92.

Honours: *Elite League* Winners 2014-15, 2010-11, 2008-09, 2003-04; Play-off Champions 2013-14, 2008-09, 2007-08, 2003-04; Knockout Cup 2005-06.
See *The Ice Hockey Annual 2010-11* for earlier Honours.

SHEFFIELD STEELERS *left to right, back row:* Colton Fretter, Luke Ferrara, Ben O'Connor, Daniel Bois, Cullen Eddy, Mark Thomas, Gord Baldwin, Phil Hill, Rod Sarich, Mike Forney, Darrel Hay, Jason Hewitt, Tyler Mosienko; *front row:* Neil Abel (asst. coach), Dustin Kohn, Jonathan Phillips, Andrew Jaszczyk, Frank Doyle, Geoff Woolhouse, Mathieu Roy, Robert Dowd, Gerad Adams (head coach).

Photo: Dean Woolley

SHEFFIELD STEELDOGS

PLAYER	*ALL COMPETITIONS					ENGLISH PREMIER LEAGUE					PLAY-OFFS				
Scorers	GP	G	A	Pts	Pim	GP	G	A	Pts	Pim	GP	G	A	Pts	Pim
Lubomir Korhon (I)	42	22	30	52	18	40	21	29	50	18	2	1	1	2	0
Tom Squires	50	22	24	46	40	48	22	24	46	38	2	0	0	0	2
Ben Morgan	50	4	38	42	20	48	4	37	41	18	2	0	1	1	2
Andrew Hirst	50	17	18	35	50	48	16	18	34	38	2	1	0	1	12
Janis Ozolins (I)	27	21	12	33	26	25	21	12	33	24	2	0	0	0	2
Jeff Legue (I) 2	20	20	12	32	16	20	20	12	32	16					
Lloyd Gibson	48	12	16	28	92	46	12	15	27	82	2	0	1	1	10
Greg Wood	46	7	21	28	83	44	7	21	28	81	2	0	0	0	2
Lee Haywood	48	4	21	25	101	46	4	21	25	97	2	0	0	0	4
Steven Duncombe	48	6	14	20	94	46	6	14	20	94	2	0	0	0	0
Ashley Calvert	49	6	14	20	96	47	6	14	20	96	2	0	0	0	0
Craig Elliott	35	3	16	19	88	33	3	15	18	86	2	0	1	1	2
Lewis Bell	48	1	7	8	63	46	1	7	8	49	2	0	0	0	14
Andre Payette (I)	32	2	4	6	265	30	2	4	6	255	2	0	0	0	10
Stanislav Lascek (I) 3	3	1	5	6	33	3	1	5	6	33					
Tim Smith	47	1	5	6	59	45	1	5	6	34	2	0	0	0	25
Cameron Brownley 1	41	2	1	3	76	39	1	1	2	76	2	1	0	1	0
Callum Pattison	32	1	1	2	257	31	1	1	2	232	1	0	0	0	25
Thomas Barry	38	0	0	0	30	36	0	0	0	20	2	0	0	0	10
Dalibor Sedlar (N)	50	0	0	0	8	48	0	0	0	8	2	0	0	0	0
Winning shots		1	1				1	1				0	0		
Bench penalties					10					10					0
TEAM TOTALS	50	153	259	412	1525	48	150	255	405	1405	2	3	4	7	120
Netminders	GP	Mins	SOG	GA	Sv%	GP	Mins	SOG	GA	Sv%	GP	Mins	SOG	GA	Sv%
Dalibor Sedlar	50	2823	1943	194	90.0	48	2703	1837	183	90.0	2	120	106	11	89.6
Brad Day	48	191	141	17	87.9	48	191	141	17	87.9					
Winning shots				1					1					0	
Empty net goals		2	2				2	2				0	0		
TEAM TOTALS	50	3014	2086	214	89.7	48	2894	1980	203	89.7	2	120	106	11	89.60

Also appeared: George Crawshaw, Cole Shudra, Charlie Thompson.

Also played for: 1 Edinburgh Capitals; 2 Sheffield Steelers; 3 Milton Keynes Lightning.

Shutouts: Day – cup: 2 Nov v Billingham Stars (27 saves).

*All competitions = league and play-offs only. EIHA did not record player statistics for the English Challenge Cup.

(I) ITC holder

SHEFFIELD STEELDOGS *left to right, standing:* Steven Packwood (equipment), Janis Ozolins, Cole Shudra, Craig Elliott, Lloyd Gibson, Ashley Calvert, Lee Haywood, Tom Squires, Lubomir Korhon, Tom Barry, Cam Brownley, Lewis Bell, Andrew Hirst, Shirley Packwood (manager); *front row:* Dalibor Sedlar, Steve Duncombe, Andre Payette, Greg Wood, Ben Morgan, Brad Day.

photo: Jake Oakley

A Legue up and down

ROGER WILLIAMS

In a determined attempt to move up the English Premier League in 2014-15, and with the help of their sponsor Bradford Breweries, the Steeldogs added Steelers' legend **Jeff Legue** to their otherwise familiar line-up.

The next part of their improvement plan called for pre-season preparations. First, the whole club competed in a weekend tournament in Dunkirk, France, hosted by Les Corsaires Dunkerque.

Then came the more traditional Wars of the Roses games, which ended with victory over Manchester Phoenix for the third year in a row.

But it was all in vain as **Andre Payette**'s team again struggled to put together any significant run of wins in the league.

There were notable victories over the Phoenix, Basingstoke Bison and Swindon Wildcats, but losses to Bracknell Bees, Milton Keynes Lightning and Peterborough Phantoms frustrated the Steeldogs as these games were considered winnable.

Only a few weeks into the campaign at home to the Phoenix, Legue was injured in an altercation with **Robin Kovář** which kept him out for a month. Payette and last season's top scorer **Lubomir Korhon** also missed games.

The depleted line-up was reinforced in December by the return of popular Latvian **Janis Ozolins,** their top scorer from 2010-12.

But the joy was short-lived as it was followed by Legue's return to the Steelers. This was all the more frustrating as he and Ozolins had clicked so well on the Steeldogs' attack.

A small consolation came in the English Challenge Cup where the Steeldogs played the majority of their games without imports. This enabled them to show off the depth of their locally trained talent, and in particular gave an opportunity to 16-year-old **Cole Shudra**. The son of the Steelers' legend **Ron Shudra** displayed a hockey maturity beyond his years.

Sheffield ended the season being dominated by high-rollers Telford Tigers in the playoff quarter-finals, and Payette paid the price for the disappointing season with the club releasing him.

PLAYER AWARDS

Players' Player	Lee Hayward
Player of the Year	Lloyd Gibson
Most Valuable Player	Dalibor Sedlar
Coach's Player	Greg Wood
British Player of the Year	Tom Squires
Most Improved Player	Tom Squires
Unsung Hero	Ashley Calvert
Entertainer of the Year	Ben Morgan

LEADING PLAYERS

Dalibor Sedlar *born 17 December 1987, Czech Republic*
In a defence that often lacked structure, the team's MVP kept his team-mates in many games. Played the entire season – bar 191 minutes.

Tom Squires *born 10 January 1991, Sheffield*
Rediscovering the form that earned him a spell in the Elite League with Hull, he outshot import Korhon, scoring most league goals with 'Dogs.

MOST PROMISING PLAYER

Cam Brownley *born 3 February 1997, Sheffield*
Made an impact in his first full season with his pace and shot showing promise. Benefited from a couple of Elite League games in Edinburgh.

FACT FILE 2014-15

English Premier League	Eighth
Play-offs	Quarter-finalists
English Challenge Cup	Third in qualifying round

HISTORY

Founded: 1994, playing out of the Queens Road, Sheffield rink. Transferred to iceSheffield in 2003. Renamed Steeldogs in 2010 when the club was taken over by **Shane Smith.**
Leagues: English Premier League 2005-15; English National League 2002-05; English Conference 2000-03, 1994-98; English League Div One 1998-2000.
Honours: English National League North, ENL play-offs and ENL Cup 2004-05; English National League North 2002-03.

SWINDON WILDCATS

PLAYER	* ALL COMPETITIONS					ENGLISH PREMIER LEAGUE					PLAY-OFFS				
Scorers	GP	G	A	Pts	Pim	GP	G	A	Pts	Pim	GP	G	A	Pts	Pim
Aaron Nell	49	39	43	82	40	47	39	43	82	40	2	0	0	0	0
Jonas Höög (I)	35	18	44	62	20	33	16	44	60	20	2	2	0	2	0
Tomasz Malasinski (I)	44	32	23	55	69	42	32	22	54	65	2	0	1	1	4
Jan Kostal (I)	50	22	24	46	14	48	21	23	44	12	2	1	1	2	2
Adam Harding	50	14	30	44	30	48	14	28	42	30	2	0	2	2	0
Henri Sandvik (I)	28	8	14	22	20	28	8	14	22	20					
Lee Richardson	50	6	16	22	12	48	6	16	22	10	2	0	0	0	2
Stephen Whitfield	48	2	14	16	70	46	2	13	15	70	2	0	1	1	0
Tomas Kana (I)	14	9	7	16	83	12	8	5	13	45	2	1	2	3	38
Sam Bullas	50	6	9	15	50	48	6	9	15	48	2	0	0	0	2
Toms Rutkis (I)	21	4	8	12	4	21	4	8	12	4					
Floyd Taylor	37	3	8	11	14	35	3	8	11	14	2	0	0	0	0
Ollie Betteridge	26	3	7	10	10	26	3	7	10	10					
Kenton Smith	28	2	7	9	60	28	2	7	9	60					
Alex Symonds	46	2	7	9	100	44	2	7	9	100	2	0	0	0	0
Callum Buglass	42	0	9	9	2	40	0	8	8	0	2	0	1	1	2
Shane Moore	46	1	5	6	113	44	1	5	6	113	2	0	0	0	0
Adam Finlinson	12	2	3	5	14	12	2	3	5	14					
Stevie Lyle (N)	50	0	4	4	6	48	0	4	4	6	2	0	0	0	0
Loris Taylor	9	1	2	3	4	7	1	2	3	4	2	0	0	0	0
Glenn Billing	18	0	3	3	0	18	0	3	3	0					
Sam Oakford	2	0	1	1	2	2	0	1	1	2					
Michael Stratford	22	0	1	1	0	22	0	1	1	0					
Ben Nethersell	13	0	0	0	2	13	0	0	0	2					
Winning shots		2		2			2		2			0		0	
Bench penalties					12					12					0
TEAM TOTALS	50	176	289	465	751	48	172	281	453	701	2	4	8	12	50
Netminders	GP	Mins	SOG	GA	Sv%	GP	Mins	SOG	GA	Sv%	GP	Mins	SOG	GA	Sv%
Stevie Lyle	50	2992	1810	148	91.8	48	2873	1748	142	91.9	2	119	62	6	90.3
Michael Crisp	47	16	13	3	76.9	47	16	13	3	76.9					
Winning shots			0					0					0		
Empty net goals			5	5				5	5				0	0	
TEAM TOTALS	50	3008	1828	156	91.5	48	2889	1766	150	91.5	2	119	62	6	90.3

Also appeared: Luc Johnson, Kyle Smith.

Shutouts: Lyle (4) – league: 1 Oct at Telford Tigers (37 saves), 8 Nov v Telford Tigers (54);
        cup: *4 Oct v Wightlink Raiders (8), 1 Nov at Wightlink Raiders (25).
    Crisp - cup: *4 Oct v Wightlink Raiders (14).   * shared

*All competitions = league and play-offs only. EIHA did not record player statistics for the English Challenge Cup.
(I) ITC holder

Höög back but Sandvik out

BEN CALLAGHAN

After a strong 2013-14 season, Wildcats' coach Ryan Aldridge made only a few changes to his English Premier League roster in the summer.

Among the key players he re-signed were GB netminder **Stevie Lyle**, forwards **Aaron Nell** and **Lee Richardson**, and imports **Henri Sandvik** and **Jan Kostal**.

The coach's biggest, and perhaps most surprising, move was to let go of high scoring **Jonas Höög** and replace him with Polish international **Tomasz Malasinski**.

He also released Finnish defenceman **Aku Pekkarinen** and snapped up Canadian **Kenton Smith** from the Elite's Braehead Clan.

Höög wasn't out for long. By late October the team were struggling for an offensive spark and Aldridge turned to the local hero.

"He's desperate to get back playing," said the coach. "I think he's probably learnt from not coming back and being at home."

The Swede linked up again with his old line-mate Nell, the team put nine goals past Invicta Dynamos in the cup, and then blanked Telford Tigers at the Link Centre.

This was Lyle's second shutout of the eventual league winners in just a few weeks. The Wildcats ended the campaign as the only team to whitewash the Tigers.

Their best streak for a few years started in mid-November, despite them being without their GB juniors for a week. They chalked up ten victories in a row, and qualified for the cup semi-finals for the first time.

The club received a nasty shock in January, not long before the signing deadline, when Sandvik, their best player of 2013-14, suddenly quit for a career in Norway.

His replacement, ex-NHL forward **Tomas Kana**, was a more physical player but he couldn't prevent them from crashing out of the cup with a heavy loss to the Phoenix in Altrincham.

The defeat was felt for a few weeks and the team struggled, eventually settling for fifth place, tied on points with Peterborough Phantoms.

Against the Phantoms in the play-offs, they battled hard, but in vain, to lose each leg by a single goal to the forthcoming champions.

PLAYER AWARDS

Players' Player	Stevie Lyle
Player of the Year	Steve Whitfield
Coach's Player	Lee Richardson
Best Forward	Tomasz Malasinski
Best Defenceman	Steve Whitfield
Best British Forward (Dave Richardson Award)	
	Aaron Nell
Most Improved Player	Adam Harding

LEADING PLAYERS

Tomasz Malasinski born 23 August 1986, Poland
Lethal finisher with great skill and professionalism. Regularly recognised by his national team.

Steve Whitfield born 12 October 1990, Swindon
Defenceman whose finest talent is blocking shots. In the Swindon system since his early teens, he won two club awards and is still improving his skills.

MOST PROMISING PLAYER

Toms Rutkis born 9 November 1997, Riga, Latvia
Six-foot teenager with skill, speed and an eye for goal has played in England's junior system since 2009. The club's most exciting prospect since Aaron Nell.

'The History of Swindon Wildcats' by Stuart Latham is on sale in the Swindon branch of Waterstones.

FACT FILE 2014-15

English Premier League	Fifth
Play-offs	Quarter-finalists
English Challenge Cup	Semi-finalists

HISTORY

Founded: 2001 as Lynx. Reverted to original name of Wildcats in 2004. Previous clubs in the Link Centre were *Phoenix* 2000-01, *Chill* 1997-2000, *IceLords* 1996-97 and *Wildcats* 1986-96.

Leagues: *Wildcats* - English Premier League 2004-15 and British League, Div One 1986-96;

Honours: *Wildcats* - Autumn Trophy 1991-92.

SWINDON WILDCATS *left to right, back row:* Pete Bradford (equipment), Mark Thorne (equipment), Alex Symonds, Adam Harding, Kenton Smith, Callum Buglass, Sam Bullas, Tomasz Malasinski, Tomas Kana, Floyd Taylor, Steven Bradford (equipment), Ollie Betteridge, Kate Davis (physio); Michael Crisp, Shane Moore, Lee Richardson, Aaron Nell, Ryan Aldridge (head coach), Jan Kostal, Stevie Whitfield, Jonas Höög, Stevie Lyle.

photo: Nicky Pearce

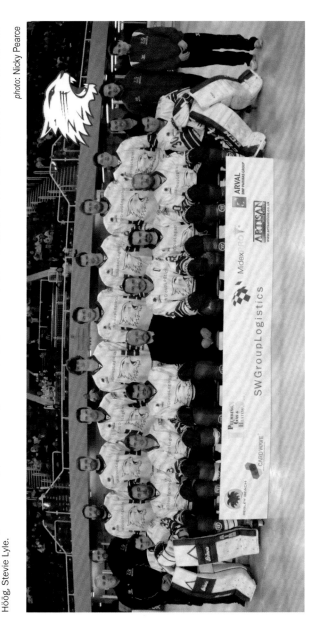

TELFORD TIGERS

PLAYER	*ALL COMPETITIONS					ENGLISH PREMIER LEAGUE					PLAY-OFFS				
Scorers	GP	G	A	Pts	Pim	GP	G	A	Pts	Pim	GP	G	A	Pts	Pim
Peter Szabo (I)	51	28	61	89	32	48	28	59	87	28	3	0	2	2	4
Jason Silverthorn (I)	48	39	41	80	70	45	38	39	77	70	3	1	2	3	0
Joe Miller	46	24	35	59	38	43	24	35	59	36	3	0	0	0	2
Max Birbraer (I)	51	22	33	55	46	48	21	33	54	46	3	1	0	1	0
Jonathan Weaver	46	10	49	59	40	43	9	45	54	24	3	1	4	5	16
Scott McKenzie	47	26	22	48	18	44	23	20	43	16	3	3	2	5	2
Sam Zajac	50	8	37	45	84	47	8	35	43	82	3	0	2	2	2
Nathan Salem	46	21	20	41	36	43	18	19	37	34	3	3	1	4	2
Daniel Davies	51	17	20	37	2	48	17	19	36	2	3	0	1	1	0
Rick Plant	50	11	25	36	53	47	10	20	30	53	3	1	5	6	0
Martin Ondrej (I)	51	6	18	24	48	48	6	18	24	44	3	0	0	0	4
Blahoslav Novak (I)	49	12	10	22	102	46	11	8	19	98	3	1	2	3	4
Rupert Quiney	44	4	8	12	69	41	3	8	11	69	3	1	0	1	0
Callum Bowley	50	2	4	6	12	47	2	4	6	12	3	0	0	0	0
Daniel Scott	38	3	2	5	58	35	3	2	5	56	3	0	0	0	2
Rick Skene	7	1	4	5	0	7	1	4	5	0					
Adam Taylor	46	1	5	6	6	43	1	4	5	6	3	0	1	1	0
Daniel Rose	48	2	1	3	16	45	2	1	3	16	3	0	0	0	0
Marcus Maynard	51	0	3	3	14	48	0	2	2	14	3	0	1	1	0
Owen Bennett	48	0	1	1	61	45	0	1	1	57	3	0	0	0	4
James Smith	17	1	0	1	2	15	0	0	0	2	2	1	0	1	0
Winning shots		1		1			1		1			0		0	
Bench penalties					40					38					2
TEAM TOTALS	51	239	399	638	847	48	226	376	602	803	3	13	23	36	44
Netminders	GP	Mins	SOG	GA	Sv%	GP	Mins	SOG	GA	Sv%	GP	Mins	SOG	GA	Sv%
Thomas Murdy	51	2105	1043	82	90.8	48	1925	966	75	92.2	3	180	77	7	90.9
Sam Gospel	48	947	473	41	91.3	48	947	473	41	91.3					
Winning shots				3					3					0	
Empty net goals			0	0				0	0					0	0
TEAM TOTALS	51	3052	1516	126	91.7	48	2872	1439	119	91.7	3	180	77	7	90.9

Also appeared: Macaulay Haywood.

Shutouts: Murdy – league: 12 Oct v Swindon Wildcats (20 saves), 24 Jan at Guildford Flames (37),
1 Feb v Swindon Wildcats *(game abandoned at 48.47)*, 21 Feb v Manchester Phoenix (36);
play-offs: 27 March at Sheffield Steeldogs (29).

*All competitions = league and play-offs only. EIHA did not record player statistics for the English Challenge Cup.
(I) ITC holder.

TELFORD TIGERS *left to right*, *back row*: Danny Rose, Scott McKenzie, Blahoslav Novak, Nathan Salem, Joe Miller, Callum Bowley, Sam Zajac, Peter Szabo; *middle row*: Jason Silverthorn, Owen Bennett, Rick Plant, Martin Ondrej, Max Birbraer, Rupert Quiney, Marcus Maynard, Adam Taylor, Dan Scott, Jonathan Weaver, Dan Davies, Andy Phillips (equipment); *front row*: Thomas Murdy, Tom Watkins (head coach), Wayne Scholes (Red Hockey CEO), Paul Thomason (general manager), Karl Creamer (asst. coach), Sam Gospel.

photo: Steve Brodie

Tigers see double

JAMES SHAW

Unsurprisingly, in their first full season under the Red Hockey banner, the Tigers started out as firm favourites for the English Premier League's treble.

Returning coach **Tom Watkins** shook up the team that had finished sixth in 2013-14, releasing all his imports and bringing in one of GB's finest home-grown defenders, **Jonathan Weaver** from the Elite League.

He was joined by two other Elite alumni, Canadian forward **Jason Silverthorn** from Hull, who was appointed captain, and Cardiff's popular winger **Max Birbraer.**

When Slovakian sniper **Peter Szabo** arrived, there were only days left until the start of the season. But as it turned out, Watkins had unearthed a diamond.

MK Lightning were duly dispatched in the first league game but it was just a harbinger of great things to come.

Laying the foundations for the league title was an 11-game winning streak. This gave the Tigers an early, healthy lead at the top of the standings which they never relinquished.

They claimed their first ever league title on 1 March after losing only nine games all season, though they were three times pushed to overtime before taking the points.

Interestingly, the losses offered hope to other teams, some of whom were chasing a bizarre £5,000 prize for second place.

The Tigers followed up a few days later with home and away defeats of Manchester Phoenix to claim the Cup and their first double of major honours.

Coach Watkins refused to let complacency set in as he aimed the club's sights on the play-offs and the Grand Slam. Just 24 hours after they won the Cup, he ordered his side back into training,

Lowly Sheffield Steeldogs were pushed aside in the quarter-finals, but in Coventry against Peterborough Phantoms the Tigers learned what it means to be 'the team to beat'.

Before a partisan Peterborough crowd and with Phantoms' keeper standing on his head, Telford's season came to a shuddering halt.

PLAYER AWARDS

Players' Player	Jonathan Weaver
Most Valuable Player	Peter Szabo
Player of the Year	Sam Zajac
Coach's Player	Sam Zajac
Best Forward	Nathan Salem
Best Defenceman	Sam Zajac
Best Plus/Minus	Sam Zajac
Personality of the Year	Dan Scott
Most Improved Player	Sam Gospel

LEADING PLAYERS

Peter Szabo born 22 March 1981, Nitra, Slovakia
His skill, speed and agility led to his capture of the league's points scoring crown.

Sam Zajac born 23 June 1989, Whitley Bay.
Defenceman's biggest asset is his heart - he's always willing to stand up for his team-mates. Also made a big contribution offensively.

MOST PROMISING PLAYER

James Smith born 29 June 1994, Dundee
Still working his way through the development system in the NIHL's second division where he tallied 109 points in 30 games, he showed maturity in his handful of senior games.

FACT FILE 2014-15

English Premier League	Winners
Play-offs	Semi-finalists
English Challenge Cup	Champions

HISTORY

Founded 2001 as Wild Foxes. Renamed Tigers in 2005 and owned by Red Hockey Ltd since October 2013. Did not play in season 2009-10. *Previous teams in Telford were Royals 1997-2001 and Tigers 1985-99.*
Leagues *Tigers* - English Premier League 2010-15, 2005-09; Brit. Nat'l Lge 1997-99, Premier League 1996-97, British League, Div One 1985-96. *Wildfoxes* - English Premier League 2002-05; English National League South 2001-02; *Royals* - English (National) League 1997-2001.
Honours: *Tigers* – English Premier League 2014-15; English Challenge Cup 2014-15.

LEAGUE ORGANISATION

Senior ice hockey in season 2014-15 was run by two separate organisations, the Elite League, under licence from the governing body, Ice Hockey UK; and the English Ice Hockey Association which controls the English Premier League (EPIHL) and the National League (NIHL).

The **Elite Ice Hockey League Ltd** (EIHL), a limited liability company, is run by its member clubs with each having one seat on the league's board.

There were no restrictions on the origin of the players and there is no wage cap.

Team rosters were limited to 20 skaters plus two netminders with a maximum of 12 professional players. Two players had to be eligible for the GB under-20 team.

Each side was allowed to ice up to 12 non-British trained players, i.e. those requiring an International Transfer Card (see panel), in any one game but could sign an unlimited number during the season. Such players could be alternated week by week.

Each team was allowed to register up to 11 work permit holders (see panel) during the year. Note – the league's rules are not made public. This information is from our own sources.

The **English Ice Hockey Association** (EIHA), a company limited by guarantee, runs the English Leagues, designated 'development' leagues, which comprise clubs with differing financial resources.

The teams with the most ice time and largest budgets compete in the **English Premier League** with the remainder entering one of the **National League**'s two regional divisions.

Each Premier League team could dress a maximum of four non-British trained players (usually those requiring an ITC - see panel) per game but ice only three at any one time. Other players had to have completed two years playing at under-19 level under the auspices of any UK home nation.

National League teams could dress two non-British trained players but ice only one at any one time.

Players requiring a work permit were not allowed to play in any EIHA-controlled league and all non-British-trained players had to hold an EU passport. There is no wage cap; as in the Elite League, players' wages were limited solely by their club's resources.

IMPORTS

The strict definition of an 'import' is a player who requires a work permit (see below).

Any other player is legally entitled to play in this country as an EU citizen.

However, each of our leagues, and the world governing body, the IIHF, impose their own regulations which our clubs are obliged to follow. The leagues' requirements are shown above. Details of the IIHF's requirements for an International Transfer Card are shown below.

International Transfer Card (ITC)

A signed International Transfer Card (ITC) is required by any player who has been a member of another national federation under the world governing body, the International Ice Hockey Federation (IIHF).

It is left to the clubs to decide how many of these players they wish to employ.

Work Permit Holders

Work permits are required by players originating from outside the European Union area who do not qualify for an EU passport and cannot acquire any other form of dispensation to play in the UK.

Each year the sport's representatives - Ice Hockey UK, the Elite League and the appropriate government department - meet to agree the criteria for Work Permit holders in ice hockey.

For season 2014-15 the criteria were that players from North America must have played in 75 per cent of their team's games at university level or above; Europeans had to have played 75 per cent of their games in a professional league from a country which competed in the World Championships (Division I and above) in the previous season.

The information provided on this page is necessarily brief. For more on the rules in force for the current season, go to www.icehockeyuk.co.uk and click on Documentation/Work Permits.
The IIHF's transfer regulations are at www.iihf.com/iihf-home/the-iihf/statutes-bylaws (bylaw 407 on page 54).

ELITE LEAGUE

FINAL STANDINGS

Elite League	GP	W	OW	OL	L	GF	GA	Pts	Pct
(2) Sheffield Steelers SHE	52	30	5	4	13	193	134	74	71.15
(5) Braehead Clan BRH	52	33	2	3	14	190	136	73	70.19
(9) Cardiff Devils CAR	52	29	5	4	14	210	151	72	69.23
(4) Nottingham Panthers NOT	52	23	6	7	16	166	141	65	62.50
(1) Belfast Giants BEL	52	25	2	6	19	177	148	60	57.69
(6) Coventry Blaze COV	52	17	7	3	25	127	145	51	49.04
(8) Hull Stingrays HUL	52	16	4	9	23	154	192	49	47.12
(7) Fife Flyers FIF	52	18	4	3	27	170	180	47	45.19
(10) Edinburgh Capitals EDI	52	13	7	6	26	135	215	46	44.23
(3) Dundee Stars DUN	52	6	8	5	33	123	203	33	31.73
Erhardt Conference									
Nottingham Panthers	32	13	5	4	10	94	81	40	62.50
Sheffield Steelers	32	15	3	3	11	97	94	39	60.94
Cardiff Devils	32	17	1	2	12	114	103	38	59.38
Belfast Giants	32	13	2	4	13	97	94	34	53.13
Coventry Blaze	32	8	3	1	20	75	105	23	35.94
Gardiner Conference									
Braehead Clan	32	25	1	1	5	135	69	53	82.81
Fife Flyers	32	15	2	1	14	120	102	35	54.69
Hull Stingrays	32	11	3	5	13	104	123	33	51.56
Edinburgh Capitals	32	10	4	4	14	87	119	32	50.00
Dundee Stars	32	4	5	4	19	84	117	22	34.38

Teams played an inter-locking schedule: eight times against teams in the same Conference and four times against teams in the other Conference. League positions decided on total points gained in all games.
Scoring system: two points for a regulation time Win (W) or Overtime Win (OW), one point for an Overtime or shootout Loss (OL).
Positions of tied teams decided on the number of regulation time Wins (W), then total Wins (W/OW). (No individual stats are awarded from the shootout.)
Pct. = percentage of points gained to points available.
Figure in brackets on left in League table indicates position in season 2013-14.

LEADING POINTS SCORERS

	GP	G	A	Pts	Pim
Mathieu Roy SHE	52	36	43	79	42
Michael Forney SHE	52	33	34	67	63
Neil Trimm BRH	52	26	41	67	28
Joey Martin CAR	50	21	46	67	45
Stefan Meyer BRH	51	31	35	66	20
Leigh Salters BRH	50	30	33	63	106
Matt Keith BRH	51	18	44	62	59
Carl Lauzon HUL	52	28	33	61	78
Jake Morissette CAR	52	23	38	61	12
Brent Walton CAR	51	21	38	59	32

LEADING NETMINDERS

	GPI	Mins	SoG	GA	Sav%
Craig Kowalski NOT	21	1199	562	44	92.2
Brian Stewart COV	52	3115	1774	139	92.2
Kyle Jones BRH	52	3093	1530	132	91.4
Mattias Modig NOT	30	1697	863	76	91.2
Frank Doyle SHE	33	1985	932	87	90.7
Carsen Chubak BEL	36	2160	979	95	90.3

Qualification: one-third of team's games (1,040 mins).

LEADING BRITISH SCORERS

The Ice Hockey Annual Trophy	GP	G	A	Pts	Pim
Ben O'Connor SHE	48	8	39	47	32
Craig Peacock BEL	50	23	18	41	24
Robert Lachowicz NOT	52	14	25	39	14
Colin Shields BEL	51	13	26	39	14
Robert Farmer NOT	48	12	24	36	170
Robert Dowd SHE	47	19	16	35	70
Jonathan Phillips SHE	52	4	28	32	49
Matthew Myers CAR	37	14	14	28	40
Jonathan Boxill NOT	52	6	20	26	62
Ashley Tait COV	44	3	23	26	18

www.eliteleague.co.uk

FAIR PLAY

Team Penalties	GP	Pim	Ave
Hull Stingrays	52	661	12.7
Coventry Blaze	52	702	13.5
Sheffield Steelers	52	761	14.6
Belfast Giants	52	825	15.9
Edinburgh Capitals	52	853	16.4
Fife Flyers	52	934	18.0
Nottingham Panthers	52	974	18.7
Dundee Stars	52	1085	20.9
Cardiff Devils	52	1113	21.4
Braehead Clan	52	1212	23.3
Totals	520	9120	17.5

SIN-BIN

Most Penalised Players	GP	Pim	Ave
Zach Fitzgerald BRH	44	304	6.91
Brad Plumton DUN	50	313	6.26
Chris Frank BRH	42	229	5.45
Matt Nickerson FIF	46	192	4.17
Honourable mention			
Joe Grimaldi EDI	14	102	7.28

SPECIAL TEAMS

Powerplay
best   Clan   61g on 274 opps. = 22.3%
worst Stars   25g on 202 opps. = 12.4%

Penalty kill
best   Giants   30ga on 217 tsh = 86.2%
worst Capitals   55ga on 238 tsh = 76.9%

tsh – times short-handed.
ops – powerplay opportunities

LEAGUE AWARDS

Coach of the Year
Ryan Finnerty Braehead Clan *(photo: Al Goold)*
Player of the Year & Best Forward
Mathieu Roy Sheffield Steelers
Best Defenceman
Andrew Hotham Cardiff Devils
Best Netminder
Brian Stewart Coventry Blaze
British Player of the Year
Ben O'Connor Sheffield Steelers

ALL-STARS

First Team
Goal   BRIAN STEWART, Coventry
Defence   ANDREW HOTHAM, Cardiff
                BEN O'CONNOR, Sheffield
Forwards   MICHAEL FORNEY, Sheffield
                JOEY MARTIN, Cardiff
                MATHIEU ROY, Sheffield

Second Team
Goal   KYLE JONES, Braehead
Defence   SCOTT AARSSEN, Braehead
                TYSON MARSH, Cardiff
Forwards   STEFAN MEYER, Braehead
                LEIGH SALTERS, Braehead
                BRENT WALTON, Cardiff

RESULTS CHART

	BEL	BRH	CAR	COV	DUN	EDI	FIF	HUL	NOT	SHE
Giants	X	31/10 4-1	3/10 3-2	27/9 4-2	11/10 7-1	12/9 8-2	28/9 1-6	10/1 2-4	16/11 2-1	30/11 4-3so (7)
	X	27/12 6-1	4/10 5-2	19/12 3-1	30/12 9-3	21/2 4-6	24/1 5-2	27/2 3-2	23/1 0-4	2/1 5-3
	X		8/11 7-4	20/12 3-2					14/3 2-3so (26)	3/1 6-3
	X		6/2 6-3	20/3 2-0					15/3 1-5	22/2 4-5ot (R)
Clan	28/12 5-2	X	29/11 7-3	18/10 4-2	20/12 3-4so (10)	25/10 3-1	10/10 4-3	7/12 6-4	15/10 4-3ot (D)	21/11 0-2
	7/2 1-0	X	14/2 0-3	8/11 4-2	3/1 2-1	17/12 2-4	6/12 2-1	31/1 2-3	27/2 4-2	22/11 5-3
		X				17/1 6-2	24/1 7-3	10/1 5-1	11/2 3-2so (21)	
		X				21/2 3-0	14/3 5-1	1/3 5-2	21/3 9-4	
Devils	9/11 3-2	20/9 5-4ot (C)	X	25/10 6-3	16/11 5-4	23/11 10-0	4/1 8-5	6/9 3-2ot (A)	2/11 1-2	19/10 5-2
	6/12 4-1	14/12 6-5ot (J)	X	27/12 3-1	7/3 12-0	18/3 6-3	22/2 3-1	30/12 7-0	21/12 5-2	25/1 0-6
	7/12 5-3		X	10/1 4-5					17/1 7-2	8/2 4-0
	1/3 3-2		X	1/2 4-5ot (O)					22/3 7-2	15/3 6-3
Blaze	28/10 2-7	5/10 3-2	12/10 1-3	X	13/9 4-0	19/10 3-2so (4)	7/9 4-2	15/3 3-2so (28)	7/12 3-4	29/11 6-2
	2/11 5-1	9/11 3-4	22/11 3-8	X	25/1 2-1	7/3 5-0	21/12 6-4	22/3 1-2so (30)	4/1 2-1so (12)	14/12 2-4
	14/2 3-2		26/12 4-5	X					28/1 4-3so (18)	11/1 2-3
	15/2 3-2		18/1 0-5	X					22/2 2-1	1/3 5-3
Stars	5/9 1-4	12/10 0-4	30/11 1-3	19/9 1-2	X	15/11 2-3	19/10 3-5	14/9 4-5ot (2)	26/10 3-4ot (G)	2/11 4-2
	11/1 3-2so (14)	21/12 1-4	15/2 2-4	7/2 1-2	X	29/11 1-2so (6)	28/12 2-3	9/11 3-4	28/2 3-2	18/1 3-2so (16)
		1/2 1-3			X	6/12 2-3	8/2 3-0	14/12 2-1ot (K)		
		22/2 0-5			X	21/3 3-5	15/3 4-8	8/3 6-1		
	BEL	BRH	CAR	COV	DUN	EDI	FIF	HUL	NOT	SHE

RESULTS CHART, contd

	BEL	BRH	CAR	COV	DUN	EDI	FIF	HUL	NOT	SHE
Capitals	21/12 2-5	11/10 0-4	21/9 3-2so(2)	13/12 3-2	7/12 3-2	X	16/11 4-3	30/11 3-2so (8)	9/11 5-3	1/11 2-10
	18/1 3-6	26/10 4-9	13/2 2-1so (22)	8/2 2-1ot (Q)	23/12 4-5so (11)	X	14/12 5-6so (9)	28/12 3-6	1/3 3-5	1/2 2-3ot (P)
			4/1 0-5		10/1 1-2so (13)	X	31/12 0-2	25/1 4-3		
			15/3 2-1		22/3 4-3so (31)	X	7/2 5-2	22/2 5-4so (23)		
Flyers	25/1 5-4so (17)	15/11 6-2	19/12 0-5	6/9 0-1	25/10 5-0	2/11 5-2	X	1/11 8-3	12/10 1-2	13/9 4-5so (1)
	21/3 1-3	13/12 2-8	31/1 3-2	17/10 1-2ot (E)	27/12 7-5	8/11 4-1	X	17/1 3-6	22/11 3-5	7/12 1-4
			2/1 2-4		14/2 5-2	11/1 9-3	X	21/2 5-0		
			22/3 2-3		14/3 3-4so (27)	28/2 5-1	X	7/3 1-3		
Stingrays	20/9 2-3	7/9 6-8	24/1 2-3ot (N)	6/12 5-3	5/10 2-5	13/9 2-5	26/10 3-1	X	29/11 0-4	21/12 3-4
	13/12 3-2	28/9 0-2	14/3 4-5	18/3 0-1so (29)	8/11 4-6	18/10 2-0	18/1 2-3	X	8/2 5-2	28/2 2-9
			2/11 6-2		22/11 5-3	27/12 3-2	1/2 3-4so (20)	X		
			11/1 1-4		1/3 4-3so (24)	10/3 5-4so (25)	15/2 5-4	X		
Panthers	25/10 4-3ot (F)	25/1 6-3	13/9 3-1	1/11 3-1	18/10 5-1	21/10 5-2	11/10 3-4so (3)	27/9 1-6	X	8/11 7-2
	14/12 3-6	7/3 6-0	15/11 2-3so(5)	30/11 3-1	23/11 3-4ot (H)	3/1 6-1	20/12 1-5	4/3 4-3	X	27/12 3-2ot (L)
	31/1 4-3so (19)		11/1 4-3ot (M)	31/12 3-2					X	14/2 2-3
	1/2 1-0		21/2 2-3	16/1 5-0					X	20/3 3-4ot (S)
Steelers	21/9 3-2	16/11 4-1	18/10 5-3	23/11 3-2ot (I)	15/10 6-3	#22/10 6-2	#14/9 8-1	#25/10 4-1	6/12 3-2	X
	15/11 4-2	#4/3 2-0	12/12 4-1	24/1 2-1	31/1 6-0	11/2 5-3	#9/11 6-1	20/12 5-2	26/12 0-4	X
	17/1 0-1so (15)		11/3 11-0	21/2 1-2					10/1 1-4	X
	7/3 4-3		21/3 2-1	14/3 2-0					7/2 4-2	X
	BEL	BRH	CAR	COV	DUN	EDI	FIF	HUL	NOT	SHE

The *Erhardt Conference* is named in honour of **Carl Erhardt**, who captained Britain to their famous Triple Crown triumph of Olympic, World and European titles in 1936.
The *Gardiner Conference* is named after **Charlie Gardiner**, the Edinburgh-born goaltender who was skipper of the NHL's Chicago Blackhawks when they won the Stanley Cup in 1934.

NOTES ON RESULTS CHART

Score shown in **bold**. *First figure is date of game.* # *at iceSheffield.*
References in brackets refer to overtime goals (OT) and game winning shots in shootouts (SO), details of which are shown below.

NED LUKACEVIC scored four game-winning penalty shots for Fife Flyers.

GAME WINNING SHOTS (so)

1 SHE Darrell Hay
2 EDI Greg Collins
3 FIF Ned Lukacevic
4 COV Jereme Tendler
5 CAR Joey Martin
6 EDI Greg Collins
7 BEL Evan Cheverie
8 EDI Daniel Naslund
9 FIF Ned Lukacevic
10 DUN Igor Gongalsky
11 DUN Sean Ringrose
12 COV Jakub Sindel (*24th shot*)
13 DUN Chris Blight
14 DUN John Dolan
15 BEL Mike Kompon
16 DUN Sean Ringrose
17 FIF Ned Lukacevic
18 COV Jereme Tendler
19 NOT Chris Lawrence
20 FIF Ned Lukacevic
21 BRH Leigh Salters
22 EDI Riley Emmerson
23 EDI Dennis Rix
24 HUL Jordan Mayer
25 HUL Carl Lauzon
26 NOT Chris Higgins
27 DUN Ryan Grimshaw
28 COV Ben Arnt
29 COV Ryan O'Marra
30 HUL Will Frederick
31 EDI Jay King

OVERTIME WINNING GOALS (ot)

A CAR Jake Morissette   ps   60.46
B HUL Jordan Mayer (unass.)   60.17
C CAR Joey Haddad (Morissette, Hotham) 63.36
D BRH Neil Trimm (Meyer, Pitt)   pp   60.46
E COV Rory Rawlyk (O'Marra, Tendler) pp 63.39
F NOT Bruce Graham (Robinson)   63.46
G NOT Nathan Robinson (unass.)   64.38
H DUN Matt Ryan (Lust)   60.54
I SHE Mathieu Roy (Fomey, O'Connor)pp 60.32
J CAR Andrew Hotham (Culligan, Walton) 60.21
K DUN Shane Lust (Quick)   pp   61.29
L NOT Chris Lawrence (Wild, Farmer) pp   60.38
M NOT Max Parent (Doucet, Schmidt)   62.46
N CAR Brent Walton (Culligan, Hotham)   62.18
O COV Cale Tanaka (Jorgensen, Sindel)   64:45
P SHE Gord Baldwin (Petruska, Mosienko) 61:24
Q EDI Rene Jarolin (Petran, Emmerson)   63.04
R SHE Cullen Eddy (unass.)   61.09
S SHE M Roy (O'Connor, Mosienko) pp 64.47

ELITE LEAGUE ROUND-UP

"You never like to see another team celebrate winning a trophy in your building, so we were determined to make sure it was us that celebrated this time." *Jeff Legue (above), after scoring the league title-winning goal in Sheffield Steelers 2-1 win over Cardiff Devils on 21 March.* Yorkshire Post

Steelers back on top

The last time **Sheffield Steelers** won the Elite League, in 2010-11, they were deadlocked on points with **Cardiff Devils**. A tie-break of most wins had to be invoked before **Paul Ragan's** team were crowned.

The title race was almost as close this time, but **Tony Smith's** side avoided another cliff-hanger by beating the Devils in their final head-to-head. Even then their margin of league supremacy was only one point over the much improved **Braehead Clan**.

Netminders **Josh Unice** and **Frank Doyle**, who had eight shutouts between them, GB defenceman **Ben O'Connor**, and **Mathieu Roy**, the league's runaway scoring leader, were the stars of the Steelers.

Coach of the Year **Ryan Finnerty** and cool keeper **Kyle Jones** were the key men for the Clan, who moved up from the middle of the pack to come within a skate's edge of first place.

Both teams were rewarded with their first games in the Champions Hockey League.

The Devils shot up the table from ninth place, almost entirely due to being under a refreshing new ownership, though **Joey Martin's** 67 points and **Andrew Hotham's** defensive skills will have helped.

Nottingham Panthers weren't helped by bolstering their roster for their ill-fated European games.

LEAGUE RECORDS

Most Points in one game: 6 - shared by **Matt Keith** BRH, **Jake Morissette** CAR and **Ray Sawada** BEL.
Most powerplay goals: 16 - **Mathieu Roy** SHE
Most shorthanded goals: 4 -
     Carl Lauzon HUL/**Guillaume Doucet** NOT
Most game winning goals: 7 - **Mathieu Roy** SHE
Most shutouts: 7 - **Kyle Jones** BRH

Out of 26 players listed, barely a dozen skated the entire season. Worse, **David Clarke**, their top scorer in 2013-14, missed two-thirds of the year through injury.

Defending champs **Belfast Giants** also found playing in Europe did little for their domestic form. New dual duty manager-coach **Steve Thornton** had his work cut out.

Coventry Blaze were so chuffed with their goalie **Brian Stewart's** performances that they handed him four awards - including Best Defenceman! Need we say more?

Hull Stingrays were chuffed just to reach the play-offs, especially as they had a rookie coach, **Omar Pacha**, and a squad of young players straight out of university.

Fife Flyers also made it into the play-offs, but viewed it much less cheerfully as their coach **Todd Dutiaume** had set his squad higher targets.

Flyers' big rivals **Edinburgh Capitals** were even more miserable as they missed out on the post-season peregrinations by just one point. Inconsistency and indiscipline were the downfall of **Richard Hartmann's** men.

Without **Dan Bakala**, their award-winning goalie of 2013-14, *Dundee Stars* were just a shadow of that third place side.

PAST WINNERS

2013-14	Belfast Giants
2012-13	Nottingham Panthers
2011-12	Belfast Giants
2010-11	Sheffield Steelers
2009-10	Coventry Blaze
2008-09	Sheffield Steelers
2007-08	Coventry Blaze
2006-07	Coventry Blaze
2005-06	Belfast Giants
2004-05	Coventry Blaze
2003-04	Sheffield Steelers

PLAY-OFFS

Eight of the ten Elite League sides qualified for the Play-offs on the following basis:
- the league winner was seeded 1,
- the winner of the conference which didn't produce the league winner was seeded 2,
- the remaining six places were taken in order from the final league table.

In the quarter-finals - played home and away - seed 1 faced seed 8, seed 2 played seed 7, and so on. Overtime and penalties were used after the second leg, if necessary.

For the finals weekend in Nottingham, the seedings for the semi-final and final were determined by the original quarter-final ranking, with the highest-placed team left in the Play-offs ranked as the top seed.

In the first semi-final the highest seed played the lowest, with the remaining teams meeting in the second semi-final.

The winners went head-to-head in the final and the losers met to decide third place.

QUARTER-FINALS

27/29 March 2015
Belfast-Cardiff   1-0h, 7-3a
Giants win 8-3 on aggregate
28/29 March 2015
Coventry-Nottingham   3-3a, 2-1h
Blaze win 5-4 on aggregate
Hull-Braehead   2-3a, 3-1ot h
Stingrays win 5-4 on aggregate
Sheffield-Fife   3-2a, 3-3h
Steelers win 6-5 on aggregate

SEMI-FINALS

4 April 2015, National Ice Centre, Nottingham
Sheffield-Hull   3-2   (0-0,2-1,1-1)
Belfast-Coventry   2-3so (1-1,1-0,0-1,0-0)

THIRD PLACE

Belfast-Hull   8-6   (2-2,3-3,3-1)

FINAL

6 April 2014, National Ice Centre, Nottingham
Sheffield-Coventry   2-4   (0-1,0-3,2-0)

COVENTRY BLAZE win the Elite League Play-off Championship

LEADING PLAY-OFF SCORERS

inc. third place play-off	GP	G	A	Pts	Pim
Mathieu Roy SHE	4	4	2	6	0
Nathan Robinson BEL	4	3	3	6	0
Eric Galbraith HUL	4	5	0	5	4
Adam Keefe BEL	4	3	2	5	2
Ryan O'Marra COV	4	1	4	5	2
Colin Shields BEL	4	1	4	5	0

LEADING PLAY-OFF NETMINDERS

	GPl	Mins	SoG	GA	Sv%
Brian Stewart COV	4	245	163	8	95.1
David Brown HUL	4	214	163	10	93.9
Carsen Chubak BEL	3	185	73	5	93.2

Qualification: played 120 minutes.

THE FINAL FOUR

Belfast Giants

Carsen Chubak, Andrew Dickson; Jeff Mason, Cody Brookwell, Kevin Phillips, Robby Sandrock, Calvin Elfring, David Phillips; Nathan Robinson, Adam Keefe *capt*, Colin Shields, Raymond Sawada, Darryl Lloyd, Mike Kompon, Evan Cheverie, Mark Garside, Craig Peacock, Mark McCutcheon, Kevin Westgarth.
Manager-Coach: Steve Thornton.

Coventry Blaze

Brian Stewart, Connor Ranby; Mark Smith, Mike Egener, James Jorgensen, James Griffin, Justin DaCosta, Steven Chalmers, Craig Cescon; Ben Arnt, Dale White, Cale Tanaka, Russell Cowley, Steve Goertzen, Ashley Tait *capt*, Ryan O'Marra, Derek Lee, Jereme Tendler, Ross Venus, Gareth O'Flaherty.
Coach: Ryan Finnerty. *Asst. coach*: Frank Morris.

Hull Stingrays

David Brown, Jeff Lil; Omar Pacha, Dominic Osman, Jamie Chilcott, Tom Stubley, Brendan Jamison, Yan Turcotte, Cory Tanaka, Thomas Ralph, Sam Towner, Carl Lauzon, Zach Hervato, Will Frederick, Eric Galbraith, Jordan Mayer.
Coach: Omar Pacha. *Asst. coach*: Carl Lauzon.

Sheffield Steelers

Josh Unice, Andy Jaszczyk; Cullen Eddy, Rod Sarich, Dustin Kohn, Mark Thomas, Darrell Hay, Ben O'Connor; Jeff Legue, Mike Forney, Mathieu Roy, Jason Hewitt, Jonathan Phillips *capt*, Tyler Mosienko, Phil Hill, Colton Fretter, Robert Dowd.
Coach: Gerad Adams. *Asst. coach*: Neil Abel.

PLAY-OFF FINALS

Semi-Finals 4 April 2015, National Ice Centre

SHEFFIELD-HULL   **3-2**   (0-0,2-1,1-1)

Scoring:

0-1 HUL	Galbraith (Frederick, Hervato)		31.41
1-1 SHE	Hay (Dowd, Mosienko) pp		34.51
2-1 SHE	Fretter (Eddy, Mosienko)		37.51
2-2 HUL	Tanaka (unass.)		48.40
3-2 SHE	Roy (unass.)	pp	59.56

Netminding:

Unice SHE	8-13-10 31	save%	93.55
Brown HUL	13-17-15 45	save%	93.33

Penalty minutes: Steelers 12, Stingrays 16.
Goals/powerplays: Steelers 2/5, Stingrays 0/3.
Men of Match: Dowd SHE, Lauzon HUL.
Referees: Dean Smith, Matt Thompson.
Lines: Beresford, Young.   *Attendance:* 6,924.

BELFAST-COVENTRY   **2-2ot**   (1-1,1-0,0-1,0-0)

Stingrays win 3-2 after penalty shootout.
Ben Arnt scores winning shot.

Scoring:

1-0 BEL	Mason (Kompon, Phillips)		11.21
1-1 COV	DaCosta (Tait, Cowley)		11.50
2-1 BEL	Sawada (Mason, Cheverie)		29.15
2-2 COV	Tendler (Goertzen, O'Marra)		41.52

Netminding:

Murphy BEL	4- 6-10-8 28	save%	92.86
Stewart COV	12-12-14-3 41	save%	95.12

Penalty minutes: Giants 0, Blaze 2.
Goals/powerplays: Giants 0/1, Blaze 0/0.
Men of Match: Robinson BEL, Tendler COV.
Referees: Tom Darnell, Mike Hicks.
Lines: Dalton, Staniforth.   *Attendance:* 6,924.

Final 5 April 2014, National Ice Centre

SHEFFIELD-COVENTRY   **2-4**   (0-1,0-3,2-0)

Scoring:

1-0 COV	Goertzen (Egener, O'Marra)		03.01
2-0 COV	Tendler (O'Marra, Goertzen)		20.29
3-0 COV	Venus (Cowley)		29.17
4-0 COV	Tait (unass.)		30.44
4-1 SHE	Roy (unass.)		43.26
4-2 SHE	Roy (Forney, Eddy)	sh	47.03

Netminding:

Unice SHE	5-12- 3 20	save%	80.00
Stewart COV	12-12-13 37	save%	94.59

Penalty minutes: Steelers 4, Blaze 4.
Goals/powerplays: Steelers 0/2, Blaze 0/2.
Men of Match: Mosienko SHE, Stewart COV.
Referees: Tom Darnell, Mike Hicks.
Lines: Dalton, Young.   *Attendance:* 6,952.

VIEWS OF THE PLAY-OFF WEEKEND

'I enjoyed the weekend. However, the production of the whole thing was a letdown.

▼ 'Video scoreboard: Why no replays? Or even streaming the game live like in the NHL. Rink teams have replay facilities, so why can't the league's main showpiece? [Simply, the NIC s scoreboard can't do this - Ed.]

'Personally, I can't understand why they can't hook up a projector on the stage wall and have a replay screen there.

▼ 'Game presentation: No pyrotechnics or ticker-tape when Coventry won. Some half-arsed cheerleaders for the final. Why not have them for the whole weekend?

▼ 'You shouldn't need other teams' mascots for the entertainment. However, the dance-off was entertaining.

▼ 'Nothing to do between the 3rd/4th game and the final. It's Easter Sunday. Nothing was open in the city unless you wanted fast food or had friends to drink with. I was alone on the Sunday, had family on the Saturday, so just sat in my seat for 2 hours while waiting for the final. Surely there was something that could have filled that gap, kids' game, etc.? It wasn't like they had anything to set up for the final.'

'natoono' on www.thehockeyforum.co.uk, reflecting some of the Annual*'s thoughts.*

VIDEO REVIEW

Editor comments - No information was provided to fans or the media regarding the video review system at the finals weekend.

As this system has never been used before by the league, and it turned out to have a major influence on the outcome of both semis, this seems to us to have been a mistake.

Better late than never, the *Annual* is happy to pass on the information we managed to glean at Nottingham.

● All goals were reviewed. In the second semi, even a goal that had been missed on the ice was reviewed by the off-ice team, then awarded after the fact. This rather bemused the 7,000 uninformed spectators, however.

● The reviews were conducted by an off-ice team of game officials, i.e. those who had been appointed for the weekend but were not on the ice for that game.

● The review team sat at TV monitors behind the timekeepers' and announcers' area and were able to communicate easily with their on-ice colleagues.

PAST PLAY-OFF WINNERS

2013-14	Sheffield Steelers
2012-13	Nottingham Panthers
2011-12	Nottingham Panthers
2010-11	Nottingham Panthers
2009-10	Belfast Giants
2008-09	Sheffield Steelers
2007-08	Sheffield Steelers
2006-07	Nottingham Panthers
2005-06	Newcastle Vipers
2004-05	Coventry Blaze
2003-04	Sheffield Steelers

Blaze win 'the video finals'

Chuck Weber, the new coach of Coventry Blaze, cemented his place in Elite League history by taking his team from sixth place in the regular season to the Play-off Championship.

The weekend produced the most thrilling and controversial play-off hockey for years.

After the first two periods of the final, the Blaze remarkably held a commanding 4-0 lead over the league-winning Steelers.

But they only just survived a dramatic third session when Sheffield's skilful and quick-thinking attacker Mathieu Roy pulled two back but then had his hat-trick effort mysteriously disallowed with a minute to go.

The first semi, when seventh place Hull Stingrays came close to upsetting the Steelers, was notable for video review being used for the first time in Elite League games. (See previous page for details).

Robert Dowd's first 'goal' for Sheffield was disallowed for a borderline high stick, but Roy's powerplay winner was ruled legitimate, despite Hull's protests that Omar Pacha's holding penalty was unnecessary.

Cory Tanaka's equaliser for the Stingrays was upheld after a third consultation.

A fourth review was needed in the Giants-Blaze semi after Justin DaCosta's tying goal for the Blaze appeared to hit the post but actually went through the goal net. The shot counted but, oddly, the officials failed to check the netting.

▲ Roy's three goals at the weekend brought his season totals to a league-leading 46 goals and 101 points. Another puzzle - when his fourth 'goal' in the final was disallowed, the officials did not request a video review.

CHALLENGE CUP

Open to all Elite League teams, the Challenge Cup was inaugurated by the Superleague in season 1997-98 when it was sponsored by a national newspaper and known as The Express Cup.

The teams in 2013-14 were divided into two groups with each team playing twice - once at home and once away - against each of the others in their group.

The top four teams in each group went through to the second round (quarter-finals). After the first round, all ties were played home and away - first in group A versus fourth in group B, and so on - with aggregate scores deciding the successful teams.

Five minutes overtime and penalty shots, as necessary, were played in the event of an aggregate draw at the end of the second leg.

In the final - also played over home and away legs - the team finishing highest in the Qualifying Round received choice of home leg.

Ten of the 40 first round games and two of the quarter-finals counted for league points.

The draw for the subsequent stages took place live at Sheffield's Motorpoint Arena, during the first interval of the Steelers' game against Nottingham Panthers on 6 December.

The draw determined the match-ups for the semi-final stages, and the home and away teams for the stand-alone final.

QUALIFYING ROUND STANDINGS

Group A	GP	W	OW	OL	L	GF	GA	Pts
Braehead Clan	8	5	2	0	1	28	18	14
Fife Flyers	8	4	1	2	1	27	14	12
Belfast Giants	8	4	1	2	1	31	21	12
Dundee Stars	8	2	1	0	5	19	32	6
E'burgh Capitals	8	0	0	1	7	12	32	1
Group B								
Sh'ld Steelers	8	5	1	1	1	25	17	13
Cardiff Devils	8	5	1	0	2	29	17	12
Nott'm Panthers	8	3	1	0	4	18	24	8
Coventry Blaze	8	2	0	2	4	18	26	6
Hull Stingrays	8	1	1	1	5	24	30	5

Points allocated as in league. Teams tied on points separated by most goals scored.

CHALLENGE CUP ACTION *above* Steelers v Devils in the Final at Sheffield;
below Devil **Chris Culligan** sweeps the puck home against the Blaze in their semi-final.
photos courtesy: Sheffield Star, South Wales Echo.

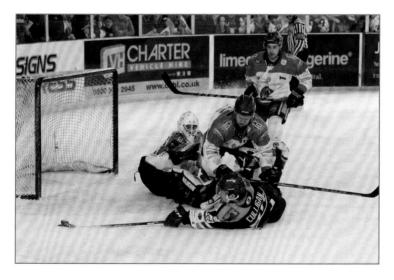

QUALIFYING ROUND RESULTS

Group A	BEL	BRH	DUN	EDI	FIF
Belfast		3-4ot (A)	7-1*	8-2*	1-6*
Braehead	4-3so (1)		3-0	3-1*	4-3*
Dundee	1-4*	4-7		6-4	2-1ot (B)
Edinburgh	1-2	0-3	2-3		1-2so (3)
Fife	2-3ot (E)	4-0	4-2	5-1	

Group B	CAR	COV	HUL	NOT	SHE
Cardiff		4-3	7-2	5-2	2-3
Coventry	0-4		4-3	4-3	2-3ot (C
Hull	2-3	4-3ps (4)		2-3ot (D)	2-3
Nottingham	3-1*	2-1	1-6*		2-1
Sheffield	2-3so (2)	3-1	#6-3	4-2	

* also league game   # at iceSheffield

Overtime scoring (ot)
A BRH Neil Trimm (Pitt) 60.34.
B DUN Igor Gongalsky (McCluskey) 63.38
C SHE Tyler Mosienko (Fretter, Thomas) 64.55
D NOT Nathan Robinson (Graham, Jacina) 62.52
E BEL Calvin Elfring (Mason, Kompon) 61.37

Winning penalty shots (so)
1   Derek Roehl BRH.
2   Joey Martin CAR
3   Bobby Chaumont FIF
4   Zach Hervato HUL

QUARTER-FINALS
9 Dec   Fife-Nottingham   2-7   (1-0,4-1,2-1)
7 Jan   Nottingham-Fife   4-6   (3-3,1-1,0-2)
Nottingham Panthers win 11-8 on aggregate
6 Jan   Belfast-Cardiff   3-4   (0-0,1-3,2-1)
14 Jan Cardiff-Belfast   4-2   (0-2,2-0,2-0)
Cardiff Devils win 8-5 on aggregate
14 Jan Coventry-Braehead 1-3   (0-1,1-1,0-1)
21 Jan B'head-Coventry   1-3ot (1-1,0-0,0-2)
COV **Ben Arnt** converts winning shot,
Coventry Blaze win 5-4 aggregate
8 Jan   Dundee-Sheffield   0-3   (0-2,0-1,0-0)
14 Jan Sheffield-Dundee   11-1 (3-0,3-1,5-0)
Sheffield Steelers win 14-1 on aggregate

SEMI-FINALS
First semi-final, first leg, 18 February 2015
COVENTRY-CARDIFF   1-4 (0-1,1-3,0-0)
Scoring: COV Sindel 1g; Tait, Tanaka 1a. CAR
Walton, Myers, Tahtinen, Lord 1g; Clarkson,
Batch, Hudson, Morissette, Culligan, Marsh,
Martin 1a. *Shots*: Stewart COV 26 (84.6%),
Bowns COV 39 (97.4%). *Pims*: COV 2, CAR 10.
G/PP: COV 0/5, CAR 1/1. *Refs*: Darnell, Hicks.
Lines: Beresford, Kavanagh. *Att*: 2,444.

Second leg, 25 February 2015
CARDIFF-COVENTRY   5-3 (3-1,0-2,2-0)
Scoring: CAR Martin 2g; Myers, Walton 1+1;
Culligan 1g; Lord, Richardson 2a; Clarkson,
Haddad, Morissette, Clarkson 1a. *Shots*: Bowns
CAR 21 (85.7%), Stewart COV 35 (85.7%). *Pims*:
CAR 14, COV 26 (Egener 2+10 slash). *G/PP*:
CAR 2/6, COV 1/5. *Refs*: Darnell, Hicks. *Lines*:
Beresford, Kavanagh. *Attendance*: 1,930.
CARDIFF DEVILS win 9-4 on aggregate

Second semi-final, first leg, 19 February 2015
SHEFFIELD-NOTTINGHAM   1-3 (0-2,1-1,0-0)
Scoring: SHE Roy 1g; Petruska, Forney 1a. NOT
Doucet 1+1; Mosey, Lawrence 1g; Jacina,
Lachowicz, Cohen 1a. *Shots*: Unice/Woolhouse
SHE 29 (89.7%), Kowalski NOT 37 (97.3%).
Pims: SHE 17 (Eddy 5m-fight), NOT 17 (Schmidt
5m-fight).   *G/PP*: SHE 0/4, NOT 0/4. *Refs*:
Darnell, Hicks. *Lines*: Kavanagh, Staniforth.
Attendance: 4,606.

Second leg 24 February 2015
NOTTINGHAM-SHEFFIELD 4-6 (0-3,3-0,1-3,0-0)
Teams tied 7-7 on aggregate. **Tomas Petruska**
scores winning shot for **Steelers**.
Scoring: NOT Boxill 1+1; Farmer, Lawrence,
Mosey 1g; Lachowicz, Berube, Parent, Graham,
Cohen 1a. SHE Fretter, Mosienko 1+2; Hay, Roy
1+1; Dowd, O'Connor 1g; Baldwin 2a; Forney 1a.
Shots: Kowalski 44 (86.4%), Gospel SHE 33
(87.9%). *Pims*: NOT 24, SHE 28. *G/PP*: NOT
1/9, SHE 2/7. *Refs*: Darnell, Smith. *Lines*:
Kavanagh, Staniforth. *Attendance*: 4,519.
SHEFFIELD STEELERS win 8-7 on aggregate

"Part of my thinking in borrowing Sam was that
he was a Nottingham boy who knew the rink and
some of the shooters." *Steelers' coach* **Gerad
Adams** *on icing Telford Tigers' goalie* **Sam
Gospel** *in their tie at Nottingham.*

FINAL

Motorpoint Arena, Sheffield, 8 March 2015
SHEFFIELD-CARDIFF   1-2 (0-0,0-2,1-0)
Scoring:
1-0 CAR   Lord (Martin, Hudson) pp   21.07
2-0 CAR   Culligan (Hendrikx, Batch)   22.55
1-2 SHE   Eddy (unassisted)   52.38
Netminding:
Unice SHE   9-6- 5 20   save% 90.00
Bowns CAR   7-7-11 25   save% 96.00
Penalty minutes: Steelers 4, Devils 4.
Goals/powerplays: Steelers 0/2, Devils 1/2.
Men of Match: Not recorded.
Refs: Tom Darnell, Mike Hicks.
Lines: Andy Dalton, Lee Young.
Attendance: 7,328.

Cardiff Devils win the Challenge Cup

THE WINNING TEAM

Cardiff Devils
Ben Bowns, Mike Will; Carl Hudson, Mark Richardson, Tyson Marsh (capt), Andrew Hotham, Josh Batch, Trevor Hendrikx; Matthew Myers, Chris Jones, Brent Walton, Luke Piggott, Joey Hadddad, Markku Tahtinen, Jake Morissette, Chris Culligan, Andrew Lord, Joey Martin, Doug Clarkson.
Coach: Andrew Lord. *Asst. coach:* Neil Francis.

LEADING CUP SCORERS

	GP	G	A	Pts	Pim
Michael Forney SHE	13	9	8	17	18
Bobby Chaumont FIF	10	9	8	17	2
Brent Walton CAR	13	7	10	17	10
Mathieu Roy SHE	12	6	10	16	8
Joey Martin CAR	13	5	11	16	4

LEADING CUP NETMINDERS

	GPI	Mins	SoG	GA	Sv%
Frank Doyle SHE	10	598	292	17	94.2
Ben Bowns CAR	12	722	375	25	93.3
Kyle Jones BRH	10	606	317	22	93.1

Qualification: 300 minutes.

Telford Tigers' goalie **SAM GOSPEL**, who was borrowed by Sheffield Steelers for their Cup tie victory in Nottingham.

Devils win trophy after 9 years

Cardiff Devils won their first major silverware for nine years, knocking out a strangely subdued Sheffield Steelers in their own barn.

In a game where defences ruled, there was little to choose between these rivals in their eighth head-to-head of the season.

Steelers were knocked back in the sixth minute by a hamstring injury to **Tomas Petruska** which hobbled their top line.

The second blow fell when Devils' player-coach **Andrew Lord** and **Chris Culligan** scored in under two minutes at the start of the middle stanza.

On the local newspaper's website, reporter *Terry Phillips* wrote: 'After the final whistle, captain **Tyson Marsh** and his team-mates were doing the Ayatollah, spraying champagne at each other and the fans, while owners **Steve King**, **Craig Shostak** and **Brian Parker** were running around the ice hugging everybody in a Devils shirt. "What an amazing night." said King.

In the two-leg semis, the Devils beat Coventry Blaze home and away, and the Steelers knocked out old rivals Panthers, each team winning in the other's barn.

The second leg of Steelers-Panthers produced the most drama with Sheffield forced to ice an EPIHL goalie when all three of their own back-stoppers were injured.

Facing a 3-1 deficit from the first game, the Steelers fought to a 7-7 draw on aggregate. Their stand-in netminder **Sam Gospel** stopped all three Panthers' efforts in the shootout while Petruska recovered to convert the winner.

ENGLISH PREMIER LEAGUE

FINAL STANDINGS

		GP	W	OW	OL	L	GF	GA	Pts	Pct.
(6)	Telford Tigers TEL	48	36	3	3	6	226	119	81	84.4
(3)	Guildford Flames GUI	48	25	5	4	14	177	144	64	66.7
(2)	Basingstoke Bison BAS	48	24	4	5	15	170	155	61	63.5
(9)	Peterborough Phantoms PET	48	21	6	2	19	167	163	56	58.3
(5)	Swindon Wildcats SWI	48	24	4	0	20	172	150	56	58.3
(1)	Manchester Phoenix MAN	48	17	4	7	20	179	165	49	51.0
(4)	Milton Keynes Lightning MIL	48	16	2	6	24	152	186	42	43.8
(7)	Sheffield Steeldogs SHE	48	12	6	2	28	150	203	38	39.6
(8)	Bracknell Bees BRK	48	7	0	5	36	108	216	19	19.8

Positions of tied teams are decided by the results between them.
Scoring system: two points for a regulation time Win (W) or Overtime Win (OW), one point for an Overtime or shootout Loss (OL). (No individual stats are awarded from the shootout.)
Positions of tied teams decided on the number of regulation time Wins (W), then total Wins (W/OW).
Pct. = percentage of points gained to points available.
Figure in brackets indicates position in 2013-14.

LEADING POINTS SCORERS

	GP	G	A	Pts	Pims
Peter Szabo TEL	48	28	59	87	28
Aaron Nell SWI	47	39	43	82	40
Frantisek Bakrlik MAN	45	37	44	81	132
Jason Silverthorn TEL	45	38	39	77	70
Robin Kovar MAN	48	29	45	74	89
Milan Kousterek MIL	48	38	31	69	122
Ciaran Long BAS	45	33	31	64	94
David Longstaff GUI	48	15	47	62	18
Jonas Höög SWI	33	16	44	60	20
Joe Greener BAS	46	28	31	59	134

LEADING NETMINDERS

	GP	Mins	SoG	GA	Save%
T Murdy TEL	48	1925	966	75	92.2
Stevie Lyle SWI	48	2873	1748	142	91.9
S Fone MAN	44	1608	1021	86	91.6
J Hadfield GUI	47	1730	936	79	91.6
Janis Auzins PET	46	2768	1716	146	91.5

Qualification: One-third of team's games

Aaron Nell *most goals*

SIN-BIN

Players' penalties	GP	Pims	Ave
Andre Payette SHE	30	255	8.50
Callum Pattinson SHE	31	232	7.48
Greg Pick PET	34	136	4.00
Grant McPherson MIL	44	171	3.89
James Galazzi BRK	46	166	3.61

OFFICIAL WEBSITE
www.eiha.co.uk/leagues/englishpremier

ENGLISH PREMIER LEAGUE

RESULTS CHART

	BAS	BRK	GUI	MAN	MIL	PET	SHE	SWI	TEL
Bison	X	1/11 **4-2**	4/10 1-2so (3)	20/9 **3-2**	8/11 **3-2**	13/9 **6-4**	11/10 **5-3**	15/11 **2-1**	27/9 2-1so (2)
	X	31/1 **4-0**	21/12 **2-3**	18/10 **4-3**	24/1 **5-4**	6/12 **2-4**	7/2 **6-1**	28/12 **1-2**	29/11 **2-4**
	X	14/2 **5-1**	28/2 5-4so (17)	17/1 **3-2**	15/3 **6-4**	10/1 **4-3**	21/2 **3-2**	7/3 **3-5**	3/1 3-2so (10)
Bees	12/10 **4-3**	X	26/10 **4-1**	13/9 **1-3**	21/9 **1-3**	20/9 **1-2**	15/11 **4-3**	19/10 **1-4**	4/10 **3-11**
	20/12 2-3so (8)	X	28/12 **3-6**	8/11 **3-1**	4/1 **4-3**	16/11 **0-2**	30/11 **1-5**	11/1 **3-1**	15/2 **1-4**
	8/3 **3-5**	X	8/2 **2-4**	24/1 **3-8**	21/2 **3-4**	1/2 **1-4**	22/3 **6-8**	18/1 **2-3**	22/2 3-4so (16)
Flames	2/11 **6-3**	6/12 **3-1**	X	5/10 **6-3**	14/9 **5-3**	19/10 **5-1**	29/10 **11-1**	21/9 **2-4**	11/10 **1-7**
	11/1 **3-4**	26/12 4-3ot (F)	X	22/11 **4-3**	18/1 **6-4**	9/11 **5-3**	4/1 2-3so (11)	21/2 **6-2**	24/1 **0-4**
	18/2 **4-3**	1/1 **5-2**	X	14/3 **4-3**	1/3 4-3ot (K)	7/2 5-4so (15)	15/2 **5-2**	8/3 **6-3**	21/3 **1-2#**
Phoenix	9/11 **8-3**	7/12 **7-0**	16/11 **5-3**	X	23/11 3-2so (6)	28/9 **3-2**	21/9 **4-6**	14/9 3-4so (1)	26/10 2-3ot (D)
	4/1 **4-3so** (12)	15/3 **5-4**	25/1 5-6so (13)	X	21/12 **5-3**	30/10 **3-4**	9/10 2-3ot (N)	8/2 **5-2**	27/12 **1-6**
	1/2 4-3so (14)	21/3 **6-1**	22/2 **5-2**	X	15/2 **5-1**	1/3 **3-5**	8/1 **8-2**	22/3 **6-5**	11/1 **3-5**
Lightning	25/10 **6-4**	11/10 **4-0**	1/11 **3-2**	27/9 **1-4**	X	4/10 5-4so (4)	18/10 1-2ot (B)	9/11 **2-3**	15/11 **3-6**
	13/12 **2-1**	17/1 **8-4**	30/11 **4-1**	31/1 **5-4**	X	22/11 **3-4**	10/1 **7-2**	10/12 **3-11**	7/2 **1-2**
	21/3 **1-3**	7/3 **5-4so** (18)	20/12 **1-2**	28/2 **5-4**	X	14/2 **5-3**	22/2 **3-1**	25/1 **3-6**	14/3 **6-3**
Phantoms	21/9 **0-3**	25/10 4-3ot (C)	27/9 2-1ot (A)	29/11 **5-4**	12/10 **3-1**	X	14/9 **5-3**	5/10 **4-2**	18/10 **1-4**
	30/11 **2-5**	3/1 **4-0**	15/11 **5-4**	20/12 2-1so (9)	2/11 **5-6**	X	8/2 **6-2**	7/12 **3-4**	31/1 **3-2**
	15/2 **2-5**	21/1 **5-3**	15/3 **5-4**	8/3 3-2so (19)	22/3 **4-1**	X	14/3 4-3ot (L)	22/2 **2-5**	28/2 **4-5**
Steeldogs	19/10 **2-5**	5/10 **3-7**	7/12 **2-3**	3/10 **4-7**	20/9 **6-2**	26/10 **6-2**	X	28/9 **3-1**	13/9 **3-4**
	14/12 **7-4**	21/12 **4-1**	17/1 **1-5**	3/1 **4-3ot** (H)	11/1 2-1ot (I)	8/11 2-3so (5)	X	22/11 **1-5**	1/11 **2-8**
	25/1 6-5ot (J)	1/3 **5-1**	14/2 **1-4**	18/1 **1-2**	1/2 **5-3**	27/12 **5-3**	X	15/3 **1-4**	31/12 **2-3**
	BAS	**BRK**	**GUI**	**MAN**	**MIL**	**PET**	**SHE**	**SWI**	**TEL**

RESULTS CHART, contd

	BAS	BRK	GUI	MAN	MIL	PET	SHE	SWI	TEL
Wildcats	26/10 **2-4**	27/12 **4-2**	20/9 **2-4**	6/12 **4-2**	29/10 **5-4ot** (E)	11/10 **2-7**	25/10 **2-5**	X	8/11 **4-0**
	1/1 **3-2ot** (G)	7/2 **10-1**	18/10 **2-5**	10/1 **4-2**	16/11 **1-3**	24/1 **1-5**	29/11 **5-4**	X	13/12 **5-4**
	14/3 **4-8**	28/2 **5-1**	3/1 **1-3**	14/2 **4-2**	18/2 **5-1**	21/3 **6-2**	31/1 **7-4**	X	17/1 **3-5**
Tigers	16/11 **6-1**	14/9 **6-1**	25/10 **4-1**	30/11 **5-6so** (7)	5/10 **7-4**	23/11 **7-4**	9/11 **8-2**	1/10 **0-4**	X
	18/1 **6-5**	2/11 **3-2**	14/12 **4-1**	28/12 **6-2**	19/10 **7-1**	4/1 **4-5**	6/12 **7-2**	12/10 **3-0**	X
	1/3 **7-1**	25/1 **8-5**	22/3 **4-3ot** (M)	21/2 **3-0**	8/2 **6-2**	7/3 **6-4**	8/3 **5-3**	1/2 **5-0ab***	X
	BAS	BRK	GUI	MAN	MIL	PET	SHE	SWI	TEL

Score shown in **bold**. First figure is date of game.
The first result for each home team also counted towards the English Challenge Cup.
References in brackets refer to overtime goals (OT) and game winning shots in shootouts (SO), details of which are shown below.
* With both teams' agreement, referee allowed clock to run down from 48.47 after Telford player was injured with the Tigers leading 5-0.
# Game abandoned in 31st minute due to a crack in the Spectrum ice near one goal. Result was allowed to stand as more than half the game had been played.

OVERTIME WINNING GOALS (ot)

A	PET Edgars Apelis (J Ferrara)		63.18
B	SHE Lubomir Korhon (Morgan)	pp	64.59
C	PET Marc Levers (unass.)	dp	63.37
D	TEL Jason Silverthorn (Davies)		64.02
E	SWI Jan Kostal (Smith)	pp	60.46
F	GUI Matt Towe (Kvetan, Campbell)		64.26
G	SWI Jan Kostal (Malasinski)	sh	63.49
H	SHE Janis Ozilins (Duncombe)		61.14
I	SHE Lee Hayward (unass.)		61.23
J	SHE Korhon (Hayward, Wood)		62.24
K	GUI Longstaff (Savage, Kutny)		64.25
L	PET Luke Ferrara (Kumeliauskas)		62.19
M	TEL Max Birbraer (Davies)	pp	64.17
N	SHE Lloyd Gibson (Korhon)		no record

GAME WINNING SHOTS (so)

1	SWI Tomasz Malasinski
2	BAS Ciaran Long
3	GUI Branislav Kvetan
4	MIL Milan Kostourek
5	PET Darius Pliskauskas
6	MAN Tony Hand MBE
7	MAN Frankie Bakrlik
8	BAS Ciaran Long
9	PET Darius Pliskauskas
10	BAS Tomas Karpov
11	SHE Tom Squires
12	MAN Adam Walker
13	GUI Vladimir Kutny
14	MAN Michal Psurny
15	GUI Marcus Kristoffersson
16	TEL Dan Davies
17	BAS Grant Rounding
18	MIL Blaz Emersic
19	PET Donatas Kumeliauskas

FAIR PLAY

Team Penalties	GP	Pims	Ave
Manchester Phoenix	48	618	12.9
Swindon Wildcats	48	701	14.6
Telford Tigers	48	803	16.7
Guildford Flames	48	825	17.2
Peterborough Phantoms	48	868	18.1
Basingstoke Bison	48	933	19.4
MK Lightning	48	937	19.5
Bracknell Bees	48	1195	24.9
Sheffield Steeldogs	48	1405	29.3

Tigers Win at Planet Ice Peterborough

'Peterborough Phantoms were powerless to prevent the English Premier League title being won at Planet Ice last night (28 February).

'The city rink was the scene for big-spending, table-topping Telford Tigers' inevitable crowning ... as they edged a ding-dong duel by the odd goal in nine.

'But their 5-4 success ultimately proved academic as a loss for second-placed Guildford in Basingstoke ended the Flames' faint hopes of snatching the silverware.

'News of the result in Hampshire ... was the trigger for the travelling army of Tigers' fans to erupt in delight with a couple of minutes of their own team's contest remaining.

'Wild celebrations on and off the ice were tough for Phantoms to watch ....

www.peterboroughtoday.co.uk, 1 March 2015

Cash Boost for Runner-up

'IMP-UK have today announced that they will give a cash boost of £5,000 to the team finishing in second place at the end of the English Premier League season in 2015.

'Hockey fans may remember that IMP-UK [Ice Media Productions] were responsible for bringing British ice hockey back on to TV screens seven years ago with the support of NASN and Setanta, and were also the first media company in the UK streaming British and North American ice hockey live ...

'The cash boost could benefit any of the top teams currently within the league.'

From a post on www.thehockeyforum.co.uk on 5 December 2014 by 'sledgewomble'.

ENGLISH PREMIER LEAGUE REPORT

Wayne's World

This was the most memorable season for *Telford Tigers* since Canadians **Kevin Conway** and **Tim Salmon** helped them win their first league title in 1987-88.

Coach **Tom Watkins** took full advantage of the funding from **Wayne Scholes**' Red Hockey to put together a side that leapt up the table from last to first in two seasons.

Watkins' key signings were GB defenceman **Jonathan Weaver** and Slovakian **Peter Szabo**, who ended as the league's top scorer.

Paul Dixon was constantly tinkering with *Guildford Flames*' line-up. But the 2012-13 winners were at a loss against the Tigers, scoring just seven goals in six games (all defeats) against them.

By contrast, **Doug Sheppard** made few changes to his *Basingstoke Bison* who beat the Tigers twice at home, but still finished a massive 20 points behind them.

Fourth and fifth placed *Peterborough Phantoms* and *Swindon Wildcats* never seriously challenged the leading sides but both took points off the Tigers. **Ryan Aldridge**'s Wildcats not only beat Telford three times, their GB netminder **Stevie Lyle** also shut them out twice.

Apart from Lyle, Swindon's outstanding performer was the league's ace goal sniper **Aaron Nell**, while keeper **Janis Auzins**, was the go-to guy for the Phantoms.

Tony Hand MBE's defending champion *Manchester Phoenix* began to feel the financial pinch in Altrincham's 'temporary' rink. In his last season, the Old One himself did more than his bit, averaging an assist per game. But injuries, especially to GB d-man **Luke Boothroyd**, took their toll.

In spite of returning to play in their expensively refurbished rink, *Milton Keynes Lightning* failed to find any form, though Czech forward **Milan Kostourek** ended second among the league's net-finders.

Sheffield Steeldogs' chances were hit when three of their best forwards, **Jeff Legue, Janis Ozilins** and **Lubomir Korhon**, played in only parts of the schedule.

Red Hockey stepped in to rescue *Bracknell Bees* only days before they finished their worst season for years.

PLAY-OFFS

The leading eight of the nine English Premier League sides qualified for the Play-offs.

In the quarter-finals, which were played over two legs, home and away, over one weekend, seed 1 faced seed 8, seed 2 played seed 7, and so on. Overtime and penalties were used after the second legs if necessary.

At the end of each round, the teams were reseeded.

For the finals weekend at Coventry's Skydome Arena, the seedings were determined by the original quarter-final ranking, so the highest placed team left in the competition was ranked as the highest seed.

The highest seed played the lowest seed in the first semi-final, with the remaining seeds playing in the second semi-final.

QUARTER-FINALS

27-29 March 2015
Manchester-Basingstoke   4-5h, 4-2a
Phoenix win 8-7 on aggregate
Milton Keynes-Guildford   3-2h, 4-3a
Lightning win 7-5 on aggregate
Peterborough-Swindon   4-3a, 2-1h
Phantoms win 6-4 on aggregate
Telford-Sheffield   5-0a, 6-3h
Tigers win 11-3 on aggregate

SEMI-FINALS

Coventry Skydome, 4 April 2015
TELFORD-P'BOROUGH   2-4   (1-2,0-1,1-1)
Scoring:
0-1 PET   Koulikov (L Ferrara)   01.56
1-1 TEL   Birbraer (Davies)   pp 11.14
1-2 PET   L Ferrara (Bebris, Pliskauskas) pp 19.58
1-3 PET   Pliskauskas (unass.)   30.42
2-3 TEL   Plant (Weaver, McKenzie)   41.56
2-4 PET   Pliskauskas (L Ferrara, J Ferrara) 57.09
Netminding:
Murdy TEL 13- 6-10 29   save% 86.21
Auzins PET 14-16- 8 38   save% 94.74
Penalty minutes: Tigers 20 (Weaver 2+10 ch-b),
Phantoms 33 (Bebris 5+game – hi-stick).
Goals/powerplays: Tigers 1/4, Phantoms 1/5.
Referee: Pickett. Lines: Cook, Korsaks.
Attendance: 2,600.

M KEYNES-MANCHESTER   4-7   (2-2,1-3,1-2)
Scoring:
0-1 MAN   Thompson (Archer, Kovář)   02.47
1-1 MIL   Huppe (Bowers)   08.49
1-2 MAN   Thompson (Archer, Kovář)   09.17
2-2 MIL   Hook (Emersic)   11.04
2-3 MAN   Kovář (Bakrlik, Walker)   21.02
3-3 MIL   Huppe (Carr, Kostourek)   26.48
3-4 MAN   Kovář (Archer)   36.59
3-5 MAN   Walker (Bakrlik, Hand)   39.18
4-5 MIL   Wiggins (Jamieson, McPherson) 46.34
4-6 MAN   Bakrlik (unass.)   en   59.11
4-7 MAN   Archer (unass.)   en   59.22
Netminding:
Wall MIL   16-14-14 44   save% 84.09
Fone MAN   12 9-10 31   save% 87.10
Penalty minutes: Lightning 4, Phoenix 4.
Goals/powerplays: Lightning 0/2, Phoenix 0/2.
Referee: Stefan Hogarth.
Lines: Lalonde, von Haselburg Palyvou.
Attendance: 2,600.

FINAL

Coventry Skydome, 5 April 2015
P'BOROUGH-MANCHESTER   5-2   (3-1,0-1,2-0)
Scoring:
1-0 PET   Baranyk (McGiffin, Bebris)   02.13
2-0 PET   Robson (Bebris)   pp   04.05
3-0 PET   Baranyk (Bebris)   13.17
3-1 MAN   Archer (Burlin, Hand)   pp   18.15
3-2 MAN   Bakrlik (Graham)   37.59
4-2 PET   Levers (Pliskauskas, Bebris) pp 52.33
5-2 PET   J Ferrara (Kumeliauskas)   59.21
Netminding:
Auzins PET 14-13-10 37   save% 94.59
Fone MAN   14- 8-11 33   save% 84.85
Penalty minutes: Phantoms 8, Phoenix 10.
Goals/powerplays: Phantoms 2/5, Phoenix 1/4.
Referee: Tim Pickett. Lines: Cook, A N Other.
Attendance: 2,600.

PETERBOROUGH PHANTOMS
are Play-off Champions

LEADING PLAY-OFF NETMINDERS

	GPI	Mins	SoG	GA	Sv%
Janis Auzins PET	4	240	138	8	94.2
Stephen Wall MIL	3	179	122	10	91.8
Thomas Murdy TEL	3	179	77	7	90.9

Qualification: played 80 minutes

LEADING PLAY-OFF SCORERS

	GP	G	A	Pts	Pim
Robin Kovář MAN	4	4	4	8	4
Frantisek Bakrlik MAN	4	4	3	7	4
James Archer MAN	4	2	5	7	4
Edgars Bebris PET	4	1	6	7	27
Darius Pliskauskas PET	4	3	3	6	2
Rick Plant TEL	3	1	5	6	0
Scott McKenzie TEL	3	3	2	5	2
Luke Ferrara PET	4	2	3	5	2
Jonathan Weaver TEL	3	1	4	5	16
Nathan Salem TEL	3	3	1	4	2

THE FINAL FOUR

MANCHESTER PHOENIX
Steve Fone, Declan Ryan; Luke Boothroyd, James Neil, Ben Wood (captain), Joe Graham, Johan Burlin; Tony Hand, James Archer, Bobby Chamberlain, Michal Psurny, Adam Walker, Jared Dickinson, Jacob Heron, Robin Kovář, Shaun Thompson, Frantisek Bakrlik, Jack Watkins. *Coach*: Tony Hand.

MILTON KEYNES LIGHTNING
Stephen Wall, Jordan Hedley; Lewis Christie, John Connolly, Michael Farn, Petr Horava, Leigh Jamieson, Nidal Phillips, Ben Russell; Blaz Emersic, Grant McPherson, Lewis Hook, Jordan Cownie, Adam Carr (capt), Chris Wiggins, Curtis Huppe, Ross Bowers, Milan Kousterek. *Coach*: Nick Poole. *Manager*: Vito Rausa.

PETERBOROUGH PHANTOMS
Janis Auzins, Dan Lane; Jason Buckman, Robert Ferrara, Cameron McGiffin, Thomas Norton, Greg Pick, Scott Robson; Milan Baranyk, Edgars Bebris, James Ferrara (capt), Luke Ferrara, Slava Koulikov, Donatas Kumeliauskas, Marc Levers, Darius Pliskauskas, Will Weldon, Bradley Moore, Martins Susters, Mason Webster, Josh Wicks. *Coach*: Vyacheslav (Slava) Koulikov. *Manager*: Jon Kynaston.

TELFORD TIGERS
Thomas Murdy, Sam Gospel; Marcus Maynard, Martin Ondrej, Rupert Quiney, Daniel Scott, Daniel Rose, Jonathan Weaver, Sam Zajac; Rick Plant, Peter Szabo, Owen Bennett, Jason Silverthorn (capt), Max Birbraer, James Smith, Daniel Davies, Joe Miller, Adam Taylor, Callum Bowley, Scott McKenzie, Blahoslav Novak, Nathan Salem. *Head coach*: Tom Watkins. *Manager*: Paul Thomason.

PAST PLAY-OFF CHAMPIONS

2013-14	Basingstoke Bison
2012-13	Manchester Phoenix
2010-11	Guildford Flames
2008-09	Peterborough Phantoms
2007-08, 09-10, 11-12	Slough Jets
2006-07	Bracknell Bees
2002-06	Milton Keynes Lightning
2001-02	Invicta Dynamos
2000-01	Romford Raiders
1999-00	Chelmsford Chieftains
1997-99, 92-93	Solihull Blaze
1993-97	*Wightlink* Raiders
1991-92	Medway Bears) *British Lge*
1990-91	Lee Valley Lions) *entry*
1989-90	Basingstoke Beavers) *playoffs*

Haunted by Phantoms

Hanging over the league's final competition of the year was the bitter dispute in Altrincham between the rink operator Silverblades and the **Manchester Phoenix** owner **Neil Morris**. (See *Review of the Year*.)

Tony Hand's team tried not to let this unwelcome blow worry them, but they had a torrid time keeping the **MK Lightning** at bay in the second semi-final.

It was only in the last period that they finally put their stamp on the game with two strikes into an unguarded Lightning net.

Earlier, **Peterborough Phantoms** threw everything at the newly crowned league champs, backed by a noisily anti-**Telford Tigers** crowd. "Some of the hits were as big as Elite League ones," said a fan, admiringly.

The Phantoms' key performances came from the Baltic Boys, Latvian netminder **Janis Auzins** (94.7%) and Lithuanian forward **Darius Pliskauskas** (two goals, three points).

After expending so much energy on the Saturday, **Slava Khoulikov**'s squad surprisingly took a 3-0 lead in the 14th minute of the final.

With fears for their future haunting their opponents, Peterborough wiped Manchester's marksman **Robin Kovář** off the scoresheet, powerplay unit scored twice and their Latvian, **Edgars Bebris**, set up four of their five goals.

At the final whistle, captain **James Ferrara** held aloft Peterborough's first silverware for six years.

ENGLISH CHALLENGE CUP
sponsored by *Red Touch Media*

Following the withdrawal of Slough Jets from the English Premier League (EPIHL), the league invited the top six teams from the third tier National League (NIHL) to join their nine sides in a new, regionalised cup competition.

Games between teams from the different leagues were played under the following rules:
- The use of non-EIHA trained players was restricted to one on the ice at any one time.
- EPIHL clubs' player-coaches could not ice.
- The EPIHL clubs' non-EIHA players were replaced by their under-23s.
Tied games were decided by playing a five-minute overtime period followed, if necessary, by a penalty shootout.

FIRST ROUND STANDINGS

South	GP	W	OW	OL	L	GF	GA	Pts
S'don Wildcats	14	9	2	0	3	58	29	22
G'ford Flames	14	10	1	0	3	68	28	22
MK Lightning	14	10	0	2	2	69	34	22
Bas'stoke Bison	14	10	0	1	3	66	33	21
Bracknell Bees	14	6	0	0	8	46	47	12
Ch'ford Ch'tains	14	3	0	0	11	34	58	6
Invicta Dynamos	14	3	0	0	11	39	98	6
W'link Raiders	14	2	0	0	12	24	77	4
North								
Telford Tigers	12	10	1	1	0	84	26	23
M'ch'ter Phoenix	12	8	1	1	2	79	35	19
She'd Steeldogs	12	8	0	0	4	64	37	16
P'boro' Phant's	12	6	0	0	6	47	47	12
Bl'burn Hawks	12	4	0	0	8	47	63	8
Solway Sharks	12	3	0	0	9	25	81	6
Billingham Stars	12	1	0	0	11	23	80	2

SEMI-FINALS

First semi-final, first leg, 28 January 2015
SWINDON-MANCHESTER   3-3 (1-1,2-1,0-1)
Second leg, February 2015
MANCHESTER-SWINDON   10-5 (2-0,5-2,3-3)
Phoenix win *13-8 on aggregate.*

Second semi-final, first leg, 4 February 2015
GUILDFORD-TELFORD   3-4 (3-1,0-0,0-3)
Second leg, 11 February 2015
TELFORD-GUILDFORD   5-2 (1-0,4-0,0-2)
Tigers win *9-5 on aggregate.*

TOM MURDY, the Tigers' winning goalie

FINALS

First leg, 12 March 2015
MANCHESTER-TELFORD   1-3 (1-1,0-3,0-0)
Scoring:
0-1 TEL   McKenzie (Novak)   19.13
0-2 TEL   Salem (Silverthorn)   22.43
0-3 TEL   McKenzie (unass.)   38.32
1-3 MAN   Bakrlik (Wood, Hand)   46.13
Netminding: Fone MAN 49 (93.9%), Murdy TEL 44 (97.7%). *Pims:* MAN 6, TEL 8.
Goals/powerplays: MAN 0/4, TEL 0/3.
Ref: Hogarth. *Lines:* Hamilton, Hetherington.
Second leg, 19 March 2015
TELFORD-MANCHESTER   5-2 (1-2,3-0,1-0)
Scoring:
0-1 MAN   Kovar (Neil, Bakrlik)   pp   02.00
0-2 MAN   Bakrlik (Kovar)   02.28
1-2 TEL   Szabo (Silverthorn, Salem)   05.54
2-2 TEL   Birbraer (Weaver, Szabo) pp   24.54
3-2 TEL   Szabo (Salem, Ondrej)   35.13
4-2 TEL   Novak (Maynard, Scott)   36.54
5-2 TEL   Novak (McKenzie, Plant)   49.19
Netminding: Murdy TEL 20 (90.0%), Fone MAN 48 (89.6%). *Pims:* TEL 20 (Quiney 10-misc.), MAN 14. *Goals/powerplays:* TEL 1/5, MAN 1/3.
Referee: Pickett. *Lines:* Gillingham, Marshall.

TELFORD TIGERS win the
English Challenge Cup *8-3 on aggregate.*

THE WINNING TEAM

Telford Tigers

Thomas Murdy, Sam Gospel; Marcus Maynard, Sam Zajac, Martin Ondrej, Daniel Rose, Daniel Scott, Jonathan Weaver, Rupert Quiney, Rick Skene; Rick Plant, Peter Szabo, Owen Bennett, Jason Silverthorn (capt), Max Birbraer, Daniel Davies, Joe Miller, Adam Taylor, Callum Bowley, Scott McKenzie, Blahoslav Novak, Nathan Salem.
Head coach: Tom Watkins. *Asst. coaches*: Karl Creamer, Barry Hollyhead. *Manager*: Paul Thomason.

Tigers dominate

As widely predicted, *Telford Tigers* won their second trophy of the season with a comfortable two-leg victory over *Manchester Phoenix*.

The Tigers dominated the first leg in Altrincham with only the Phoenix's netminder **Stephen Fone** keeping his side in the game.

Any complacency **Tom Watkins's** team might have felt was shaken at the start of the second leg when the Phoenix tied the overall score 3-3. But it was their last hurrah with **Peter Szabo** (2), **Blahoslav Novak** (2) and **Max Birbraer** scoring five unanswered goals.

The Tigers had earlier won the Battle of the Bulging Wallets when they beat *Guildford Flames* home and away in their semi.

Cup holders *Basingstoke Bison* couldn't get past the qualifying round with a fourth place finish.

■ The trophy was presented to the Tigers by former Liverpool FC player **Jamie Carragher**. Tigers' owner **Wayne Scholes** is apparently a great fan of the Premiership team and his Red Touch Media sponsored Carragher's XI in a charity match at Anfield in March 2015.

■ The second leg of the final at Telford ice rink was streamed online by *Premier Sports* and www.247.tv with commentary from BBC Radio Shropshire. More in *Review of the Year*.

■ Telford Tigers are owned by Red Hockey Ltd, which is itself owned by US-based technology company Red Touch Media.

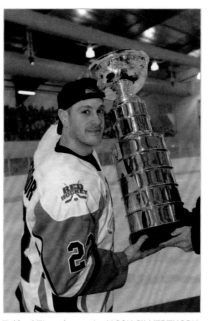

Telford Tigers' captain **JASON SILVERTHORN** with the Stanley Cup, sorry, the winners' trophy, which was commissioned by the sponsor Red Touch Media.

PAST PREMIER CUP WINNERS

2013-14	Basingstoke Bison
2012-13	Guildford Flames
2011-12	Guildford Flames
2010-11	Slough Jets
2009-10	Guildford Flames
2008-09	Peterborough Phantoms
2007-08	Bracknell Bees
2006-07	Guildford Flames
2005-06	Bracknell Bees
2004-05	Romford Raiders
2003-04	Peterborough Phantoms
2002-03	Peterborough Phantoms
2001-02	Romford Raiders
2000-01	Isle of Wight Raiders
1999-00	Chelmsford Chieftains
1998-99	Milton Keynes Kings

NATIONAL LEAGUE

OFFICIAL WEBSITE
www.eiha.co.uk/nihl

FINAL STANDINGS

Div One South	GP	W	L	D	GF	GA	Pts
Ch'ford Ch'ftains	36	26	5	5	163	79	57
Invicta Dynamos	36	25	11	0	202	140	50
Str'tham R'skins	36	23	11	2	187	141	48
W'link Raiders	36	20	9	7	164	107	47
Br'cknell Hornets	36	17	15	4	151	135	38
MK Thunder	36	16	15	5	127	118	37
S & G Devils	36	13	22	1	151	175	27
London Raiders	36	9	24	3	120	191	21
Oxford City Stars	36	7	25	4	143	230	18
Cardiff NL Devils	36	7	26	3	100	192	17

Div One North (Moralee)	GP	W	L	D	GF	GA	Pts
Bl'kburn Hawks	24	21	0	3	155	45	45
Billingham Stars	24	15	8	1	105	67	31
Solway Sharks	24	15	9	0	120	88	30
Sheff'ld Spartans	24	9	9	6	90	85	24
Sutton Sting	24	9	12	3	82	85	21
Whitley Warriors	24	7	14	3	80	99	17
M''ter Minotaurs	24	0	24	0	53	216	0

Teams tied on points are separated by the results in games between them.

LEADING NETMINDERS

South & North	GP	Min	SoG	GA	Sv%
James Flavell BIL	14	817	600	37	93.8
Euan King CHE	21	1259	636	41	93.5
Stuart Ashton BLA	12	679	276	20	92.7
Gary Russell SOL	13	699	426	31	92.7
Mark Lee INV	17	949	576	43	92.5
Damien King MIL	35	2030	1338	103	92.3
M Colclough WIG	28	1618	948	73	92.3
Mark Watson BIL	11	619	362	28	92.3
Daniel Brittle BLA	13	758	319	25	92.2

Qualification: 480 minutes played

LEADING SCORERS

South	GP	G	A	Pts	Pim
Callum Best STR	36	35	55	90	60
Juraj Huska INV	36	46	41	87	32
Callum Fowler INV	33	29	58	87	107
Steven Fisher STR	35	31	42	73	116
Jaroslav Cesky WIG	34	31	38	69	110

North	GP	G	A	Pts	Pim
Luke Brittle BLA	24	35	37	72	47
Adam Brittle BLA	24	24	44	68	26
Richard Bentham SOL	24	21	28	49	72
Jared Owen BLA	24	16	25	41	60
Oliver Barron SHE	24	26	13	39	51

PLAY-OFFS

QUARTER-FINALS

Chelmsford-London   0-5a, 0-5h
Forfeit to London after Chieftains iced an ineligible player

Invicta-Solent & Gosport   3-3a, 8-7h
Dynamos win 11-10 on aggregate

Milton Keynes-Streatham   2-2a, 7-2h
Thunder win 9-4 on aggregate

Wightlink-Bracknell   5-3h, 6-2a
Raiders win 11-5 on aggregate

SEMI-FINALS

South

Invicta-Milton Keynes   3-1a, 6-4h
Dynamos win 9-5 on aggregate

Wightlink-London   12-6h, 8-3a
Wightlink win 20-9 on aggregate

North *at Dumfries Ice Bowl*

Billingham-Solway   9-6

Blackburn-Sheffield   4-2

FINALS

South

Wightlink-Invicta   3-2h, 6-4a

WIGHTLINK RAIDERS
win NIHL South Play-off title
9-6 on aggregate

North *at Dumfries Ice Bowl*

Blackburn-Billingham   6-3

BLACKBURN HAWKS
win NIHL North (Moralee) Play-off title

-124-

CHELMSFORD CHIEFTAINS

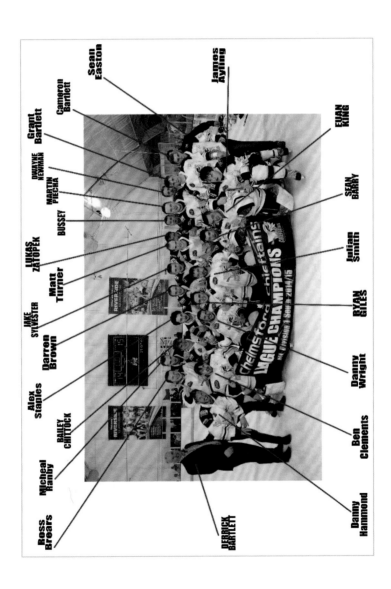

Sean Easton

James Ayling

Cameron Bartlett

Grant Bartlett

EVAN KING

DWAYNE NEWMAN

MARTIN PIECHA

SEAN BARRY

BUSSEY

LUKAS ZATOPEK

Julian Smith

Matt Turner

JAKE SYLVESTER

RYAN GILES

Darren Brown

Alex Staples

Danny Wright

BAILEY CHITTOCK

Ben Clements

Micheal Hanby

Danny Hammond

Ross Brears

DERRICK BARTLETT

NATIONAL LEAGUE SOUTH by Dave Carr

King sparkles for Chiefs

After **Chelmsford Chieftains**' total dominance of the previous year, it was a relief that the 2014-15 campaign was far more open.

While coach **Dwayne Newman** and his side clinched a third successive division title, they failed to retain the cup or play-off championship.

Unsurprisingly for a team organised by a former defenceman, the Essex side were stingy at the back, with Czech import **Lukas Zatopek** a key player on the blue line and **Euan King** on sparkling form between the pipes.

Conceding fewer than half the goals of their nearest rivals, it was no wonder that they triumphed over the 38-game regular season, with a few blowouts of other teams on the way.

Runners-up **Invicta Dynamos** were, by contrast, a swashbuckling outfit surrounded by drama on and off the ice. With arguably the division's most exciting line-up of forwards, including **Callum Fowler**, local legend **Andy Smith** and Slovak **Juraj Huska**, few 'Mos fans could argue with the fare on offer for the ticket price.

The revolving door of players out of the club put paid to their chances of matching the consistency of the Chieftains, but when **Kevin Parrish**'s team clicked they were a joy to watch.

They managed to pick up an elusive piece of silverware in the Cup competition, edging Chelmsford over two legs in the final.

But their hopes for an end-of-season double were dashed by **Wightlink Raiders**, the division's fourth place finishers.

Jeremy Cornish proved once again his ability to coach a seemingly unspectacular outfit to glory, with a sensational second leg win in front of a packed crowd at Invicta's Silverblades rink.

The Raiders were unfancied to win the two-leg final, but a spectacular cameo from the well-travelled Czech **Jaroslav Cesky** edged them over the line to the delight of their sizeable travelling support.

Streatham Redskins challenged strongly before slipping up late on. **Warren Rost**'s line-up boasted **Callum Best**, the division's player of the year and top scorer. The former Guildford Flame was in mesmerising form for the Londoners all season, combining with American **Sean** Scarbrough and **Steve Fisher** to form a formidable attacking trio.

Milton Keynes Thunder bounced back from dead last to become one of the division's most talked about teams. This was mainly due to some sensational performances by goalie **Damien King** and good work at the other end by captain **Jamie Line**.

Thunder's coach **Paul Gore** was rightly recognised at the end of the year by his peers, scooping the Coach of the Year award, ahead of Solent Devils' player-coach **Alex Murray**.

Solent were another much improved team. Canadian **Andrew Magee** was a key figure, as was their returning goalie **Christian Cole**, who had lasted only a few months at Wightlink at the start of the season.

PLAYER AWARDS

Player of the Year   **Callum Best**, Streatham
Coach of the Year   **Paul Gore**, MK Thunder
ALL-STAR TEAM
Goal: **Damien King**, M Keynes. Defence: **Lukas Zatopek** Chelmsford, **Dom Hopkins** Streatham. Forwards: **Callum Fowler, Juraj Huska** Invicta; **Callum Best**, Streatham.
Voted for by the division's coaches and players.

At the bottom of the pile, **London Raiders** just pulled away from trouble, thanks mainly to the fortunate mid-season captures of **Liam Chong** and **Alan Lack**. Both players were of a higher league pedigree and only found their way to the Lee Valley Ice Centre due to personal circumstances.

London's revival left Oxford and Cardiff to fight over the single relegation place. Ultimately, **Darren Elliott** and his City Stars condemned the Welsh side to Division Two thanks to some dramatic late results.

The relegation drama created so much enthusiasm in Oxford that the local radio station sent a commentator and pundit to the vital end-of-season clash in Cardiff against London. The Devils lost a heart-breaker as the winner came from their former player **Stephen Deacon**.

But they won a reprieve when the Division Two winners, **Bristol Pitbulls**, were unable to accept promotion.

Dave Carr, a regular columnist with www.prohockeynews.com, has occasionally been spotted on Streatham Redskins' blueline.

BLACKBURN HAWKS *left to right, back row:* Nick Riley (equipment), Mike Harris (asst. manager), Daniel MacKriel, Matt Viney, Aaron Davies, Jordan Bannon, Tom King, Jake Nurse, David Miekle, Richard Ravey, Chris Butler, Pavel Slowik, Richard Hughes, Ollie Lomax, Mark Kinder (manager); *front row:* Daniel Brittle, Luke Brittle, Chris Arnone, Jared Owen, Craig Rogers, Adam Brittle, Stuart Ashton.

Photo: Ella Thornton

NATIONAL LEAGUE NORTH (MORALEE)

Tigers' loss is Hawks' win

CHRIS MACKENZIE

Blackburn Hawks celebrated their 25th anniversary season by capturing the Moralee Division's league and play-off titles.

While it was the second play-off crown for Jared Owen's side, their wonderful unbeaten run of 21 wins and three draws in the regular season secured the first division title in their history.

Much of their success was down to the changes at the EPIHL's *Telford Tigers*, following their take-over by Red Hockey.

Five Telford-born players moved to the Hawks, including brothers **Adam** and **Luke Brittle**, who topped the scoring, and player-coach Owen, who was voted Coach of the Year.

Local men anchored the team's defence - **Chris Arnone**, who was also selected as an All-Star, and netminder **Stuart Ashton**, who started the year at Division Two's *Widnes Wild*.

Billingham Stars, who won the division in 2011-12 and ended third in 2013-14, had to settle for runners-up place this time, a huge 14 points behind Blackburn. **Michael Elder, Chris Sykes** and Winnipegger **Thomas Stuart-Dant** all had fine seasons up front while **Andrew Munroe** was impressive on defence.

Just one point behind the Stars were the 2013-14 winners *Solway Sharks*. After a poor start, coach **Martin Grubb** signed two imports - New Zealand forward **Josh Hay** and Belgian blueliner **Jens Engelen** – and the results came. Hay played nine games before Grubb axed him and brought back Slovakian **Pavol Melichercik**.

Dumfries's own **Alan Crane**, the team's captain, and **Struan Tonnar**, along with tricky Ayr-born forward **Stevie Moore** were the Scottish side's top performers.

Sutton Sting and *Sheffield Spartans* battled for fourth and the final play-off spot, a tussle which went down to a winner-takes-all game at iceSheffield at the end of the season. There the Spartans claimed a surprisingly comfortable 7-1 victory to advance to the play-off finals.

Whitley Warriors were not only out of the play-offs after a dismal sixth place finish but coach **Simon Leach** also had to lead his crew through the pain of a relegation play-off against Division Two's *Widnes Wild*. But as expected the Warriors had too much for the Wild over two legs and came away with an emphatic 20-5 aggregate victory. Whitley's flying teenage winger **Callum Queenan** is one to watch as he earned the division's Young Player of the Year award and was selected for GB's under-18 World Championship side.

Manchester Minotaurs, the second team at the Altrincham rink behind the EPIHL's troubled Phoenix, failed to gain a single point all season.

For the second year in a row, the play-offs were held at the Dumfries Ice Bowl over an April weekend. Sheffield had the most difficult game as they faced the Hawks.

PLAYER AWARDS

Player of the Year	**Adam Brittle**, Blackburn
Coach of the Year	**Jared Owen**, Blackburn
Best Young Player	**Callum Queenan**, Whitley
Fans' Favourite	**Chris Arnone**, Blackburn

All-Star Team
Goal: **Dimitri Zimozdra**, Sutton. *Defence*: **Chris Arnone**, Blackburn; **Jonathan Kirk**, Sheffield. *Forwards*: **Adam Brittle, Luke Brittle**, Blackburn; **Richard Bentham**, Solway.
Sponsored by www.prohockeynews.com

Martin White's Spartans had twice drawn with the division champs, so they started the game in a positive frame of mind. Their confidence was justified as they held the Hawks 2-2 until the 57th minute. Then **Aaron Davies** made it 3-2 Blackburn, and with only five seconds left, Luke Brittle fired into an empty net for a 4-2 Hawks' victory.

The second semi between the Stars and the Sharks was a free-scoring affair. With the game knotted at 3-3 early in the second, Billingham cut loose with five goals before the interval from Elder (2), Sykes, **Ben Davison** and **James Moss**. The defending play-off champion Sharks never recovered from the onslaught.

The final between the Stars and the Hawks was a repeat of the 2014 semi-final. With Billingham holding a narrow 3-2 lead after 41 minutes, their opponents woke up and beat keeper **James Flavell** three times in 75 seconds.

Aaron Davies, Luke Brittle and **Tom King** did the damage with **Jordan Bannon** later adding a sixth for good measure.

▲ A history of Blackburn Hawks' first 25 seasons is on Wikipedia.

TRIBUTES

ALLAN WOODHEAD

Allan Woodhead was a hugely respected figure in Grimsby sporting circles, especially in ice hockey.

He first became secretary of the town's ice hockey club in 1951 when the Redwings played in the Ladysmith Road rink. That building closed in 1956 but when the Cromwell Road rink opened in the 1970s he resumed his old post and was instrumental in re-forming the team.

The Buffaloes entered the amateur Southern League (there was no pro league in Britain in the 1970s) and attracted a sell-out crowd of 1,300 for their first game on 21 February 1975. (**Martin Weddell**, who went on to become CEO of **John Nike**'s Bracknell organisation, played on Grimsby's blueline.)

Mr Woodhead was a keen believer in youth sports and helped to create a strong junior organisation at Cromwell Road. Grimsby Dynamos won the Southern Junior League in their first year of competition.

This early success could not be built on, unfortunately, as the ice surface is well below standard size. The current rink is only 120 by 60 feet, which is even smaller than the Cromwell Road one.

Allan was a big supporter of sport for all. He worked with the sledge (disabled) ice hockey club, who award a trophy each year in his honour, and he was treasurer of Cleethorpes and Grimsby Riding for the Disabled.

He played several sports himself, including badminton (he was a founder member of the Grimsby Badminton League), golf (he was a member of Cleethorpes Golf Club), tennis and table tennis.

His wife Glenys has run a local riding school since 1986 and their son Ian has won medals at the European dressage championships. Ian's daughters represent Great Britain in dressage and eventing.

During World War Two, Allan served in the General Headquarters of the Middle East Land Forces in Egypt, employed in what he described as business of a 'highly secret nature'. On his return to civilian life, he worked for a local firm, staying on until he was 70.

Of all his sporting interests, it was his position as secretary of the ice hockey club that made him happiest, said Glenys. Allan held the post for almost 60 years until his health deteriorated. He contracted Parkinson's disease a few years ago.

Glenys added: "From all of the cards people have sent me, nearly everyone has said that Allan had helped them in some way. He just loved his work and he loved people."

Allan Woodhead was born in Grimsby on 8 May 1929 and died on 31 May 2015, aged 86.

ROWLEY WALKER

A player with the original Grimsby Redwings, **Rowley Walker** died in November 2014, age 91.

The *Grimsby Telegraph* reported – 'At his funeral, his daughter Nadine said: "On the ice he was fast and full of menace, frequently fighting and earning the nickname of the Sin Bin King."

'As an electrician, he was still signing certificates the week before he died. He was featured by Yorkshire Television as the oldest qualified electrician still working in England.

'This prompted an inspection from regulators who couldn't believe he could still be competent. Nadine said: "He sent the first inspector away with a flea in his ear for being condescending. He offered to have another inspection which, of course, he duly passed."'

BEN BEER, a goalie on Cardiff's recreational team, the Ice Hounds, died in September 2014 of pancreatitis. He was 25.

Ben was the son of **Anthony** and **Elaine Beer**. Anthony, a big Cardiff Devils' fan and a member of the old British Ice Hockey Writers Association, wrote the book 'It's Funny When You Win Everything' (Rover Publications, 1994), the story of the Devils' first decade.

The club have named a trophy in Ben's honour, and the Devils paid their own tribute with applause before one of their home games.

JOAN WILSON, the secretary of Liverpool Leopards and the Southern Ice Hockey Association in the 1970s, died on 26 February 2015 after a long illness. Joan's husband Bill, who was also closely involved in the sport, predeceased her.

BARRY GAGE

Defenceman **Barry Gage** was a founder and later captain of London Phoenix (Richmond) Flyers.

In 1983-84 he was part of the Southampton Vikings team that won Division One of the (Heineken) British League.

In all, he played 15 seasons (1976-91) for sides in Chelmsford, Richmond, Southampton and Streatham, appearing in a total of 370 games and scoring 290 points (56 goals).

GB defenceman **Robin Andrew**, one of his contemporaries, paid tribute on his Facebook page: "I respected Barry as an opponent and later when he was my teammate.

"He was the reason I got the opportunity to play hockey in Nottingham. I had retired from Streatham [in 1984] and he asked me to fill in for an injured import at Southampton. We went to Nottingham with only seven skaters and ... **Charlie Colon** in the nets and beat them 3-1 in front of 3,500 fans."

Among the other Facebook tributes paid to him were: "One of my first teammates when I came to the UK" – **Gary Stefan**; "He was a big part of Flyers' history" – **Geoff Dadswell**; "He taught me a lot about playing defence" – **Stevie Heath**; "A great defenceman and a really nice guy. I'll always cherish the memories I have of my time with the Flyers (1979-82) and he was a huge part of it" – **David Howden**.

Barry Gage died on 27 January 2015 from a brain tumour, aged 53, leaving his wife Maria.

ROD HINKS

Canadian winger **Rod Hinks** played in the Elite League with Newcastle Vipers (2006-07) and Cardiff Devils (2008-09).

Drafted by New York Islanders in 1993, he played most of his professional career in Europe, scoring 16 points (eight goals) for Villach in 2001-02 when they won the Austrian championship.

Rod died after suffering a heart attack at his home in Burlington, Ontario on 18 September 2014, aged 41, leaving sisters Joleen and Laurie and two nephews.

JONATHAN ADAMS

Canadian **Jon Adams**, who played a season with the Blackburn Hawks, died in Newmarket, Canada in July 2015, aged 25.

York Regional Police in Ontario released a statement on 9 July saying: "Jonathan Adams was found this afternoon deceased in a forested area near Dufferin and Davis Drive. His death is not being treated as suspicious at this time. Condolences to his family and many friends."

Adams was a member of the Hawks during the 2013-14 season, scoring 16 goals and 28 points in 16 games in the NIHL's Moralee Division. According to www.eliteprospects.com he also played for King Wild and South Muskoka Shield in Canada's GMHL and had a brief stint with Malungs IF in Sweden.

DAVE HOWELL

Sad news reached us just before press-time that former referee **Dave Howell** died following a heart attack in March 2014. He was 72.

Dave, who lived in the Liverpool area, officiated at games all over northern England in the 1970s and 1980s in the days when we had few rinks and even fewer referees. He is survived by his wife Sue and three daughters.

PLAYERS FROM THE GOLDEN ERA

BOB (DOC) BRODRICK

'Doc' Brodrick was the captain and assistant coach of Streatham in their all-conquering 1949-50 season. In that year, **Red Stapleford**'s men won the National League and National Tournament, and beat the world champions, Canada's Edmonton Mercurys. Robert James Brodrick BA, MD, CM, had two ambitions in life – one was to be a hockey player, the other to be a doctor. Hence his nickname.

Born and raised in Montreal, Canada, he learned to play on outdoor rinks before being picked to play for the local Royals at senior and junior levels.

To realise his other ambition he studied medicine at Montreal's McGill University. While there he played four seasons (1943-47) with the Redmen, captaining the side when they won the Canadian Inter-Collegiate Championship.

After graduating, he came to Britain to pursue a post-graduate specialist course, again combining this with his other love by turning out for Streatham for two seasons (1948-50).

Brodrick and Streatham twice beat the Edmonton Mercurys in a three-match series. The other game was drawn. As Canada, the Mercurys won the 1950 World Championships in London, beating **Lou Bates**'s GB 12-4 along the way.

After he retired as a player, 'Doc' was the medical director of the Montreal Expos baseball team for 25 years (1969-1994) and later president of the Major League Baseball Physicians' Association.

Brodrick enjoys a third claim to hockey fame. On his stay here he was impressed with the enthusiasm of the British players. This led him to write a book, *Ice Hockey* (Nicholas Kaye Ltd, 1951), which set out the skills needed to become a top class player.

'Doc' Brodrick was born on 1 September 1922 and died on 22 February 2015, aged 92.

VIC HOWE

Victor (Vic) Howe was the younger brother of hockey legend **Gordie Howe** and played in 33 NHL games with the New York Rangers.

But what many British fans may not know is that the right winger spent his last season, 1956-57, in London with Harringay Racers of the old British National League, scoring 32 points (15 goals) in 32 games.

Between these stints, the Canadian spent most of his career in minor leagues throughout North America. After retiring from the sport, he moved to Moncton, New Brunswick and became a constable with the Canadian National Railway Police.

Vic Howe was born on 2 November 1929 in Saskatoon, Saskatchewan and died on 31 January 2015, aged 85.

JOHN MAHAFFY

Montreal native **John Mahaffy**, who died aged 96 on 2 May 2015, played briefly for Streatham in the English National League in season 1938-39.

During his 20 seasons in North America starting in 1934, the 5ft 7in centreman played in the NHL for Montreal Canadiens and New York Rangers during World War Two, and enjoyed a post-war career in the American Hockey League.

At the time of his death, he was the oldest surviving Montreal Canadien. John's more illustrious team-mate, Hall of Famer **Elmer Lach**, 97, predeceased him by two months.

▲*Note for NHL buffs* – When we checked in July 2015, Boston Bruins' legend **Milt Schmidt**, who turned 97 on 5 March 2015, was the oldest former NHL player still with us.

AL SENIOR

Quebecer **Al Senior** was a prolific goal scorer with Ayr Raiders of the Scottish National League for three seasons, 1946-49.

The 6ft right-winger's best campaign was 1947-48 when his 78 goals and 126 points in 60 games earned him a berth on the *Ice Hockey World*'s first All-Star team. In his three years in Scotland, he scored 154 goals in 176 games.

Allan Longley Senior was born on 5 July 1925 in Verdun, Quebec and died on 28 March 2015 in Victoria, British Columbia, aged 89.

HAROLD (HAL) KEWLEY

Lawrence Harold (Hal) Kewley spent three seasons in Britain during the heyday of the professional Scottish National League (SNL) in 1950-53.

He played right wing on three different teams – Ayr Raiders (1950-51), Fife Flyers (1951-52) and Paisley Pirates (1952-53). His most prolific season was his first when he made the top ten scoring chart with 93 points (34 goals) in 66 games for the Raiders.

The youngest of six brothers, Canadian Hal came to this country with two siblings, Herb, who died in 2002, and Keith who survives him. A third brother, netminder Danny, was in Paisley Pirates line-up in 1947-48.

After leaving Scotland, Hal joined the team in Bolzano, Italy, where the arena apparently still displays his player profile. He returned to his native land in 1956 and remained involved in the sport for the rest of his long life, coaching youngsters.

Hal Kewley was born in North Bay, Ontario on 31 March 1930 and died on 10 May 2015, aged 85, leaving Marie, his wife of 58 years, and a large family.

▲ Keith Kewley was inducted into Britain's Hall of Fame in 2005. His biography can be found at www.ihjuk.co.uk.

With grateful acknowledgements to the Grimsby Telegraph, Nottingham Post *and the Society for International Hockey Research, www.sihrhockey.org.*

'WINK' WILSON

Richard (better known as Wink or Dick) Wilson was the grandfather of Brock Wilson and Jordan Fox. All three men were members of Nottingham Panthers. Wink turned out for them in the 1958-59 season, registering 19 points (nine goals) in 23 games.

Wilson and Fox were a key part of the Panthers side that won the Challenge Cup in 2011-12, with Fox staying on to become part of the Grand Slam-winning team the next year.

Wink returned to the city in 2012 to watch his grandsons play and to drop the ceremonial puck at the opening face-off.

"They treated him like a god," recalled Brock, "rolling out the red carpet for him. Jordy and I both got to do the ceremonial face-off and Wink had tears in his eyes."

Wink took a degree in business at Michigan Tech where he played for the Huskies in the 1950s. Later he provided advice to the Panthers' coach Corey Neilson, an old friend.

One of Wink's sons, Rik Wilson, played 251 games in the NHL for St Louis Blues. His father Roy and other son, Dave, also enjoyed successful playing careers.

Wink Wilson was born in Schumacher, Ontario on 4 April 1936 and died on 18 January 2015, aged 78.

COLIN WELFARE

Brighton-born goalie Colin Welfare briefly featured in the amateur Southern League where he was voted to the All-Star B team in season 1971-72.

In his first and only season of ice hockey, he back-stopped Sussex Tigers in four games to help them win the league title.

The Tigers were captained by ex-Brighton Tiger and GB defenceman Roy Shepherd, and included Brighton's internationals Rupe Fresher, Mike O'Brien and John Cook.

Colin learned to play through grice hockey – a form of ice hockey on grass which was popular in the south of England in the 1960s and 1970s. He died on 9 July 2015, aged 73.

WORLD CHAMPIONSHIPS

2015

IIHF

ICE HOCKEY
WORLD
CHAMPIONSHIP
THE NETHERLANDS
Eindhoven
Division I - Group B

13-19 April 2015

MEN'S SENIORS

FINAL STANDINGS

	GP	W	OW	OL	L	GF	GA	Pt
Korea KOR	5	4	0	0	1	30	11	12
Britain GB	5	3	1	0	1	13	10	11
Lithuania LTU	5	3	0	0	2	11	12	9
Croatia CRO	5	2	0	1	2	17	20	7
Estonia EST	5	1	0	0	4	10	21	3
Netherlands NED	5	1	0	0	4	9	16	3

Win (W) - 3 points
Overtime or shootout Win (OW) - 2 pts
Overtime or shootout Loss (OL) - 1 pt.
The positions of tied teams are decided on goal difference in the game between them.
Korea promoted to Division I, Group A;
Netherlands relegated to Division IIA.

BRITAIN'S WORLD RANKING: 24th

The IIHF World Rankings are based on the past four years' results - 100 per cent of 2015, 75 per cent of 2014, and 50 per cent and 25 per cent of the first two years respectively.
Britain's second place in Division IB in 2015 left them officially two places lower than 12 months previously.
In 20 internationals since 2012, Britain have won 9 (two in OT) and lost 11.

RESULTS

	KOR	LTU	CRO	EST	NED
GB	3-2	2-3	3-2ot	2-1	3-2
KOR		5-0	9-4	7-3	7-1
LTU			1-4	6-1	1-0
CRO				5-2	2-5
EST					3-1

BRITAIN'S POINTS SCORERS

	GP	G	A	Pts	Pim	S	P/M
Ben O'Connor	5	3	2	5	6	24	+1
Jonathan Weaver	5	0	3	3	0	10	+3
Mark Richardson	5	2	0	2	0	3	0
Robert Farmer	5	2	0	2	2	14	+1
Craig Peacock	5	1	1	2	0	8	+2
Russell Cowley	5	1	1	2	2	4	0
David Phillips	5	1	1	2	4	8	+3
Colin Shields	5	0	2	2	0	16	+1
Robert Dowd	5	0	2	2	4	11	+2
Chris Blight	5	1	0	1	0	3	+1
Paul Swindlehurst	5	1	0	1	2	3	0
Mark Garside	5	1	0	1	8	5	0
Rob Lachowicz	5	0	1	1	0	14	0
Matthew Myers	5	0	1	1	2	11	0
Jack Prince	5	0	1	1	2	7	+2
Mark Thomas	5	0	1	1	4	2	+1

S - Shots on goal P/M - plus-minus.

BRITAIN'S NETMINDING

	GPI	Mins	SoG	GA	Sv%
Ben Bowns	5	299	122	10	91.80
TEAM TOTALS	5	300	122	10	91.80

FAIR PLAY

Penalty minutes per team:
1 Estonia 47, **2 Britain 50**, 3 Netherlands 64, 4 Korea 68, 5 Lithuania 79, 6 Croatia 146.

BRITAIN

Goal: Ben Bowns CAR; Stevie Lyle SWI.
Defence: David Phillips BEL; Mark Richardson CAR *asst capt*; Russell Cowley COV; Paul Swindlehurst DUN; Ben O'Connor, Mark Thomas SHE; Jonathan Weaver TEL.
Forwards: Mark Garside, Craig Peacock, Colin Shields BEL; #Matt Haywood BRH; #Josh Batch, Matthew Myers CAR; @#Chris Blight DUN; #Jonathan Boxill, Robert Farmer, Robert Lachowicz NOT; Robert Dowd *asst capt*, Jonathan Phillips SHE *capt*; #Jack Prince (Un. of Alabama-Huntsville).
Head Coach: Peter Russell (Okanagan Hockey Academy UK). *Asst. coaches*: *Richard Hartmann EDI, Tom Watkins TEL.
General manager: Andy Buxton COV.
New cap (5). @ British-Canadian (1).
*Hartmann was sacked by his club and didn't attend the games. Ex-GB coach **Paul Thompson** assisted unofficially from the stands.*

BRITAIN'S SPECIAL TEAMS

Powerplay 6th – Britain scored 2 goals on 16 man advantages for **12.50%**. (Korea 1st with 31.82%).
Penalty kill 1st – Britain conceded 3 goals on 23 shorthanded situations for **86.96%**.

BRITAIN's GAME SUMMARIES

13 April, Ice Sport Arena, Eindhoven, N'lands

GB- CROATIA   3-2ot (0-1,0-0,2-1,1-0)

Scoring:

0-1 CRO	Glumac (unass.)	sh	16.57
0-2 CRO	Perkovich (Sertich)	pp	46.52
1-2 GB	O'Connor (Myers)	pp	52.57
2-2 GB	Richardson (Dowd)		59.55
3-2 GB	Richardson (O'Connor)		60.11

Netminding:
Bowns GB   12-8-10-0 30 *save%* 93.33
Dekanich CRO   14-9-12-1 36 *save%* 91.67
Penalty minutes: Britain 10, Croatia 24 (Waugh 2+10 ch-behind).
Goals/powerplays: Britain 1/6, Croatia 1/4.
Men of Match: Bowns GB, Dekanich CRO.
Referee: Warschaw USA.   *Attendance:* 750.

This was a fiery baptism for the new coach and his revamped team against one of the championship favourites.

Last year, the Croats shutout the Brits. And at 2-0 down in the last period, it looked like going the same way again, though GB had played better than that score line.

Richardson: "That was some ending. Credit the guys for not giving up. We knew we could compete with them, we just had to keep going and going. Our passion was there for all to see."
Dowd: "Starting with a win is so important. It's the difference between being in the flow and in the hunt for a gold medal, or having to play catch-up hockey."

Indeed, Myers was unlucky to have had his goal disallowed at 15.30 when Croatia's AHL keeper Dekanich went unpenalised after knocking his net off its moorings.

Glumac was the Croatian danger man, deking Bowns moments later on a short-handed breakaway after the keeper had foiled his earlier attempt.

Then in the middle period ex-NHL forward Murray put the puck across the GB goal line only to have it nullified after a video review showed that Bowns' net had been dislodged.

Croatia's second goal, from Perkovich, pushed GB to greater efforts, and when Jacmenjak knocked down Boxill off the puck, O'Connor crashed home from the blueline on the powerplay.

Then came Richardson's memorable 16 seconds. He swept the puck into the net during a scramble in the slot, then after the break he snared a long, pinpoint pass from O'Connor and beat Dekanich with a hard shot from the right face-off circle.

Now it was important for GB to remember not that they'd beaten an important rival but that they'd dropped a point.

▼ Britain's lack of depth showed with the top lines often being over-played. Glumac's breakaway goal came when defender O'Connor was at the end of a long shift and he couldn't catch the speedy Croat.

► GB's World Championship record v Croatia (since 2001) – four wins, one loss (in 2014).

WORLD CHAMPIONSHIPS

BRITAIN *left to right, back row:* Steve Small (asst. manager), Jonathan Boxill, Ben O'Connor, Jack Prince, David Phillips, Robert Farmer, Josh Batch, Paul Swindlehurst, Mark Thomas, Matthew Myers, Craig Peacock, Chris Blight, Matt Haywood, Mark Garside, Tom Murdy, Andy Buxton (general manager), Jason Ellery (equipment); *front row:* Stevie Lyle, Jonathan Weaver, Colin Shields, Peter Russell (head coach), Robert Dowd, Jonathan Phillips, Mark Richardson, Tom Watkins (asst. coach), Robert Lachowicz, Russell Cowley, Ben Bowns, Chris Ellis (media).

photo: Colin Lawson

14 April, Ice Sport Arena, Eindhoven, N'lands

ESTONIA-GB		1-2	(0-1,1-0,0-1)

Scoring:

0-1 GB	D Phillips (Weaver, Cowley)	15.36
1-1 EST	Rooba (Makrov)	33.19
2-1 GB	Farmer (Weaver, Phillips)	54.10

Netminding:

Shumikhin EST	11- 9-12 32	save%	93.75
Bowns GB	10-14- 6 30	save%	96.67

Penalty minutes: Estonia 2, GB 6.
Goals/powerplays: Croatia 0/3, GB 0/1.
Men of Match: Shumikhin EST, Farmer GB.
Referee: Salonen FIN.   *Attendance:* 500.

Estonia were the lowest ranked team in Eindhoven (a full seven places behind GB) but the young side were not expected to be pushovers.

And so it proved. Britain found it hard to make much headway against a well-coached team determined to stifle their opponents and possessing a couple of truly creative forwards.

Early on, GB had to cope with a fussy ref as well, who sent off Dowd and Haywood for minor infringements.

But when the out-raced Shields hooked Estonia's big man Rooba on a short-handed breakaway, Salonen's penalty shot call was the right one.

Russell: "No game is easy and I knew this one wouldn't be any different. Sure, we weren't at our best but we kept on going and ground it out."
O'Connor: "Estonia played very well and were stronger than we expected. I don't think we under-estimated them but it shows the lower-seeded teams are getting better every year.

"The [second] goal was a big relief, especially for me after my earlier mistake."

Only the acrobatics of Bowns kept the puck out, and less than two minutes later Dave Phillips put GB on the board with a rocket from 25 feet.

But Rooba, who plays in the Finnish league, and his linemate, Makrov, continued to be a threat. The pair combined for the equaliser after a give-away by the defence in a poor middle period for GB when Estonia outshot them 14-9.

Russell must have made an inspired dressing room pep-talk as his men revived in the last session. The winning goal was almost a carbon copy of GB's equaliser the day before.

After Dave Phillips fired the puck into a scrum in front of goal, Farmer flicked the rebound over Shumikhin.

Two games, two wins, but neither was convincing, and the toughest opponent was up next.

▲ In a game with only four minor penalties, Britain took three of them. But this only took their total sin-bin time to a weedy 16 minutes, making our angels easily the cleanest team in the tournament so far.

▶ GB's World Championship record v Estonia (since 1998) – Four wins, three losses.

16 April, Ice Sport Arena, Eindhoven, N'lands

S KOREA-GB		2-3	(1-0,1-2,0-1)

Scoring:

0-1 KOR	Woo-sang Park (DK Lee, W Kim)	19.38
0-2 KOR	K Kim (S Kim, Radunske)	20.35
1-2 GB	Farmer (unass.)	20.51
2-2 GB	O'Connor (Weaver) pp2	33.35
2-3 GB	O'Connor (penalty shot)	46.39

Netminding:

S Park KOR	12-10-8 30	save%	90.00
Bowns GB	9-14-7 30	save%	93.33

Penalty minutes: Korea 14, GB 12.
Goals/powerplays: Korea 0/6, GB 1/6.
Men of Match: Sungje Park KOR, Boxill GB.
Referee: Grumsen DEN.   *Attendance:* 500.

This was expected to be as difficult a game as the opener. Korea were ranked right behind GB and had won their first two games by a comfortable 14-4 goal diff.

HERO OR ZERO

"I've been practicing that move in training all year and it was on my mind all the time. I just haven't done it in a game before.

"There was a long wait before the shot [while they fixed the net] and my nerves were shaking. It was either hero or zero and luckily it paid off."

Ben O'Connor, #ballsofsteel, after converting his outrageous penalty shot goal.
(Readers can find the goal online at YouTube.)

Britain made a slow start, going 2-0 behind with Bowns making a rare mistake on the second. Then Farmer's wrister from the slot, which knocked the water bottle off Park's net, got them into the game.

BEN O'CONNOR scores a goal for the ages with this deft penalty shot which bamboozles Korean goalie **Sungje Park** and gives GB a 3-2 win.

A stream of Koreans into the box gifted GB two five-on-three opportunities. Only on the second – after an animated time-out talk from the coach – was O'Connor able to equalise with a howitzer from the top of the right face-off circle.

But when the history of the game – indeed, the history of our sport – comes to be written, all the above will be forgotten.

One of the most memorable moves this reporter has witnessed in a life-time of watching British ice hockey occurred at 46.39.

To re-wind briefly, Cowley was robbed on a breakaway when a desperate, chasing Korean, Yoonhwan Kim, threw his stick at the puck.

Though it missed its target, the ref correctly called a penalty shot. But the Danish official erred by allowing O'Connor (wearing 28) rather than Cowley (26) to take the shot. A jersey number confusion, perhaps.

Anyway, the Sheffield Steelers' defender took his chance coolly, pivoting in front of Park, and backhanding the puck between his own skates into the roof of the net.

Everyone in the rink was breathless in amazement. Ben couldn't stop grinning.

The goal held up for the game-winner, and GB's third victory lifted them into pole position for promotion, two points ahead of Korea.

▶ *For rules buffs* - IIHF Rule 176i states that the skater fouled must take the penalty shot. O'Connor wasn't even on the ice when Cowley's attempt was thwarted.

▶ **GB's World Championship record v Korea** (since 1991) - Five wins, one loss (in 2013).

18 April, Ice Sport Arena, Eindhoven, N'lands

GB-NETHERLANDS   3-2   (3-1,0-0,0-1)

Scoring:
0-1 NED Mason (Hagemeijer, van Oorschot) 03.09
1-1 GB Swindlehurst (O'Connor, Shields) 04.01
2-1 GB Blight (Peacock)   09.24
3-1 GB Peacock (Shields)   12.13
3-2 NED Houkes (van Lijden, Tummers)   53.58
Netminding:
Bowns GB   8-3-6 17   *save%* 88.24
Oosterwijk NED) 11 /-/ 11 *save%* 72.73
Meierdres NED)   1-9-9 19   *save%* 100.0
Penalty minutes: GB 8, Netherlands 2.
Goals/powerplays: GB 0/1, NED 0/4.
Men of Match: J Phillips GB, van Oorschot NED.
Referee: Ingram CAN.   *Attendance:* 2,500.

Probably GB's weakest display as they allowed themselves to be dragged down to the level of the Dutch who were later relegated.

But it was good to see the line of Blight-Peacock-Shields getting among the scoring points as GB struck three times in eight minutes and put the Dutch keeper Oosterwijk out of a job.

His replacement, Meierdres, stopped the rot and kept a clean sheet for the rest of the way.

Boxill: "It wasn't the best of performances for us but we got the job done. Netherlands were inspired by their home fans and put up a good fight."

With another game in less than 24 hours, GB were content to defend their lead, though the physical Dutch fought hard in the last period and were rewarded with a late second goal.

The win gave the Brits a two-point lead over Korea at the top of the table and guaranteed them a silver medal.

The game drew the only capacity crowd of the week, but Britain's colourful, 400-odd Barmy Army had no trouble making themselves heard.

▶ **GB's World Championship record v Netherlands** (since 1993) – Ten wins, one loss (in 2004).

In the first game on 19 April Korea beat Croatia 9-4. This left GB needing only one point against Lithuania to win the gold medal and promotion back to Division IA.

19 April, Ice Sport Arena, Eindhoven, N'lands

LITHUANIA-GB   3-2   (0-1,2-0,1-1)

Scoring:
0-1 GB Garside (Thomas, Lachowicz)   14.08
1-1 LTU Nomanovas (Rybakov, Visockas) 29.55
2-1 LTU Alisauskas (Kumeliauskas) pp2 37.45
2-2 GB Cowley (Weaver, Prince)   43.25
3-2 LTU Gintautas (Kieras, Alisauskas) pp 53.01
Netminding:
Armalis LTU   9-13-15 37   *save%* 94.59
Bowns GB   2- 6- 7 15   *save%* 80.00
Penalty minutes: Lithuania 33 (Kumeliauskas – match/head butt), GB 14.
Goals/powerplays: Lithuania 2/7, GB 0/5.
Men of Match: Alisauskas LTU, Weaver GB.
Referee: Salonen FIN.   *Attendance:* 1,800.
While only a one-goal defeat, with so much at stake this loss couldn't have been more crushing had it been ten goals.

Britain began purposefully. Garside beat Armalis from short range to give Russell's men an early lead, and they limited Lithuania to just two shots.

But in the second period they fell behind an opponent which showed more passion than Britain, who were clearly feeling the pressure of the occasion.

Lithuania's second goal was especially wounding as it was only the second powerplay goal Britain conceded all week. But it did come on a five-on-three man advantage.

"We've just said in the dressing room that we don't want to feel like this again. It's horrible to be so close to gold and not get over the finishing line.

"But we should be proud of what we've done this week and we're certainly moving in the right direction.

"We have a good set of guys and there's a great passion for Great Britain."
Robert Lachowicz

"I feel sorry for them. We played one heck of a game today and it made me feel proud of my country. This win means so much for us. That such a small country can defeat the likes of Britain and the Netherlands is simply amazing."
Lithuanian forward Darius Pliskauskas, who has played in the UK since 2009.

Being behind usually spurred the Brits to greater efforts and they duly recovered some of their poise in the last session.

The equaliser came with Cowley tipping-in Weaver's blueline blast.

But on only their 12th shot of the game, Lithuania went ahead with another powerplay goal, also a blueline deflection.

Lithuania nearly blew it when Kumeliauskas became so infuriated by Dave Phillips that he head-butted the defender. This foolishness – both players were wearing visors - gifted GB a powerplay for the final four minutes.

Sadly, they couldn't enjoy the gift, with O'Connor getting sent off in the final minute.
► **GB's World Championship record v Lithuania** (since 2007) – One win, three losses.

Notes and Quotes
▼ GB won one more game and finished two places higher than last year, so this can be counted as some sort of success. But it still means they will have to spend a third season in the world's third division.

▲ **Ben O'Connor** stamped his international card as GB's go-to guy. The Defenceman of the Tournament was also his side's top scorer.

► Of GB's modest total of 13 goals, eight were scored by defencemen, led by O'Connor with three.

► Key players out of GB's line-up were goalie **Stephen Murphy** and forward **David Clarke** (both injured), forward **Ashley Tait** (now 39), and defenceman **Danny Meyers** (EPIHL).

► GB conceded the fewest goals of any nation. But their scoring power was only third best, partly due to lack of shooting accuracy. According to the stats, while they were second best at putting the puck *on* the net, they were second worst at getting it *in* the net.

▲ GB's average age dropped from 28 in 2014 to 27 this time out. Seven players (eight if you include non-icing goalie **Stevie Lyle**) were over 30. **Jonathan Weaver**, the only out-player from the EPIHL, was the oldest at 38. He was one of GB's few standouts in the final loss to Lithuania.

■ GB and Swindon Wildcats goalie Lyle, 35, was in Eindhoven for his 12th World Championships, and the first time as back-up to **Ben Bowns**, who was playing in his third tournament.

Bowns said: "It's great having Stevie to learn from. We work on things together in training and I can take his advice into a game."

▼ Fans (and media) hoping to catch a glimpse of singer **Rod Stewart**'s off-spring **Liam Stewart** were disappointed. Liam, 20, had signed for ECHL side Quad City Mallards, his first pro side.

► Coach Russell called up reserve **Craig Peacock** in place of Stewart but played him sparingly. This was puzzling as Peacock was the top British goal scorer in the Elite League.

▲ GB added three more half-centurions in Eindhoven. **Dave Phillips** earned his 50th cap against Croatia, and **Russell Cowley** got his against Estonia, as did team manager **Andy Buxton**.

▼ Coach Russell's reaction to **Ben O'Connor** making such a high risk move on his penalty shot at a crucial point (tied 2-2) in the game against Korea was not recorded. You can bet it would have been had the Steeler fluffed it.

▲Playing smart – The Brits didn't often trouble the ref and when they did get into a spot of bother, they usually killed off the penalty. Yes, GB were the tournament's best penalty killers.

■ **Greg Owen** was the team's video analyst. The ex-Coventry Blaze and Basingstoke Bison forward had 41 caps for GB before retiring after the 2013 championships in Budapest. He was an assistant coach with this year's under-20s.

▲ The untiringly boisterous GB fans ensured that Britain attracted the highest crowds to the arena, apart from those following the host nation. Without them, some say those one-goal wins could have turned into defeats.

▲ *Lithuania*'s German coach **Bernd Haake** coached nine years in the German DEL.

▲ *Korea*'s first goal against GB came from **Woosang Park**, who played for Coventry Blaze in 2011-12.

▲ *Korea*'s coaching staff includes the only two men from the Asian country to play in the NHL - head coach **Jim Paek** and assistant **Richard Park**. Paek patrolled the Nottingham Panthers' blueline during the Superleague era.

Korea can afford this pair as the Korean Ice Hockey Association have pledged to invest over US$20 million into the national team programme over the next three years.

That's because *Korea* are to host the 2018 Winter Olympics in Pyongyang. After their overtime defeat by GB, Paek's pack must have been mightily relieved by their first place finish as this keeps them on target to join the world's elite 16 nations in three years.

■ Estonian defenceman **Ilja Urushev** played two games earlier in the season with Invicta Dynamos of the National League (NIHL).

■ *Croatia*'s line-up was studded with nine dual nationals. They included 6ft, 2in Canada-born goaltender **Mark Dekanich**, who was a top goalie in the AHL and is in his second season in the Russian KHL with Zagreb. Forward **Andrew Murray** has 221 NHL games on his resume.

▶"It's usually slightly easier to get into a good rhythm in [a short series like the World Championships].

"We were on the ice twice a day during our training camp, and had a pre-game skate before both games against Poland. When you're on the ice that much more, you just have to find a rhythm in your game and stick with it."

"In terms of preparation for the tournament, you have to eat even more than usual and make sure you get loads of fluids. You also have to get adequate sleep – listen to your body and do what it's telling you to do."

Ben Bowns talking to Rob McGregor in the online blog One Puck Short *before the games.*

A team of GB Prospects was put together for a game against the Romanian national side, who were on the way to their World Championship group in Iceland.

Romania won all their games in Division IIA and will meet the full GB side in the 2016 World Championships and the upcoming Winter Olympic Qualifiers.

10 April 2015 Kirkcaldy, Fife

GB PROSPECTS-ROMANIA	3-1 (0-0,2-0,1-1)

GB scorers: Long, Jones 1+1; Chamberlain 1g; Scott, Norton, Chalmers, Sullivan 1a.
GB: Ciaran Long BAS; Zach Sullivan BRH; Chris Jones, Mike Will (goal) CAR; Steven Chalmers COV; Bari McKenzie DUN; Allan Anderson FIF; Bobby Chamberlain, Joe Graham MAN; Jordan Cownie, Lewis Hook MIL; Luke Ferrara, Tom Norton PET; Adam Harding SWI; Dan Davies, Sam Gospel (goal), Nathan Salem, Dan Scott, Sam Zajac TEL; Alex Forbes (Ogden Mustangs).
Coaches: Martin Grubb (Solway), Simon Leach (Whitley Bay).
Manager: Alma Greger.

BRITAIN'S RECORD 1989-2014

2014 Division IB, Vilnius, Lithuania
Head coach: **Doug Christiansen** (Sheffield)
Croatia 0-4, Romania 4-1, Lithuania 1-2, N'lands 4-3, Poland 4-2.
World ranking: **22nd**. *Group standing:* 4th.

2013 Division IA, Budapest, Hungary
Head coach: **Tony Hand** (Manchester).
Hungary 2-4, Kazakhstan 0-5, Italy 1-5, Japan 1-4, S Korea 1-4.
World ranking: **22nd**. *Group standing:* 6th.
Relegated to Division IB.

2012 Division 1A, Ljubljana, Slovenia
Head coach: **Tony Hand** (Manchester).
Slovenia 2-3, Austria 3-7, Ukraine 4-3ot, Japan 0-5, Hungary 5-4.
World ranking: **21st**. *Group standing:* 5th.

2011 Division 1/B, Kiev, Ukraine
Head coach: **Paul Thompson** (Coventry)
Ukraine 5-3, Kazakhstan 1-2, Estonia 7-0, Lithuania 5-2, Poland 3-2.
World Ranking: **21st**. *Group standing:* 2nd.

2010 Division I/B, Ljubljana, Slovenia
Head coach: **Paul Thompson** (Coventry)
Croatia 4-1, S Korea 2-1, Slovenia 3-4ot, Hungary 0-2, Poland 1-2.
World Ranking: **23rd**. *Group standing:* 4th.

2009 Division I/B, Torun, Poland
Head coach: **Paul Thompson** (Coventry).
Ukraine 2-4, Italy 2-5, Romania 8-0, Netherlands 3-2, Poland 2-1ot.
World Ranking: **25th**. *Group standing:* 3rd.

2008 Division I/A, Innsbruck, Austria
Head coach: **Paul Thompson** (Coventry)
Poland 1-2so, Austria 5-10, S Korea 4-1, Netherlands 8-1, Kazakhstan 1-3.
World Ranking: **29th**. *Group standing:* 4th.

2007 Division I/B, Ljubljana, Slovenia
Head coach: **Paul Thompson** (Coventry)
Japan 4-3, Lithuania 2-3, Slovenia 0-4, Hungary 2-4, Romania 6-1.
World Ranking: **29th**. *Group standing:* 4th.

2006 Division I/A, Amiens, France
Head coach: **Rick Strachan** (Hull).
Hungary 3-4, France 0-1, Germany 0-8, Japan 2-4, Israel 12-0.
World Ranking: **31st**. *Group standing:* 5th.

2005 Division 1/A, Debrecen, Hungary
Head coach: **Rick Strachan** (Hull)
Poland 0-2, Norway 3-8, Japan 3-5, Hungary 3-0, China 10-0.
World Ranking: **25th**. *Group standing:* 4th.

2004 Division I/A, Oslo, Norway
Head coach: **Chris McSorley** (Geneva)
Hungary 3-5, Norway 4-4, Belarus 4-5, Netherlands 1-4, Belgium 6-0.
World Ranking: **29th**. *Group standing:* 5th.

2003 Division I/B, Zagreb, Croatia
Head coach: **Chris McSorley** (Geneva)
France 2-2, Italy 2-4, Estonia 3-4, Croatia 7-1, Norway 2-3.
World Ranking: **21st**. *Group standing:* 5th.

-141-

Britain's Record 1989-2014, *contd*

2002   Division I/B, Ljubljana, Slovenia
Szeskesfehervar/Dunaujvaros, Hungary
Head coach: **Chris McSorley** (Geneva)
Denmark 3-5, Hungary 1-4, Romania 5-2,
China 8-3, Norway 1-2.
World Ranking: **20th**. *Group standing*: 4th.

2001   **Pool B**, Ljubljana, Slovenia
Head coach: **Chris McSorley** (London)
Estonia 6-2, Croatia 10-1, Slovenia 3-3,
China 12-1, Kazakhstan 11-2.
World Ranking: **18th**. *Group Standing*: 2nd.

2000   **Pool B**, Katowice, Poland
Head coach: **Peter Woods** (Superleague)
Estonia 5-6, Sl'v'nia 3-3, N'lands 9-0, P'land 6-4
Denmark 5-4, Kazakhstan 3-1, Germany 0-5.
World Ranking: **19th**. *Group standing*: 3rd.

1999   **Pool A Qualifying Tournament**
Sheffield Arena, England, 11-14 November 1999
Head coach: **Peter Woods** (Superleague)
Ukraine 2-2, Latvia 0-0, Kazakhstan 1-1.
GB standing: 3rd. *Play-off*: Norway 1-2.

1999   **Pool B**, Copenhagen/Odense, Denmark
Head coach: **Peter Woods** (Superleague)
Slovenia 2-1, Kazakhstan 1-0,
Germany 2-3, Estonia 6-2, Poland 4-3,
Hungary 4-2, Denmark 5-5.
World Ranking: **18th**. *Group standing*: 2nd.

1998   **Pool B**, Ljubljana/Jesenice, Slovenia
Head coach: **Peter Woods** (Superleague).
Ukraine 1-6, Denmark 7-1, Estonia 4-5,
Slov'ia 3-5, Poland 4-3, Norway 3-4, N'lands 10-3.
World Ranking: **22nd**. *Group standing*: 6th.

1997   **Pool B**, Katowice/Sosnowiec, Poland
Head coach: **Peter Woods** (Basingstoke)
Poland 3-4, Kazakhstan 2-4,
Netherlands 8-2, Denmark 9-1, Austria 2-2,
Switzerland 2-3, Belarus 2-6.
World Ranking: **18th**. *Group standing*: 6th.

1996   **Pool B**, Eindhoven, Netherlands
Head coach: **Peter Woods** (Basingstoke).
Latvia 5-6, Switzerland 2-7, Poland 4-2,
Netherlands 6-2, Japan 3-3, Denmark 5-1,
Belarus 4-2.
World Ranking: **16th**. *Group standing*: 4th.

1995   **Pool B**, Bratislava, Slovakia
Head coach: **George Peternousek** (unatt.)
Slovakia 3-7, Romania 0-2, Neth'lands 3-2,
Denmark 2-9, Japan 3-4, Poland 4-3, Latvia 4-8.
World Ranking: **19th**. *Group standing*: 7th.

1994   **Pool A**, Bolzano, Italy
Head coach: **Alex Dampier** (Sheffield)
Russia 3-12, Germany 0-4, Italy 2-10,
Canada 2-8, Austria 0-10, Norway 2-5.
World Ranking: **12th**. *Group standing*: 12th.

1993   **Pool B**, Eindhoven, Netherlands
Head coach: **Alex Dampier** (Sheffield).
Poland 4-3, Denmark 4-0, Japan 5-4,
Bulgaria 10-0, Netherlands 3-2,
Romania 10-4, China 14-0.
World Ranking: **13th**. *Group standing*: 1st.

1992   **Pool C**, Hull, England
Head coach: **Alex Dampier** (Nottingham).
Australia 10-2, S Korea 15-0, Belgium 7-3,
N Korea 16-2, Hungary 14-3.
World Ranking: **21st**. *Group standing*: 1st.

1991   **Pool C**, Copenhagen, Denmark
Head coach: **Alex Dampier** (Nottingham).
China 5-6, N Korea 7-2, Denmark 2-3,
Belgium 11-0, Hungary 3-3, Bulgaria 4-5,
S Korea 7-1, Romania 6-5.
World Ranking: **21st**. *Group standing*: 5th.

1990   **Pool D**, Cardiff, Wales
Head coach: **Alex Dampier** (Nottingham).
Australia 14-0, 13-3; Spain 13-1, 17-3.
World Ranking: **26th**. *Group standing*: 1st.

1989   **Pool D**, Belgium
Head coach: **Terry Matthews** (Whitley Bay).
New Zealand 26-0, Romania 6-6, Belgium 5-6,
Spain 8-4.
World Ranking: **27th**. *Group standing*: 3rd.

ELITE DIVISION, *Prague & Ostrava, Czech Rep.*
1 Canada, 2 Russia, 3 USA, 4 Czech Rep.,
5 Sweden, 6 Finland, 7 Belarus, 8 Switzerland,
9 Slovakia, 10 Germany, 11 Norway, 12 France,
13 Latvia, 14 Denmark, 15 Austria, 16 Slovenia.
Austria and Slovenia relegated.
DIVISION IA, *Krakow, Poland*
1 Kazakhstan (promoted), 2 Hungary, 3 Poland,
4 Japan, 5 Italy, 6 Ukraine (relegated).
DIVISION IIA, *Belgrade, Serbia*
1 Romania (promoted), 2 Belgium, 3 Serbia,
4 Spain, 5 Iceland, 6 Australia (relegated).
DIVISION IIB, *Cape Town, South Africa*
1 China (promoted), 2 New Zealand, 3 Mexico,
4 Bulgaria, 5 Israel, 6 South Africa (relegated).
DIVISION III, *Izmir, Turkey*
1 N Korea (promoted), 2 Turkey, 3 Luxembourg,
4 Hong Kong, 5 Georgia, 5 UAE, 6 Bosnia.

WORLD CHAMPIONSHIPS

BRITAIN women *left to right, back row:* Jodie Bloom, Chrissy Newman, Saffron Allen, Georgina Farman, Kim Lane, Katherine Gale, Helen Emerson, Katie Henry; *middle row:* Andy French (IHUK general sec.), Brian Miller (equipment), Holly Cornford, Louise Adams, Sophie Herbert, Beth Scoon, Sarah Hutchinson, Rachel Serrell, Leanne Ganney, Amanda Handisides, Paige Henry, Nathan Craze (goalie coach); *front row:* Lisa Calvert (team manager), Samantha Bolwell, Lauren Summers, Michelle Smith (coach), Alice Lamb, Cheryl Smith (coach), Natalie Aldridge, Nicole Jackson, Gael Moffat (sports therapist), Philippa Turner (doctor).

Photo: Colin Lawson

-143-

WOMEN'S SENIORS

Division II, Group A, Dumfries, Scotland,
30 March-5 April 2015

FINAL STANDINGS

	GP	W	OW	OL	L	GF	GA	Pt
Kazakhstan KAZ	5	5	0	0	0	30	2	15
Britain GB	5	4	0	0	1	23	5	12
S Korea KOR	5	2	1	0	2	21	8	8
Poland POL	5	1	1	1	2	17	17	6
Croatia CRO	5	1	0	0	4	9	45	3
New Zealand NZL	5	0	0	1	4	5	28	1

Kazakhstan promoted to Division I, Group B;
New Zealand relegated to Division IIB.

GB's World Ranking: 21st

RESULTS

	KAZ	KOR	POL	CRO	NZL
GB	0-2	3-1	4-0	8-1	8-1
KAZ		2-0	4-1	12-1	10-0
KOR			4-3	13-0	3-0
POL				10-3	3-2
CRO					4-2

BRITAIN'S POINTS SCORERS

	GP	G	A	Pts	Pim
Christine Newman	5	6	3	9	8
Jodie Leigh-Bloom	5	2	6	8	2
Saffron Allen	5	2	5	7	0
Katie Henry	5	5	1	6	0
Katherine Gale	5	2	2	4	4
Leanne Ganney	5	3	0	3	6

BRITAIN'S NETMINDING

	GPI	Mins	SoG	GA	Sv%
Nicole Jackson	4	239	110	4	96.4
Samantha Bolwell	1	60	18	1	94.4
TEAM TOTALS	5	299	128	5	96.1

Women take silver, too

When your biggest rival is coached by one of the legendary players from the storied days of Soviet ice hockey, you know you're in trouble.

That was the situation when GB, who'd won their first four games in convincing style, came to the final one against Kazakhstan.

Coaching the Kazakhs was **Alexander Maltsev**, now 66, who was the highest scoring forward with the Big Red Machine that dominated world ice hockey in the 1970s.

It wasn't immediately clear how the great man came to be coaching the best women players from the former Soviet republic.

But his team's five wins and goal difference of +28 showed he had mastered his new brief.

And once again, a GB side came up against a tougher opponent just when the gold medal seemed to be in their grasp.

▶ GB women's head coach **Paul Burton** and team manager **Lyn Burton** resigned from the national team after 18 months.

Their places for the 2015 games were taken by **Cheryl Smith** and **Michelle Smith**, who stepped up from their roles as assistant coaches. The Sheffield-born twins represented GB Women as players in 1995-2001.

▲ Dumfries and Galloway Council backed the event to the tune of £35,000.

BRITAIN

Goal: Nicole Jackson HUL; Samantha Bolwell GUI.

Defence: Rachel Serrell BIL; Amanda Handisides, Lauren Summers BRK; Holly Cornford, Sarah Hutchinson, Bethany Scoon HUL; Jodie-Leigh Bloom SHE; Alice Lamb SLO; Helen Emerson WHI; Georgina Farman (IFK Norrköping SWE).

Forwards: Natalie Aldridge BRK; Leanne Ganney, Christine Newman BRK; Louise Adams GUI; Kimberley Lane PET; Saffron Allen SHE; Paige Henry SOL; Katherine Gale (Toronto Un. CAN); Sophie Herbert (Brock Un. CAN); Katie Henry (IFK Norrköping SWE).

Head Coach: Cheryl Smith. *Asst. coach*: Michelle Smith. *Manager*: Andy French.

WORLD CHAMPIONSHIP AND OLYMPIC QUALIFYING RECORDS OF GB PLAYERS 2015

PLAYERS

Club	Year	Comp	GP	G	A	Pts	PIM
BATCH Josh			F		b.15-Jan-91		
Car	2015	WC	5	0	0	0	2
BLIGHT Chris			F		b. 14-Oct-82		
Dun	2015		5	1	0	1	0
BOXILL Jonathan			F		b. 25-Apr-89		
Not	2015		5	0	0	0	2
COWLEY Russell			F		b. 12-Aug-83		
Cov	2003	WC	5	0	0	0	0
Cov	2004	WC	5	0	0	0	4
Cov	2005	WC	5	0	1	1	2
Cov	2006	WC	5	1	3	4	2
Car	2007	WC	5	0	2	2	4
Cov	2008	WC	5	0	1	1	2
Cov	2008	OQ	3	1	1	2	2
Cov	2009	WC	5	0	4	4	0
Cov	2010	WC	5	0	1	1	2
Cov	2011	WC	5	1	1	2	2
Cov	2015	WC	5	1	1	2	2
		Totals	53	4	15	19	22
DOWD Robert			F		b. 26-May-88		
She	2008	OQ	3	0	0	0	0
She	2009	WC	5	1	2	3	4
She	2010	WC	5	1	1	2	6
She	2011	WC	5	2	1	3	4
Bel	2012	WC	5	5	4	9	6
Swe	2012	POQ	3	1	1	2	0
Swe	2013	FOQ	3	1	1	2	0
Swe	2013	WC	5	1	2	3	6
She	2014	WC	5	2	0	2	2
She	2015	WC	5	0	2	2	4
		Totals	44	14	14	28	34
FARMER Robert			F		b. 21-Mar-91		
Cov	2012	WC	5	0	0	0	2
Brh	2012	POQ	3	0	0	0	4
Brh	2013	FOQ	3	0	0	0	2
Brh	2013	WC	5	2	0	2	0
Not	2014	WC	5	0	1	1	2
Not	2015	WC	5	2	0	2	2
		Totals	26	4	1	5	12

Club	Year	Comp	GP	G	A	Pts	PIM
GARSIDE Mark			F		b. 21-Mar-89		
Edi	2010	WC	5	1	0	1	0
Bel	2012	WC	5	0	0	0	2
Bel	2012	POQ	3	0	0	0	0
Bel	2013	FOQ	3	0	0	0	2
Bel	2014	WC	5	1	3	4	2
Bel	2015	WC	5	1	0	1	8
		Totals	26	3	3	6	14
HAYWOOD Matthew			F		b. 27-Dec-90		
Brh	2015	WC	5	0	0	0	2
LACHOWICZ Robert			F		b. 8-Feb-90		
Not	2011	WC	5	0	2	2	0
Not	2012	WC	5	0	1	1	2
Not	2012	POQ	3	0	0	0	2
Not	2013	FOQ	3	1	0	1	0
Not	2013	WC	5	0	0	0	0
Not	2014	WC	5	0	3	3	0
Not	2015	WC	5	0	1	1	0
		Totals	31	1	7	8	4
MYERS Matthew			F		b. 6-Nov-84		
Car	2004	WC	5	1	2	3	2
Not	2005	WC	5	3	0	3	10
Not	2006	WC	5	5	0	5	16
Not	2007	WC	5	0	1	1	8
Not	2008	WC	5	0	2	2	8
Not	2008	POQ	3	0	2	2	0
Not	2009	WC	5	1	2	3	10
USA	2010	WC	5	0	0	0	2
Not	2011	WC	5	1	2	3	0
Not	2012	WC	5	1	1	2	10
Not	2012	POQ	3	0	0	0	4
Not	2013	FOQ	3	0	1	1	16
Not	2013	WC	5	0	0	0	10
Car	2014	WC	5	1	0	1	8
Car	2015	WC	5	0	1	1	2
		Totals	69	13	14	27	106

Club	Year	Comp	GP	G	A	Pts	PIM
O'CONNOR Ben			D		b. 21-Dec-88		
Cov	2008	POQ	3	0	0	0	0
Cov	2009	WC	5	1	0	1	0
Edi	2010	WC	5	1	1	2	6
Fra	2011	WC	5	3	1	4	14
Kaz	2012	POQ	3	3	1	4	0
Kaz	2013	FOQ	3	0	2	2	2
Kaz	2014	WC	5	0	2	2	2
She	2015	WC	5	3	2	5	6
		Totals	34	11	9	20	30
PEACOCK Craig			F		b. 8-Apr-88		
Bel	2010	WC	5	0	0	0	4
Bel	2012	WC	5	1	2	3	0
Bel	2012	POQ	3	2	2	4	0
Bel	2013	FOQ	3	2	0	2	0
Bel	2013	WC	5	0	0	0	4
Bel	2015	WC	5	1	1	2	0
		Totals	26	6	5	11	8
PHILLIPS David			D		b. 14-Aug-87		
Hul	2006	WC	5	1	2	3	10
Hul	2007	WC	5	0	0	0	0
Hul	2008	WC	5	0	2	2	6
Bel	2008	POQ	3	1	0	1	2
Bel	2009	WC	5	1	1	2	2
Echl	2011	WC	5	0	1	1	4
Den	2012	WC	5	0	1	1	10
Bel	2012	POQ	3	0	0	0	0
Bel	2013	FOQ	3	0	0	0	0
Bel	2013	WC	5	1	0	1	2
Bel	2014	WC	5	0	2	2	8
Bel	2015	WC	5	1	1	2	4
		Totals	54	5	10	15	48

Key
WC - World Championships
WCQ - World Pool A Qualifying
POQ - Pre-Olympic Qualifying
FOQ - Final Olympic Qualifying

PLAYERS, contd

PHILLIPS Jonathan   F   b. 14-July-82

Club	Year	Comp	GP	G	A	Pts	PIM
Car	2003	WC	5	0	1	1	6
Car	2004	WC	5	2	0	2	10
Car	2005	WC	5	0	0	0	14
Car	2006	WC	5	1	2	3	16
She	2007	WC	5	1	4	5	4
She	2008	WC	5	1	1	2	0
She	2008	POQ	3	1	2	3	2
She	2010	WC	5	2	1	3	0
She	2011	WC	5	2	0	2	2
She	2012	WC	5	1	0	1	0
She	2012	POQ	3	0	0	0	2
She	2013	FOQ	3	0	0	0	2
She	2013	WC	5	0	0	0	2
She	2014	WC	5	1	0	1	8
She	2015	WC	5	0	0	0	6
Totals			69	12	11	23	74

SHIELDS Colin   F   b. 27-Jan-80

Club	Year	Comp	GP	G	A	Pts	PIM
NAHL	2001	WC	5	6	2	8	4
UoM	2002	WC	5	2	3	5	4
UoM	2003	WC	5	4	1	5	2
UoM	2004	WC	5	0	2	2	6
ECHL	2005	WC	4	2	2	4	6
Bel	2006	WC	5	4	0	4	10
Bel	2008	POQ	3	1	1	2	0
Bel	2009	WC	5	2	4	6	14
Bel	2010	WC	5	0	1	1	2
Bel	2011	WC	3	1	2	3	0
Fra	2012	WC	5	3	4	7	0
She	2012	POQ	3	1	3	4	2
Bel	2013	FOQ	3	0	2	2	4
Bel	2013	WC	5	1	0	1	2
Bel	2014	WC	5	5	1	6	0
Bel	2015	WC	5	0	2	2	0
Totals			71	32	30	62	56

WEAVER Jonathan   U   b. 20-Jan-77

Club	Year	Comp	GP	G	A	Pts	PIM
New	1998	WC	7	1	5	6	0
Man	1999	WC	7	0	2	2	2
USA	1999	WCQ	4	0	0	0	2
Ayr	2001	WC	5	7	2	9	0
Ayr	2002	WC	3	0	0	0	0
Fif	2003	WC	5	2	1	3	4
New	2005	WC	5	2	4	6	6
New	2006	WC	5	0	1	1	8
New	2007	WC	5	1	2	3	4
Cov	2008	WC	5	2	4	6	4
Cov	2008	POQ	3	2	1	3	0
Cov	2009	WC	5	1	2	3	2
Cov	2010	WC	5	0	1	1	8
Cov	2011	WC	5	1	7	8	0
Not	2012	POQ	3	0	2	2	4
Not	2013	WC	5	0	2	2	12
Not	2014	WC	5	0	3	3	0
Tel	2015	WC	5	0	3	3	0
Totals			87	19	42	61	56

PRINCE Jack   F   b. 14-Feb-91

Club	Year	Comp	GP	G	A	Pts	PIM
UAH	2015	WC	5	0	1	1	2

SWINDLEHURST Paul   D   b. 25-May-93

Club	Year	Comp	GP	G	A	Pts	PIM
Dun	2014	WC	5	0	0	0	0
Dun	2015	WC	5	1	0	1	2
Totals			10	1	0	1	2

RICHARDSON Mark   D   b. 1-Oct-86

Club	Year	Comp	GP	G	A	Pts	PIM
Brk	2005	WC	5	1	0	1	0
Car	2006	WC	5	0	0	0	0
Car	2007	WC	5	1	0	1	0
Not	2008	POQ	3	1	1	2	0
Not	2009	WC	5	0	0	0	0
Car	2010	WC	5	0	1	1	2
Car	2011	WC	5	0	1	1	6
Car	2012	WC	5	0	2	2	2
Car	2012	POQ	3	0	0	0	0
Car	2013	FOQ	3	0	0	0	0
Car	2013	WC	5	0	2	2	0
Car	2014	WC	5	0	0	0	0
Car	2015	WC	5	2	0	2	0
Totals			59	5	7	12	10

THOMAS Mark   D   b. 23-Jul-83

Club	Year	Comp	GP	G	A	Pts	PIM
Lon	2005	WC	5	0	0	0	16
She	2006	WC	5	0	1	1	6
She	2009	WC	5	0	1	1	4
She	2011	WC	5	0	0	0	4
She	2012	WC	5	0	1	1	2
She	2012	POQ	3	0	0	0	2
She	2013	FOQ	3	0	0	0	2
She	2013	WC	5	0	0	0	2
She	2015	WC	5	0	1	1	4
Totals			41	0	4	4	42

NETMINDERS

BOWNS Ben   b. 21-Jan-91

Club	Year	Comp	GP	GPI	Mins	GA	GAA
Hul	2012	POQ	3	0	0	0	0.00
Hul	2013	FOQ	3	1	60	6	6.00
Hul	2013	WC	5	1	5	0	0.00
Hul	2014	WC	5	5	252	8	1.90
Car	2015	WC	5	5	299	10	2.01
Totals			21	12	616	24	2.34

LYLE Stevie   b. 4-Dec-79
Records for 1995-2013 in The Ice Hockey

Club	Year	Comp	GP	GPI	Mins	GA	GAA
Annual 2013-14			69	44	2456	112	2.74
Swi	2015	WC	5	0	0	0	0.00
Totals			74	44	2456	112	2.74

WORLD CHAMPIONSHIP + OLYMPIC QUALIFYING
APPEARANCES 1989-2015

PLAYERS

PLAYERS	Years	GP	G	A	Pts	PIM
ADEY Paul	1995-2001	55	28	24	52	65
BAILEY Chris	2003	4	0	0	0	25
BATCH Josh	**2015**	**5**	**0**	**0**	**0**	**2**
BENNETT Ivor	1989	4	0	1	1	2
BERRINGTON Paul	2002-03	10	2	3	5	8
BIDNER Todd	1993	4	1	1	2	4
BISHOP Mike	1995-2000	36	5	8	13	109
BLIGHT Chris	**2015**	**5**	**1**	**0**	**1**	**0**
BOBYCK Brent	1999-2000	7	0	1	1	0
BOE Vince	1999-2000	11	0	3	3	22
BOOTHROYD Luke	2008 & 13	10	0	0	0	0
BOXILL Jonathan	**2015**	**5**	**0**	**0**	**0**	**2**
BREBANT Rick	1994-2002	32	10	13	23	78
CAMPBELL Scott	1999-2003	13	0	1	1	60
CHAMBERS Greg	2008-10	18	6	20	26	37
CHARD Chris	1995	1	0	0	0	0
CHINN Nicky	1993-2000	40	6	8	14	109
CLARKE David	2000-14	79	24	32	56	76
CLARKE Gary	2008	5	0	0	0	0
CONWAY Kevin	1992-99	58	33	33	66	54
COOPER Ian	1989-2000	80	30	31	61	128
COOPER Stephen	1989-2000	61	11	27	38	54
COTE Matt	1994-2000	33	0	2	2	16
COWLEY Russell	**03-11,15**	**53**	**4**	**15**	**19**	**22**
CRAIPER Jamie	1990-92	17	12	8	20	34
CRANSTON Tim	1993-97	39	11	13	24	91
DAVIES Ben	2013-14	10	1	3	4	4
DAVIES Mathew	2014	5	0	0	0	0
DIXON Paul	1995-2004	59	4	16	20	26
DOWD Robert	**2008-15**	**44**	**14**	**14**	**28**	**34**
DURDLE Darren	1996-2000	22	3	6	9	36
EDMISTON Dean	1991-92	12	3	4	7	15
ELLIS Mike	2000-07	42	6	12	18	32
FARMER Robert	**2012-15**	**26**	**4**	**1**	**5**	**12**
FERA Rick	1993-94	17	7	17	24	34
FUSSEY Owen	2012	5	1	0	1	6
GALAZZI Mark	2003	4	0	0	0	25
GARDEN Graham	1995-2000	27	5	5	10	28
GARSIDE Mark	**2010-15**	**26**	**3**	**3**	**6**	**14**
HAND Paul	1989-92	18	7	5	12	41
HAND Tony	1989-2007	64	40	82	122	34
HARDING Mike	1999-2000	7	1	3	4	4
HAYWOOD Matthew	**2015**	**5**	**0**	**0**	**0**	**2**
HEWITT Jason	2008-14	34	1	2	3	20
HILL Phil	2009-14	35	4	2	6	6
HOAD Jeff	2002-04	14	6	5	11	14
HOPE Shannon	1992-98	53	1	8	9	88
HORNE Kyle	2001-08	25	0	3	3	10

PLAYERS, contd.	Years	GP	G	A	Pts	PIM
HUNT Simon	1995-96	11	3	1	4	26
HURLEY Darren	1999-2003	36	9	8	17	138
HUTCHINS Jeff	2011-12	9	0	3	3	6
IREDALE John	1989-93	24	6	8	14	12
JAMIESON Leigh	2004-12	23	3	5	8	32
JOHNSON Anthony	1990-93	28	15	13	28	20
JOHNSON Shane	2009	5	0	0	0	6
JOHNSON Shaun	1992-2007	21	2	8	10	8
JOHNSON Stephen	1990-93	23	10	12	22	6
JOHNSTONE Jeff	1999-2000	14	4	3	7	6
KENDALL Jason	2000	3	0	0	0	0
KELLAND Chris	1990-94	31	10	8	18	44
KIDD John	1989	4	2	1	3	0
KINDRED Mike	1995	5	0	1	1	2
KURTENBACH Terry	1993-96	29	1	7	8	6
LACHOWICZ Robert	**2011-15**	**31**	**1**	**7**	**8**	**4**
LAKE Ryan	2004	5	0	1	1	0
LAMBERT Dale	1993	4	0	0	0	4
LARKIN Bryan	1997	7	0	1	1	6
LATTO Gordon	1976-89	21	2	2	4	10
LAWLESS John	1990-91	12	5	10	15	22
LEE Phil	1989-90	8	2	0	2	0
LEE Stephen	2010,13,14	24	0	0	0	8
LEVERS Marc	2005-06	10	1	5	6	6
LIDDIARD Neil	2000-05	25	2	3	5	26
LINDSAY Jeff	1995-96	22	0	1	1	22
LITTLE Richard	1996-97	10	5	2	7	18
LONGSTAFF David	1994-2012	101	32	45	77	86
MacNAUGHT Kevin	1990-92	17	14	16	30	16
MALO Andre	1993-2000	37	2	7	9	40
MARSDEN Doug	1997	7	0	1	1	8
MASON Brian	1990-94	34	10	10	20	37
McEWEN Doug	1993-2001	49	13	13	26	32
MEYERS Danny	2004-14	59	6	12	18	32
MITCHELL Lee	2010	5	0	0	0	0
MOODY Scott	2003-06	14	1	1	2	6
MORAN Paul	2004-06	15	2	1	3	12
MORGAN Neil	1995-98	35	11	11	22	16
MORIA Steve	1995-2000	49	22	13	35	30
MORRIS Frank	1994-95	13	1	1	2	10
MORRISON Scott	1993-95	25	15	8	23	16
MULVENNA Glenn	2000	7	0	0	0	18
MYERS Matthew	**2004-15**	**69**	**13**	**14**	**27**	**106**
NEIL Scott	1981-93	37	23	12	35	18
NEILSON Corey	2011-12	10	2	4	6	35
NELL Aaron	2013	5	0	0	0	2
NELSON Craig	2002	5	0	0	0	10
ORD Terry	1989	4	0	1	1	0

WORLD CHAMPIONSHIP + OLYMPIC QUALIFYING
APPEARANCES 1989-2015

PLAYERS, contd

PLAYERS	Years	GP	G	A	Pts	PIM
O'CONNOR Ben	2008-15	34	11	9	20	30
O'CONNOR Mike	1992-94	22	4	5	9	52
OWEN Greg	2003-13	41	6	18	24	30
PAYNE Anthony	1995	6	1	0	1	0
PEACOCK Craig	10-13,15	26	6	5	11	8
PEASE James	2005-08	15	0	1	1	12
PENNYCOOK Jim	1977-89	23	10	9	19	4
PENTLAND Paul	1989	4	0	0	0	0
PHILLIPS David	2006-15	54	5	10	15	48
PHILLIPS Jonathan	2003-15	69	12	11	23	74
PHILLIPS Kevin	2005 & 10	10	0	0	0	2
PICKLES Andy	2001	5	0	1	1	2
PLOMMER Tommy	1995-96	7	3	0	3	4
POPE Brent	2003-04	8	0	0	0	37
POUND Ian	1995	7	0	0	0	10
PRIEST Merv	1996-2000	30	6	7	13	30
PRINCE Jack	2015	5	0	1	1	2
RADMALL Adam	2005-06	8	0	1	1	2
REID Alistair	1989	4	1	2	3	0
REMPEL Nathan	2007	5	3	0	3	2
RHODES Nigel	1989	4	2	0	2	2
RICHARDSON Mark	2005-15	59	5	7	12	10
ROBERTSON Iain	1991-95	27	4	3	7	2
SAMPLE Paul	2004-08	20	2	3	5	22
SARICH Rod	2013	3	0	0	0	6
SAUNDERS Lee	1995-96	8	0	1	1	0
SCOTT Patrick	1993-97	31	10	9	19	24
SHIELDS Colin	2001-15	71	32	30	62	56
SMITH Damian	1992-95	14	3	4	7	10
SMITH David	1995	5	1	0	1	0
SMITH Paul	1981-89	11	0	1	1	13
SMITH Peter	1989-91	14	7	2	9	10
SMITH Stephen	1989	4	2	1	3	2
STEFAN Gary	1990-92	17	12	10	22	28
STONE Jason	1998	6	0	0	0	0
STRACHAN Rick	1995-2002	66	7	10	17	20
SWINDLEHURST Paul	2014-15	10	1	0	1	2

PLAYERS, contd

PLAYERS	Years	GP	G	A	Pts	PIM
TAIT Ashley	1995-2014	102	23	33	56	154
TAIT Warren	2005-08	20	1	2	3	2
TASKER Michael	2001-02	10	2	3	5	8
THOMAS Mark	2005-15	41	0	4	4	42
THOMPSON Paul	1998	6	1	1	2	8
THORNTON Steve	1999-2008	29	6	23	29	14
TOWE Matt	2008 & 10	10	0	0	0	2
WAGHORN Graham	1991-96	19	1	3	4	16
WALTON Graeme	2007-09	18	0	1	1	4
WARD Colin	2004	5	3	0	3	2
WATKINS Tom	2007-09	15	4	0	4	10
WEAVER Jonathan	1998-2015	87	19	42	61	56
WEBER Randall	1998	7	0	2	2	6
WILSON Rob	1998-2004	34	11	22	33	32
WISHART Gary	2002	5	0	2	2	4
YOUNG Scott	1999-2002	16	5	4	9	56

NETMINDERS

NETMINDERS	Years	GP	GPI	Mins	GA	GAA
BOWNS Ben	2012-15	21	12	616	24	2.34
CAVALLIN Mark	2003-04	9	5	300	16	3.20
COWLEY Wayne	1999-2000	10	3	160	10	3.75
CRAZE Nathan	2010-11	6	1	14	0	0.00
FOSTER Stephen	1995-2000	31	16	855	61	4.28
GRAHAM David	1989-91	10	6	330	18	3.27
GRUBB Ricky	1995	1	1	40	5	7.50
HANSON Moray	1989-94	9	6	317	32	6.06
HIBBERT Jim	2000	1	1	20	3	9.00
LEHMAN Jody	2009	5	5	262	10	2.29
LYLE Stevie	95-13,15	74	44	2456	112	2.74
McCRONE John	1989-94	23	19	957	57	3.57
McKAY Martin	1990-94	15	8	418	28	4.02
MORRISON Bill	1995-99	33	17	1000	38	2.28
MURPHY Stephen	2001-14	61	37	2034	101	2.98
O'CONNOR Scott	1992-2003	9	5	198	4	1.21
SMITH Jeff	1990	3	1	60	2	2.00
WATKINS Joe	1999-2005	25	12	709	36	3.04
WOOLHOUSE Geoff	2012	5	0	0	0	0.00

LEADING POINTS SCORERS 1989-2015

	Years	GP	G	A	Pts
HAND Tony	1989-2007	64	40	82*	122*
LONGSTAFF David	1994-2013	101	32	45	77
CONWAY Kevin	1992-99	58	33	33	66
SHIELDS Colin	2001-15	71	32	30	62
COOPER Ian	1989-2000	80	30	31	61
WEAVER Jonathan	1998-2015	87	19	42	61
CLARKE David	2000-14	79	24	32	56
TAIT Ashley	1995-2014	102*	23	33	56

NOTES

Active players shown in **bold**.
Includes World Championships 1989-2015; Pool A
Qualifying Games in Nov 1999; and Olympic
Qualifying tournaments in 1993, 1995-96, 2000,
2008 and 2012-13.
Excl Euro Challenge games (non-IIHF) and friendlies.
GB's all-time top goal scorer is **Gerry Davey**
(1914-77) with 44 in 45 games in seasons 1932-48.
* *all-time GB team records*

WORLD JUNIOR CHAMPIONSHIPS

2015

Tallinn, 7-13 December 2014

Age limit is under 20 years on 1 Jan 2015

FINAL STANDINGS

	GP	W	OW	OL	L	GF	GA	Pts
Britain GB	5	4	1	0	0	22	13	14
Lithuania LTU	5	2	1	1	1	24	19	9
S Korea KOR	5	2	1	1	1	18	18	9
N'lands NED	5	1	1	0	3	18	16	5
Estonia EST	5	1	0	1	3	12	22	4
Romania ROU	5	1	0	1	3	18	24	4

W = win - 3 pts, OW = overtime win - 2 pts, OL = overtime loss - 1 pt.

Britain promoted to Division I, Group B; **Romania relegated** to Division II, Group B.

RESULTS

	LTU	KOR	NED	EST	ROU
GB	5-4	5-4ps	4-2	3-1	5-2
LTU		5-1	3-4	6-4	6-5
KOR			3-2	4-3	6-3
NED				7-0	3-6
EST					4-2

BRITAIN'S LEADING SCORERS

	GP	G	A	Pts	Pim
Bobby Chamberlain	5	6	6	12	10
Jordan Cownie	5	5	6	11	0
Lewis Hook	5	4	7	11	4
Ivan Antonov	5	2	1	3	2
Ollie Betteridge	5	2	0	2	0
Sam Duggan	5	2	0	2	4
Cameron Wynn	5	1	1	2	2

BRITAIN'S NETMINDING

	GPI	Mins	SoG	GA	Sv%
Jordan Hedley	1	60	20	1	95.00
Adam Goss	4	245	122	12	90.16
GB TOTALS	5	305	142	13	90.85

BRITAIN UNDER-20

Goal: *Adam Goss (Mercyhurst University, USA); *Jordan Hedley MIL. *Defence:* Declan Balmer, *Matt Selby capt BAS; Harvey Stead BRK; Scott Robson PET; Callum Buglass SWI; #Josh Grieveson (Middlesex, USA); Craig Moore capt (Ogden Utah Mustangs). *Forwards:* Cameron Wynn BAS; *#Ivan Antonov BRK; Sam Towner HUL; *Bobby Chamberlain MAN; *Jordan Cownie, *Lewis Hook MIL; *Ollie Betteridge, *Floyd Taylor SWI; #Glen Billing, #Toms Rutkis, #Michael Stratford (Okanagan UK); Alex Forbes (Ogden Utah Mustangs); *#Sam Duggan (Orebro, Sweden).

Head coach: Pete Russell (Okanagan HA).
Asst. coaches: Paul Heavey, Greg Owen (unatt.); Tom Watkins TEL. *Manager:* Alma Greger.
* played on last year's under-20s (9).
\# played on this year's under-18s (6).

ALMA GREGER

Popular GB under-20 manager **Alma Greger** stepped down following the championships after four years in the role.

Ice Hockey UK chairman **Jim Anderson** said: "Alma's excellent organising skills and attention to detail have always been second to none. She is an unsung hero, like many volunteers in the sport, and she will be sadly missed."

In her 20 years in ice hockey, Alma held several positions in her native Scotland with Kirkcaldy and Scottish Ice Hockey UK, and as national development co-ordinator for Scottish Conference junior teams.

She also managed this year's GB Prospects side (see page 140.)

CHALLENGE GAMES

The GB under-20s' three-day training camp in Helsinki, Finland ended with a 7-3 win over an under-20 side from local club *Grankulla IFK*. *Goals:* Rutkis (2), Wynn, Chamberlain, Robson, Forbes, Hook.
▶ GB under-20s beat *Nottingham Lions* of the NIHL in a challenge game on 4 November 2014.

GB UNDER-20 GAME SUMMARIES

7 Dec **N'LANDS-BRITAIN** **2-4** (0-0,0-1,2-3)
GB scorers: Cownie 1+1; Antonov, Betteridge, Chamberlain 1g; Forbes, Moore, Stratford, Hook 1a. *Shots:* Vermeulen NED 35 (88.6%), Goss GB 42 (95.2%). *Pims:* NED 6, GB 12. *GB MOM:* Goss. *Referee:* Nalivaiko BLR. *Attendance:* 97.

8 Dec **BRITAIN-LITHUANIA** **5-4** (0-2,1-0,4-2)
GB scorers: Wynn, Antonov, Duggan, Cownie, Chamberlain 1g; Robson, Hook, Rutkis 1a. *Shots:* Goss GB 25 (84.0%), Baltrunas LTU 39 (89.7%). *Pims:* GB 12, LTU 8. *GB MOM:* Wynn. *Referee:* Zviedritis LAT. *Attendance:* 133.

10 Dec **BRITAIN-ROMANIA** **5-2** (2-1,1-1,2-0)
GB scorers: Cownie 2g; Hook 1+2; Betteridge, Duggan 1g; Chamberlain 3a; Wynn, Grieveson, Taylor 1a. *Shots:* Goss GB 29 (93.1%), Adorjan ROU 38 (86.8%), *Pims:* GB 8, ROU 6. *GB MOM:* Hook. *Referee:* Tzirtziganis BEL. *Att:* 275.

12 Dec **S KOREA-BRITAIN** **4-4ot** (1-0,1-3,2-1,0-0)
GB won 5-4 *after penalty shootout.*
Cownie scored winning shot.
GB scorers: Chamberlain 3+1; Hook 1+3; Cownie 3a; Moore 1a. *Shots:* Kweongyoung/Lee KOR 39 (89.7%), Goss GB 26 (84.6%). *Pims:* KOR 6, GB 18 (Chamberlain 10m-unsports.). *GB MOM:* Chamberlain. *Ref:* Zviedritis LAT. *Att:* 310.

13 Dec **BRITAIN-ESTONIA** **3-1** (1-0,1-0,1-1)
GB scorers: Hook 2g; Chamberlain 1+2; Cownie 2a; Antonov 1a. *Shots:* Hedley GB 20 (95.0%), Seppenen EST 35 (94.3%). *Pims:* GB 4, EST 14. *GB MOM:* Hook. *Ref:* Tzirtziganis BEL. *Att:* 550.

Cool Cownie strikes for gold

Pete Russell's Brits dropped only one point – to the Jim Paek/Richard Park-coached South Koreans – to propel them back into Division IB.

Three EPIHL forwards dominated Britain's scoring – Lewis Hook, Bobby Chamberlain and Jordan Cownie. The latter, who was voted the games' best forward, coolly converted the shot which downed Korea and won the gold.

Though GB were playing at a level lower than they should have been (an admin. cock-up led to their relegation a year ago), few of their opponents were walk-overs. Only the relegated Romanians were convincingly dispatched.

Tallinn, 22-28 March 2015

Age limit is under 18 years on 1 Jan 2015

FINAL STANDINGS

	GP	W	OW	OL	L	GF	GA	Pts
S Korea KOR	5	5	0	0	0	28	7	15
Poland POL	5	4	0	0	1	18	10	12
Britain GB	**5**	**2**	**1**	**0**	**2**	**18**	**13**	**8**
Ne'lands NED	5	1	1	1	2	18	22	6
Croatia CRO	5	1	0	0	4	9	24	3
Estonia EST	5	0	0	1	4	11	26	1

S Korea promoted to Division I, Group B; **Estonia relegated** to Division II, Group B.

RESULTS

	KOR	POL	NED	CRO	EST
GB	2-4	1-4	4-3ps	7-1	4-1
KOR		4-1	6-3	7-0	7-1
POL			6-3	2-1	5-1
NED				4-2	5-4
CRO					5-4

BRITAIN'S LEADING SCORERS

	GP	G	A	Pts	Pim
Michael Stratford	5	4	2	6	4
Luc Johnson	5	2	4	6	14
Glenn Billing	5	3	2	5	4
Sam Duggan	5	3	1	4	6
Ivan Antonov	5	2	2	4	4
Lee Bonner	5	2	1	3	0

BRITAIN'S NETMINDERS

	GPI	Mins	SoG	GA	Sv%
Renny Marr	2	119	50	4	92.0
Denis Bell	3	185	97	8	91.8
GB TOTALS	**5**	**304**	**147**	**12**	**91.8**

WORLD JUNIOR CHAMPIONSHIPS

BRITAIN under-20 *left to right, back row, standing:* Pete Russell (head coach), Greg Owen (asst. coach – video), Ivan (Vanya) Antonov, Callum Buglass, Cameron Wynn, Ollie Betteridge, Matt Selby, Sam Duggan, Floyd Taylor, Paul Heavey (asst. coach), Jim Anderson (team leader); *middle row:* Lewis Hook, Bobby Chamberlain, Toms Rutkis, Alex Forbes, Craig Moore, Harvey Stead, Josh Grieveson, Michael Stratford, Jordan Cownie, Craig Cooke (equipment); *front row:* Adam Goss, Sam Towner, Glen Billing, Declan Balmer, Jordan Hedley, Scott Robson; *in front:* Alma Greger (manager).

Photo: Colin Lawson

BRITAIN UNDER-18

Goal: Renny Marr FIF; *Denis Bell-Blake TEL. *Defence*: Callum Wells CHE; Edward Knaggs MIL; Ben Nethersell, Kyle Smith, Ollie Stone (Okanagan Hockey Academy UK); Bradley Jenion (Ontario Hockey Academy); #*Josh Grieveson (Middlesex Bears, USA); Cameron Pound (CIHA, Rockland, Ontario). *Forwards*: #*Ivan Antonov, Danny Ingoldsby BRK; Owen Bradshaw CAR; Callum Queenan WHI; #*Glenn Billing, Adam Finlinson, *Luc Johnson, #Toms Rutkis, #*Michael Stratford (Okanagan Academy UK); Connor Henderson (Ontario Hockey Academy); *Lee Bonner (Iowa Wild, USA); #*Sam Duggan (Orebro HK, Sweden).
Head coach: Martin Grubb (Solway). *Asst. coaches*: James Pease (Coventry) Simon Leach (Whitley Bay). *Manager*: Ian Turner (unatt.).
*played on last year's under-18s (8).
played on this year's under-20s (6).

Bronze for Brits

Martin Grubb's under-18s won the bronze medal in Estonia, finishing two places higher than they had at home 12 months previously.

They tripped up against Poland and – like the under-20s – the Koreans, whose eyes are fixed on the 2018 Olympics.

The most memorable game was the final one against the Netherlands, which needed 17 penalty shots before Britain could claim victory.

After both sides had been blanked in the best-of-five, **Ivan Antonov** beat the Dutch keeper on GB's sixth effort, only for Muller to respond with the next shot.

Antonov missed the net on his next attempt, and Hermens' shot was saved by **Denis Bell**.

Sam Duggan hit the back of the net on GB's eighth, and Bell outwitted Lambregts.

■ The 17-shot marathon is a record for all GB teams. The tie-breaking system was introduced by the IIHF in 2008.

GB UNDER-18 GAME SUMMARIES

22 Mar **KOREA-BRITAIN** 4-2 (1-0,2-0,1-2) GB scorers: Henderson, Duggan 1g; Stratford, Finlinson, Rutkis, Antonov 1a. *Shots*: Hyounseop KOR 35 (94.29%), Marr GB 33 (90.91%). *Pims*: KOR 20, GB 8. *GB MOM*: Knaggs. *Referee*: Shrubok BLR. *Att*: 247.

23 Mar **BRITAIN-ESTONIA** 4-1 (2-1,1-0,1-0) GB scorers: Johnson 2+1; Stratford 2g; Billing, Antonov, Nethersell 1a. *Shots*: Bell-Blake GB 32 (96.88%), Valjakin EST 28 (85.71%). *Pims*: GB 24 (Johnson 2+10 – rough+unsport.) EST 12. *GB MOM*: Billing. *Ref*: Fazekas SRB. *Att*: 647.

25 Mar **POLAND-BRITAIN** 4-1 (1-0,0-1,3-0) GB scorers: Stratford 1g; Johnson 1a. *Shots*: Studzinski POL 19 (94.74%), Bell-Blake GB 30 (86.67%). *Pim*: POL 20 (Gozdziewicz 10 – unsport.), GB 16. *GB MOM*: Grieveson. *Ref*: Fazekas SRB. *Attendance*: 162.

27 Mar **BRITAIN-CROATIA** 7-1 (4-0,2-1,1-0) GB scorers: Billing 3+1; Antonov 2g; Stratford 1+1; Bonner 1g; Johnson 2a; Bradshaw, Duggan, Knaggs 1a. *Shots*: Marr GB 17 (94.12%), H Adamovic CRO 50 (86.00%). *Pim*: GB 10, CRO 10. *GB MOM*: Antonov. *Ref*: Gregersen DEN.

28 Mar **N'LANDS-BRITAIN** 3-3ot (1-1,1-1,1-1,0-0) **GB win 4-3** after penalty shootout. *Duggan* scored winning shot. GB scorers: Bonner 1+1; Duggan, Rutkis 1g; Ingoldsby, Grieveson 1a. *Shots*: Leeuwesteijn NED 38 (92.11%), Bell-Blake GB 35 (91.43%). *Pim*: GB 12, LTU 2. *GB MOM*: Bell-Blake. *Referee*: Fazekas SRB. *Attendance*: 153.

CHALLENGE GAMES

The GB under-18s beat the *NIHL Coventry Blaze* 10-1 on 3 February 2015 in the Skydome. Rutkis scored a natural hat-trick in the second period.

On 20 March, the under-18s beat a team of *Finnish juniors* 7-4 in Helsinki. *Goal scorers*: Duggan, Billing, Johnson, Queenan, Bradshaw, Stratford, Finlinson.

In both games, GB netminders Bell and Marr shared ice-time equally.

WORLD JUNIOR CHAMPIONSHIPS

BRITAIN under-18 *left to right, back row:* Ivan Antonov, Adam Finlinson, Ollie Stone, Cameron Pound, Kyle Smith, Callum Queenan, Connor Henderson, Lee Bonner; *middle row:* Mark Gallagher (trainer), Craig Cooke (equipment), Toms Rutkis, Owen Bradshaw, Ben Nethersell, Michael Stratford, Simon Leach (asst. coach), James Pease (asst. coach), Bradley Jenion, Danny Ingoldsby, Callum Wells, Edward Knaggs, Ian Turner (general manager); *front row:* Denis Bell-Blake, Glenn Billing, Josh Grieveson, Martin Grubb (head coach), Luc Johnson, Sam Duggan, Renny Marr, Gabby McGraw (physio), Jim Anderson (team leader).

Photo: Paul Sorokin.

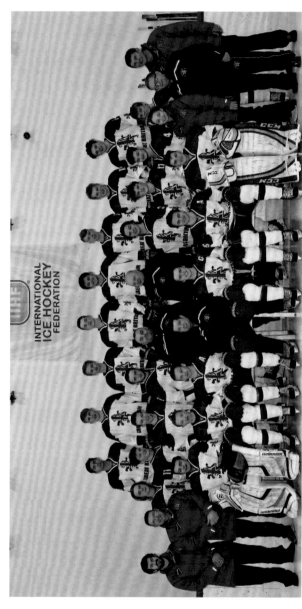

THE PLAYERS

Captain concussed

▶ Under-20 captain **Matt Selby** was concussed in the Lithuania game and underwent blood tests and a CAT scan at the local hospital.

Though this revealed no underlying issues, following IIHF concussion protocol, the Basingstoke defender was unable to take any further part in the tournament. He remained with the team but his captaincy was taken on by his fellow blueliner **Craig Moore**.

▶ Assistant coach **Tom Watkins** was unable to join the under-20s after his son Sam sustained a broken leg on 30 November, for the second time in 2014. Former GB senior forward **Greg Owen** was added to the coaching staff.

▶ This was the second year at under-20 for Bracknell Bee **Ivan** (Vanya) **Antonov** who was born in May 1997. The Moscow-born forward was one of six players who were picked for both the 20s and the 18s.

▶ Another 20/18 forward, **Toms Rutkis**, 17, of Swindon Wildcats and the Okanagan HA, holds dual Latvian-British citizenship and needed IIHF clearance before competing.

▶ Following **Pete Russell**'s appointment as head coach of the EPIHL's Milton Keynes Lightning for the 2015-16 season, his assistant Tom Watkins replaced him as head coach of GB's under-20s. Watkins remains as coach of the EPIHL's Telford Tigers and an assistant with the GB seniors.

Okanagan Hockey Academy UK

The ranks of this season's under-20s and under-18s included nine teenagers who have spent their winters in North America or Sweden.

This year, in addition, a record number of eight GB juniors were graduates of the Swindon-based Okanagan Hockey Academy (OHA), the UK branch of the famous Canadian hockey school.

It is no coincidence that **Pete Russell** has been the school's head coach since 2012.

Founded in Canada in 1963, the OHA provides seasonal hockey camps and a year-round academy programme that combines an education with athletics.

The school is fee-paying, but in return players are on the ice every day and receive coaching from professionals.

More on the OHA at www.hockeyschools.co.uk.

STILL A LONG WAY TO GO

Denmark and GB met at under-18 level in 2007 when Denmark won the group – Division IB.

Three of that team are now NHL regulars - goalie **Frederik Andersen** (Anaheim) and forwards **Mikkel Boedker** (Arizona) and **Lars Eller** (Montreal). Four other Danes played in the NHL in 2014-15.

Most of these players spent two or three seasons with Swedish and Canadian junior clubs before being drafted.

According to the IIHF, Denmark has 4,252 registered players, almost half of them under-20s (2,174).

By comparison, GB has 11,309 registered players, including 4,343 under-20s.

■ According to NHL.com, since 2007 three British-born players have been drafted by the NHL - **Thomas Larkin** (2009), **Brendan Perlini** (2014) and **Nathan Walker** (2014).

None has played for a GB team and none – at the time of writing – has played a game in the NHL.

■ There's more on Perlini in *People in the News*. Walker is an Australian citizen who was born in Cardiff (see page 26 of last year's *Annual*). Larkin, a London-born Italian, is unknown to us.

ENGLAND UNDER-16s
Another bronze in Tilburg

England's national under-16 boys team won their second bronze medal in as many years in the annual *Chris Verwijst* tournament in Tilburg, Netherlands in April 2015.

The **Robert Wilkinson**-coached side beat a Belgian under-16 club from Herentals 6-4 in the third place play-off.

England were placed third after the first round, which was played on a league basis, after shutting out German side Neusser EV 13-0 and Herentals 9-0, and beating local team Tilburg Trappers 5-1.

Defenceman **Sam Jackson** and forward **Adam Barnes** – England's top scorer with 16 points (five goals) - were voted to the tournament's All-Star team.

The competition was won by Mannheim Jungadler of Germany, who beat England 6-2 in the first round. Mannheim players took four of the top five scoring places. Barnes was third.

ENGLAND
Dean Bowater, Zach Grandy-Smith; Ryan Kemp, Lewis Baldwin, Sam Jackson, Jake Howis, Ethan Boolkah, Luke Jackson; Sean Norris, Aaron Lyons, James Royds, Harvey George, Ross Cowan, Richard Krogh, Louis Colvin, Liam Kirk, Harry Hopkins, Liam Coleman. *Head coach*: Robert Wilkinson, *asst. coach:* Sean Easton. *Manager*: Shirley Bliss.

The Wilkinson family dynasty
From season 2015-16 the team will revert to being the GB under-16s but will remain in the charge of England coach Robert Wilkinson.

The under-16s last competed in the Chris Verwijst tournament as GB in 1988-2000.

Wilkinson, 44, is the son of long-serving EIHA board director and former under-16 team manager **Bob Wilkinson**. A defenceman with Durham Wasps, Robert represented GB at under-18 and under-20 levels.

He has been coach of the England 16s throughout their existence.

ENGLAND UNDER-13s
England reach the last eight

England under-13s, coached by Slough's **Ben Pitchley**, reached the quarter-finals of their group in the Quebec International Pee-Wee Tournament in February 2015.

Results: 11 Feb v San Diego Gulls 1-3; 16 Feb v Angers Dukes 6-0; 18 Feb v Benelux Select 8-2; *Quarter-final*: 20 Feb v Acadie-Bathurst Titan 3-4.

England's top scorer (13th in group) was **Alex Graham** with seven points (four goals). **Lucas Brine**, one of the two netminders, is the son of former GB junior and Streatham Redskins keeper Gary Brine.

The Team: Lucas Brine, Bradley Windebank; Daniel Hitchings, Jack Goodchild, Bailey Challans, Danny Jackson, Thomas McFadden, Jarvis Hunt, Bradley Bowering, Jordan Griffin, Tommy Huggett, Liam Bartholomew, Max Chamberlain, Finley Howells, Dylan Hehir, Elliot Hall, Ewan Hill, Alex Graham. *Head coach*: Ben Pitchley. *Manager*: Rory Gavin.

WOMEN'S U-18 CHAMPIONSHIPS

Division I Qualifier, Katowice, Poland,
19-25 January 2015

FINAL STANDINGS

	GP	W	OW	OL	L	GF	GA	Pts
Denmark	5	5	0	0	0	29	2	15
Italy	5	4	0	0	1	11	8	12
Poland	5	3	0	0	2	21	12	9
Kazakhstan	5	1	1	0	3	6	14	5
China	5	1	0	1	3	3	19	4
Britain	5	0	0	0	5	3	18	0

Denmark promoted to the Elite Division

In their fourth year of international competition, **Sean Alderson**'s team lost all five of their games, scored only three goals and were shutout twice.

But Nottingham Leopards' keeper **Molly Brooks** emerged with credit as she performed small miracles in goal, saving 135 of the 149 shots poured on her. (This was more than three times the amount of rubber that the winning Danish netminder faced.)

With a superb save percentage of 90.60, 17-year-old Molly was voted GB's best player.

PAST WINNERS
WORLD UNDER-20s

1984 6th in Pool C in Varese, Italy
1985 5th in Pool C in Belgium
1986 3rd in Pool C in Gap, France
1987 3rd in Pool C in Esbjerg, Denmark
1988 4th in Pool C in Feltre/Belluno, Italy
1989 4th in Pool C in Bracknell, Cardiff & Swindon
1990 6th in Pool C in Eindhoven, Netherlands
1991 4th in Pool C in Belgrade, Yugoslavia
1992 3rd in Pool C in Rome, Italy
1993 5th in Pool C in Esbjerg, Denmark
1994 4th in Pool C in Odense, Denmark
1995 8th in Pool C in Puigcerda, Spain
1996 5th in Pool C in Jesenice & Bled, Slovenia
1997 4th in Pool C in Romania
1998 7th in Pool C in Estonia
1999 7th in Pool C in Lithuania
2000 3rd in Pool C in Nagano, Japan
2001 5th in Pool C in Lithuania
2002 5th in Div II in Zagreb, Croatia
   Coach: **Kevin King**.
2003 2nd in Div II (group A) in Romania
   Coach: **Kevin King**
2004 1st in Div II (group B) in Lithuania
   Coach: **Roger Hunt**
2005 6th in Div I (last in group A) in Sheffield
   Coach: **Roger Hunt**
2006 1st in Div II (group A) in Bucharest
   Coach: **Peter Russell**
2007 3rd in Div I (group B) in Torre Pellice, Italy
   Coach: **Mike Urquhart**
2008 *6th in Div I (group B) in Riga, Latvia
   Coach: **Peter Russell**
2009 2nd in Div II (group B) in Logrono, Spain
   Coach: **Peter Russell**
2010 1st in Div II (group A) in Debrecen, Hungary
   Coach: **Peter Russell**
2011 3rd in Div I (group A) in Bobruisk, Belarus
   Coach: **Peter Russell**
2012 *6th in Div 1 (last in group A) in Germany.
   Coach: **Joel Poirier**.
2013 5th in Division 1B in Donetsk, Ukraine.
   Coach: **Andre Payette**.
2014 #5th in Division IB in Dumfries, Scotland.
   Coach: **Peter Russell**.
   # relegated – ineligible player.
Bold - promoted (3)   * relegated

WORLD UNDER-18s

1979 3rd in Pool C in Sofia, Bulgaria
1980 3rd in Pool C in Frederikshaven, Denmark
1981 2nd in Pool C in Netherlands/Belgium
1982 3rd in Pool C in Billingham & Durham
1983 2nd in Pool C in Sarajevo, Yugoslavia
1984 2nd in Pool C in Murrayfield & Kirkcaldy
1985 3rd in Pool C in Feltre, Italy
1986 1st in Pool C in Barcelona, Spain
1987 7th in Pool B in Bucharest, Romania
1988 *Last in Pool B in Briancon, France
1989 2nd in Pool C in Puigcerda, Spain
1990 3rd in Pool C in Sofia, Bulgaria
1991 1st in Pool C in Sofia, Bulgaria
1992 7th in Pool B in France
1993 *8th in Pool B in Bucharest, Romania
1994 6th in Pool C in Bled, Slovenia
1995 4th in Pool C, Group 1, in Kiev, Ukraine.
1996 5th in Pool C in Maribor, Slovenia
1997 1st in Pool C in Romania
1998 8th in Pool B in Germany
1999 8th in Pool B in France
2000 *5th in Div I in Slovenia
2001 5th in Div II in Lithuania
2002 3rd in Div II in France
   Coach: **Allan Anderson**.
2003 6th in Div I in Latvia (*mistake! - should
   have been in Div II)*   Coach: **Allan Anderson**.
2004 1st in Div II in Lithuania
   Coach: **Mike Urquhart**
2005 *6th in Div I (group A) in Maribor, Slovenia
   Coach: **Mike Urquhart**
2006 1st in Div II (group B) in Lithuania
   Coach: **Mick Mishener**.
2007 *6th in Div I (group B) in Sanock, Poland
   Coach: **Mick Mishener**.
2008 2nd in Div II (group B) in Talinn, Estonia
   Coach: **Jon Rowbotham**.
2009 1st in Div II (group B) in Narva, Estonia
   Coach: **Jon Rowbotham**.
2010 5th in Div I (group B) in Krynica, Poland
   Coach: **Jon Rowbotham**.
2011 *5th (last) in Div I (group A) in Riga, Latvia
   Coach: **Mark Beggs**
2012 4th in Division IIA in Heerenveen, N'lands.
   Coach: **Mark Beggs**
2013 4th in Division IIA in Tallinn, Estonia.
   Coach: **Mark Beggs**.
2014 5th in Division IIA in Dumfries, Scotland
   Coach: **Martin Grubb**.

Junior ice hockey is alive and growing!

Junior ice hockey relies heavily on its volunteers and parents, so first I would like to thank all of you who are doing a great job, usually with little or no appreciation.

Over the last ten years I have seen the junior leagues grow substantially despite the acute lack of facilities. Communities all over Britain are crying out for ice rinks but there seems to be a built-in bureaucracy stopping this cost effective multi-sports facility from happening.

We are now at a crisis point where we cannot take any more children into our programmes because there is not enough rink time for ice hockey as well as other ice related activities.

As it is, we make our junior teams practice at unsuitable hours (11 pm-1am for under-13s!) plus a two-hour drive for most of the players. How can we improve our national standing when there are so many road blocks to success?

I urge all fans to go out and take in a junior game and see the excitement first hand. And if your town doesn't have a rink, talk to your local councillor and tell them how popular this great game is!

Troy Labelle
Coach, Streatham Junior Ice Hockey Club
(email: troy_labelle@hotmail.com)

CHAMPIONS HOCKEY LEAGUE

CHAMPIONS HOCKEY LEAGUE

2014-15
www.championshockeyleague.net

The inaugural Champions Hockey League (CHL) comprised 44 clubs from 11 national leagues in Central and Western Europe.

Britain's Elite League was one of five national leagues given a wild card to enter a team. (The others were Denmark, France, Norway and Slovakia).

Nottingham Panthers, who won the Elite League's Challenge Cup in 2013-14, agreed to take part after league champs *Belfast Giants* were forced to decline their invitation due to lack of available dates in the busy Odyssey Arena.

The complicated draw was streamed live on the internet and conducted by *Paul Romanuk*, a Canadian commentator based in London.

The teams were drawn into 11 groups, each consisting of four teams, with each club playing six games in a double round-robin.

All the Panthers' games - detailed on these pages - were screened live in the UK on *Premier Sports*.

After the first round, the top two teams in each group advanced to the knockout stage, which was played home and away.

The final was held on 3 February 2015 at the Coop Norbotten Arena in Luleå, Sweden, the home of the team with the best league record.

▲ The CHL's founding leagues – or 'original six' – are *Sweden, Finland, Czech Republic, Switzerland, Germany and Austria*.

▼ The CHL was unable to reach agreement with the Kontinental Hockey League for Russian teams to take part.

► There have been two Euro leagues in the last two decades. The first, which included teams from the UK's Superleague, lasted four seasons, 1996-2000. The second was in 2008-09. In each case, the league failed to attract sufficient crowds and investment. The second edition was also hit by the worldwide economic recession.

Nottingham won only one game in the CHL but that didn't stop the Panthers Nation from following their heroes everywhere. This was in Hamburg.   *photo: Michael Poole/Nottingham Post.*

FIRST ROUND

Group K	GP	W	OW	OL	L	GF	GA	Pts
*Lukko Rauma FIN	6	5	0	0	1	21	7	15
* Luleå Hockey SWE	6	5	0	0	1	32	6	15
Hamburg Freezers GER	6	1	0	0	5	8	21	3
Nottingham Panthers GB	**6**	**1**	**0**	**0**	**5**	**9**	**36**	**3**

* qualified for Second Round
Teams tied on points separated by goals scored in the games between them. Lukko and Luleå remained tied after using this system; Lukko were awarded first place as they finished higher in the Finnish league (third) than Lulea did in the Swedish league (sixth).

RESULTS IN GROUP K

22 Aug	**Panthers**-Lukko Rauma	2-4
	Hamburg Freezers-Luleå HF	4-1
24 Aug	**Panthers**-Luleå	1-10
	Freezers-Lukko	0-3
5 Sep	Lukko-**Panthers**	6-2
	Luleå-Freezers	6-0
7 Sep	Luleå-**Panthers**	9-1
	Lukko-Freezers	5-0
23 Sep	**Panthers**-Freezers	3-1
	Luleå-Lukko	3-1
7 Oct	Lukko-Luleå	2-0
	Freezers-**Panthers**	6-0

NOTTINGHAM PANTHERS

Line-up for Game Day One:
Craig Kowalski, Martins Raitums; Bryan Schmidt, Evan Mosey, Mike Berube, Charles Landry, Sam Oakford, Steve Lee, Colby Cohen; Robert Lachowicz, Max Parent, Chris Lawrence, Robert Farmer, Ollie Betteridge, Bruce Graham, Brandon Benedict (capt), Greg Jacina, Mark Lee, Martin Podlesak, Chris Higgins, Jonathan Boxill, Nathan Robinson.
Head coach: Corey Neilson. *Asst. coach:* Rick Strachan. *General manager:* Gary Moran.

Changes after Game Day One:
Brandon Benedict *missed Game Day Six due to concussion.*
Ollie Betteridge *dropped for Game Days Three and Four.*
David Clarke *returned from injury for Game Day Six and took over as captain from the injured Benedict.*
Colby Cohen *missed Game Days Five and Six after his contract expired (temporary replacement for Wild).*
Jordan Cownie *played on Game Days Five and Six.*
Robert Farmer *missed Game Day Six due to a foot injury.*
Dan Green *replaced* **Martins Raitums** *as back-up goalie after Game Day Two.*
Chris Higgins *missed all games after Game Day Two with injury.*
Lewis Hook *played on Game Days Five and Six.*
Mark Lee *missed all games after Game Day One with a back injury.*
Martin Podlesak *missed all games after Game Day Three for family reasons.*
Cody Wild *returned from injury to play after Game Day Two.*

Lukko were semi-finalists in the Finnish championships, Luleå were quarter-finalists in the stronger Swedish league. Hamburg won the German DEL and reached the semi-finals of the play-offs. The DEL is ranked third of the four leagues represented in group K.

The Elite League was 'odd man out' of the CHL. All the other member leagues were based in countries which compete in the Elite Division (top 16) of the World Championships. Britain was ranked 22nd in season 2014-15.

PANTHERS' LEADING SCORERS

	GP	G	A	Pts	Pims
Nathan Robinson	6	1	4	5	0
Robert Lachowicz	6	1	2	3	2
Brandon Benedict	5	2	1	3	4
Steve Lee	6	2	1	3	2
Cody Wild	4	2	1	3	2

PANTHERS' NETMINDING

	GP	Mins	SoG	GA	Save%
Craig Kowalski	6	322	215	30	86.05
Martins Raitums	1	38	29	6	79.31

ATTENDANCES

Group K	Lge pos.	Home crowds	GP	Ave
Hamburg	3	15227	3	5075
Panthers	9	11490	3	3830
Luleå	25	8622	3	2874
Lukko	27	8345	3	2781

PANTHERS' GAME SUMMARIES

Game Day One, 22 August 2014, National Ice Centre, Nottingham
PANTHERS-LUKKO RAUMA 2-4 (0-2,2-0,0-2)
Panthers' scoring:
Lee 2g; Robinson, Cohen, Farmer, Graham 1a.
Netminding
Kowalski NOT shots 44 save % 90.91
Zapolski LUK shots 22 save% 90.91
Penalty minutes: Panthers 12, Lukko 8.
Goals/powerplays: Panthers 1/4, Lukko 1/6.
Referees: Tom Darnell (GB), Shane Warschaw (Austria).
Lines: Andy Dalton (GB), Lee Young (GB).
Attendance: 4,045.

● Lukko were defeated by Tappara in the Finnish Liiga semi-finals in seven games.
● The Finns' line-up included Stanley Cup forward **Ville Niemenen**, 37.

After all games played on Day One, the Panthers stood third in Group K after Swedish side Luleå beat the Freezers 4-1 in Hamburg.

Premier Sports' TV commentators (from a studio in Dublin) were **Aaron Murphy, Neil Russell** and **Paul Adey.**

Against Lukko Rauma in their first home game, the Panthers did well in the middle period to get back to 2-2 with both goals from British d-man **STEVIE LEE** (celebrating here with **COLBY COHEN**).   *photo*: Michael Poole/Nottingham Post.

Game Day Two, *24 August 2014, National Ice Centre, Nottingham*
PANTHERS- LULEÅ HF   **1-10** (1-2,0-6,0-2)
Panthers' scoring:
Benedict 1g; Lachowicz, Cohen 1a.
Netminding
Raitums NOT   *shots* 22, *goals* 6, *save*% 78.57
Kowalski NOT   *shots* 10, *goals* 4, *save*% 71.43
Larsson LUL   *shots* 17, *goals* 1, *save*% 94.44
Penalty minutes: Panthers 16, Luleå 10.
Goals/powerplays: Panthers 1/4, Luleå 4/8.
Referees: Mike Hicks GB, Shane Warschaw AUT.
Linesmen: Dalton, Young GB. *Attendance*: 4,004

● Ex-Panthers' player and coach **Paul Adey** said on *Premier Sports* that Lulea were the best team he'd seen in Nottingham for 15-20 years.

Game Day Three, *5 September 2014, Kivikylän Areena, Rauma, Finland*
LUKKO RAUMA-PANTHERS   6-2 (4-0,1-1,1-1)
Panthers' scoring: Benedict 1+1; Mosey 1g; Robinson, Wild, Jacina 1a.
Netminding:
Zapolski LUL   *shots* 8, *saves* 7, *save*% 87.50
Setanen LUL   *shots* 7, *saves* 6, *save*% 85.71
Kowalski NOT   *shots* 35, *saves* 29, *save*% 82.86
Penalty minutes: Lukko 8, Panthers 8.
Goals/powerplays: Lukko 1/3, NOT 1/4
Referees: M Holm SWE, A Boman FIN.
Linesmen: J Saha, S Suominen FIN.
Attendance: 3,072

Game Day Four, *7 September 2014, Coop Norrbotten Arena, Luleå, Sweden*
LULEÅ-PANTHERS   **9-1** (4-0,3-0,2-1)
Panthers' scoring:
Cody Wild (unass.) 56.49.
Netminding:
Lassinantti LUL *shots* 16, *goals* 1, *save*% 93.75
Kowalski NOT   *shots* 46, *goals* 9, *save*% 80.43
Penalty minutes: Luleå 4, Panthers 20.
Goals/powerplays: Luleå 2/8, Panthers 0/1.
Referees: A Rantala FIN, T. Björk SWE.
Linesmen: E Yletyinen, J. Sandström SWE.
Attendance: 3,088.

● Luleå went on to win the CHL with a 4-2 come-from-behind victory in the final over fellow Swedish League club, Frolunda.

Game Day Five, *23 September 2014, National Ice Centre, Nottingham*
PANTHERS-HAMBURG   **3-1** (1-1,1-0,1-0)
Panthers' scoring:
Lachowicz, Robinson 1+1; Wild 1g; Lee, Graham, Mosey, Lawrence 1a.
Netminding:
Kowalski NOT *shots* 36, *goals* 1, *save* % 97.22
Caron HAM   *shots* 18, *goals* 1, *save* % 94.44
Kotschnew HAM *shots* 11, *goals* 2, *save*% 81.82
Penalty minutes: Panthers 12, Freezers 16.
Goals/powerplays: Panthers 1/6, Freezers 0/6.
Men of Match: Kowalski NOT, Pettinger HAM.
Refs: Antti Boman FIN, Mike Hicks GB.
Linesmen: Pirry, Young GB. *Attendance*: 3,441.

● This game made history for both sides. While it was the Panthers' first ever win in a major European competition, it was a loss too many for the Freezers, who sacked their coach of four years, **Benoit Laporte**.

Game Day Six, *7 October 2014, O2 World, Hamburg, Germany*
HAMBURG-PANTHERS   **6-0** (1-0,5-0,0-0)
Panthers' scoring: None.
Netminding:
Kotschnew HAM *shots* 25, *saves* 25, *save*% 100
Kowalski NOT   *shots* 40, *saves* 34, *save*% 85
Penalty minutes: Freezers 18 (Cabana 2+2+10 misc – rough), Panthers 16 (Jacina 2+2 rough).
Goals/powerplays: Freezers 1/5, Panthers 0/3.
Referees: M Krawinkel GER, D Massy SWI.
Linesmen: M Hofer, J-C Müller GER.
Attendance: 5,000 est.

REPORT

Brits, fans are Panthers' stars

The Panthers put on a brave show in the Elite League's first venture into serious Euro hockey, and emerged with one victory.

Corey Neilson's injury-hit squad, reinforced by several temporary imports, were out-classed by two of Europe's leading clubs but defeated Germany's struggling Hamburg Freezers.

Their overall goal difference was -27 and might well have been worse but for the acrobatics of netminder **Craig Kowalski.**

The performances of Panthers' Brits were universally praised. **Rob Lachowicz** scored a breakaway goal against the Freezers which would have graced any NHL highlights show.

Defender **Stevie Lee** got to wear the controversial Top Scorer jersey in game two after potting twice in the opening game.

Their Next Generation trio of **Lewis Hook,** 18, **Jordan Cownie,** 19, and **Ollie Betteridge,** 18, also stood out.

The Brits starred on a 25-man roster which was bolstered by five overseas skaters who had been signed for the duration of the CHL.

The best of these was Canadian attacker **Nathan Robinson,** 32, a Canadian with games in the NHL, AHL and German DEL to his credit.

'Robbo' is one of the game's characters: an exhibition of his artwork was staged in Nottingham.

But the other four – Canadian **Mark Lee,** American **Colby Cohen,** Czech **Martin Podlešák,** and back-up keeper **Martins Raitums** – iced in only nine games between them, as you can see from the long list of roster changes earlier in this section.

The category in which the Panthers scored best was their crowds. The attendance for their three home games was 11,490, an average of 3,830 per game, good enough for tenth place and higher than two of their opponents.

The team also got great support away from home – and it was often a long way. Around 400 fans went to Hamburg for the last game despite zero chance of any silverware.

For their performances on the ice Nottingham were eventually ranked 40th out of the 44 CHL teams, impressively ahead of Czech club Pardubice and Swiss A side Kloten, as well as Oslo, Norway and Briancon of France.

QUOTES

"It was like playing an NHL team. If an NHL team played on that rink I'm not sure they'd beat Luleå. It would certainly be one hell of a game." *Corey Neilson after Panthers' game in Sweden.*

"It's tough to adjust to such a good standard, especially for guys like me who have never played at that level." *Panthers' two-goal scorer* **Steve Lee** *after the first game.*

'Panthers have a long bus ride to northern Sweden on Saturday [6 Sept] and take on another top flight European team at Luleå on Sunday afternoon.' *On the Panthers' website after their game in Raumo, Finland. [Ed's note – it was a 500-mile (820km), 13-hour trip.]*

'Period over. 8-1 @LuleaHockey here in Nottingham. Pure domination. This aint just a team a class above. They're galaxies beyond! #CHL.' *Tweet from Panthers' fan.*

"When you're involved in professional sport your aim has to be to provide your loyal fans with the best possible fare that you can put on the menu. You must want to compete at the highest level possible.

"It did cost us financially but it brought positives for both our club and our league. Things will grow and develop as each season comes and goes and the competition will continue to grow." *Gary Moran, Nottingham Panthers' general manager.*

NOTES

▲Five British officials were selected by the league for Panthers' home games. **Tom Darnell** did Game Day One, and **Mike Hicks** was on duty for Game Days Two and Five. Brits **Lee Young, Andrew Dalton** and **Gordon Pirry** were the local linesmen.
►CHL boss **Martin Baumann** was in the NIC for the Luleå game.

► Superleague's *Manchester Storm,* coached by **John Lawless** (1996-97) and **Kurt Kleinendorst** (1997-2000), and *Ayr Scottish Eagles,* coached by **Jim Lynch** (1998-99), took part in the IIHF's European Hockey League. There's more on these games in *The Ice Hockey Annuals* for those seasons.

CONTINENTAL CUP

CONTINENTAL CUP 2014

The IIHF Continental Cup was established in 1997 as a replacement for the European Cup (inaugurated 1965).

Entry to the Cup is open to all teams that have been crowned their country's national champions (usually the play-off champions but in Britain the Elite League winners).

Costs are kept down by gathering clubs together geographically as far as possible and allowing games to be played by groups of teams in one venue, over a long weekend, rather than home and away.

Sixteen clubs took part in the 2014 version of the Cup, in three qualifying rounds played in September-November. The four successful sides competed in the Super Final in Bremerhaven, Germany.

Britain's representatives in the qualifying rounds were the Elite League winners, Belfast Giants, who were seeded into the second round.

British teams have entered the competition every year since 1983, apart from 1997 and 2003.

SECOND ROUND

Group B, Bremerhaven, Germany,
17-19 October 2014

	GP	W	OW	OL	L	GF	GA	Pts
Fischtown Pinguins	3	3	0	0	0	14	4	9
Belfast Giants	**3**	**2**	**0**	**0**	**1**	**12**	**7**	**6**
Tilburg Trappers	3	1	0	0	2	6	12	3
CSKA Sofia	3	0	0	0	3	8	17	0

3 points for a Win (W),
2 points for an Overtime or shootout Win (OW),
1 point for an Overtime or shootout Loss (OL).
The Giants won through to round 3 as the best second placed team in round 2. This followed the withdrawal from round 3 of Ukrainian team **Kompanion Kyiv** for political reasons.

BELFAST GIANTS

Stephen Murphy, Andrew Dickson; Robby Sandrock, David Phillips, Calvin Elfring, Cody Brookwell, Jeff Mason, Kevin Phillips; Mark Garside, Adam Keefe (capt), Darryl Lloyd, Ray Sawada, Mike Kompon, Mark McCutcheon, Evan Cheverie, Colin Shields, Craig Peacock.
Manager/Coach: Steve Thornton.

GIANTS' GAME SUMMARIES

17 October 2014

TILBURG-GIANTS   **1-4** (0-1,0-3,1-0)

Giants' scoring: Keefe, McCutcheon, Brookwell, Kompon 1g; Mason 2a; Lloyd, Elfring, Sawada, Shields, K Phillips, Sandrock 1a.
Netminding:
Meierdres TIL 17-15- 8 40   save% 90.00
Murphy BEL   8- 9-13 30   save% 96.67
Pims: Tilburg 10, Giants 10.
Goals/powerplays: Tilburg 0/3, Giants 2/3.
Giants' man of match: Brookwell.
Ref: Novak SVK. *Lines:* Berger, Merten GER.
Attendance: 812.

18 October 2014

GIANTS-SOFIA   **6-2** (2-1,2-1,2-0)

Giants' scoring: Lloyd 2+1; Kompon, Elfring 1+1; Garside, Mason 1g; Peacock 2a; Sawada, Sandrock, D Phillips, Keefe, McCutcheon, Shields, K Phillips 1a.
Netminding:
Murphy BEL   7-12- 3 22   save% 90.91
Klimentev SOF 24-11-18 53   save% 88.68
Pims: Giants 8, Sofia 14.
Goals/powerplays: Giants 3/7 (one s/h), Sofia 0/4.
Giants' man of match: Lloyd.
Ref: Garbay FRA. *Lines:* Muller, Seessle GER.
Attendance: 903.

19 October 2014
GIANTS-FISCHTOWN   **2-4** (2-1,0-0,1-0)
Giants' scoring: Kompon 2g; Sandrock, Sawada 1a.
Netminding:
Murphy BEL   12-14-8 34   *save%* 88.24
Langmann BRE   11- 8-7 26   *save%* 92.31
Pims: Giants 12, Pinguins 8.
Goals/powerplays: Giants 1/3, Pinguins 2/5.
Giants' man of match: Kompon.
Ref: Novak SVK. *Lines*: Berger, Merten GER.
Attendance: 1,563.

SECOND ROUND REPORT
Giants catch a break

Belfast Giants came up short in a bruising battle against their German hosts and finished runners-up in their group.

But **Steve Thornton**'s team were gifted an escape hatch to round three when the Ukrainian champs were forced to pull out of the event due to the disturbances in the capital, Kiev.

After securing comfortable victories in their opening games against the Dutch and Bulgarian league winners, the Giants met Bremerhaven's Fischtown Pinguins in an exciting final.

Going into the last three minutes the sides were tied 2-2 with Canadian **Mike Kompon** scoring both the Giants' goals.

Then came disaster when **Ray Sawada** was banished for slashing and Pinguin **Brock Hooten** scored on the resulting powerplay.

Thornton took netminder **Stephen Murphy** off in the dying moments, but the six attackers failed to stop a fourth Bremerhaven goal into the empty net with one second left to play.

To have missed out on the next round after such a close fought contest would have been heart-breaking, so the Giants could be excused for believing their good fortune in getting through was deserved, especially for their fans, as so many had followed them to the North Sea port.

"With the support we had here, we really wanted to win it for our fans," said Kompon, adding: "But you know what? We played hard and our reward is that we still get to go to France."

Highlights and lowlights

▲ Belfast's Mike Kompon tallied five points (four goals) to put him in third place in the tournament's scoring chart. The 32-year-old spent his seven seasons in Europe with Munich of the German DEL or DEL2.

▲ *Tilburg Trappers* were coached by Canadian **Paul Gardner** who spent half a season on the Braehead Clan bench in 2012-13.

▼ **Evan Cheverie** did not ice against Tilburg.

► The Giants went through to the next round after compiling a better record in their group than Romanian side Corona Brasov did in finishing second in the other group.

► In group C, former NHLer **Mike Danton** scored the game- and group-winning goal on the powerplay with just 3:30 left to play in regulation to put his Polish club **KH Sanok** into the third round. Danton was refused a visa to play for Coventry Blaze in season 2012-13.

► The winner of the Continental Cup qualifies for the Champions Hockey League (CHL) in 2014-15. But ... Bremerhaven's Fischtown Pinguins, who qualified for the Super Final after winning group D in Italy, cannot qualify as they play in DEL2, Germany's second highest league. Only teams from their country's elite league are permitted to compete in the higher CHL.

THIRD ROUND
Group E, Angers, France,
21-23 November 2014

	GP	W	OW	L	OL	GF	GA	Pts
Angers Ducs FRA	3	2	0	1	0	9	5	6
Neman Grodno BEL	3	2	0	1	0	6	4	6
Belfast Giants GB	3	2	0	1	0	7	5	6
KH Sanok POL	3	0	0	3	0	3	11	0

RESULTS
21Nov	**Giants**-Grodno	1-0 (0-0,1-0,0-0)
	Sanok-Angers	0-4 (0-1,0-2,0-1)
22Nov	Grodno-Sanok	2-0 (1-0,1-0,0-0)
	Angers-**Giants**	2-1 (2-0,0-0,0-1)
23Nov	Sanok-**Giants**	3-5 (0-1,3-2,0-2)
	Angers-Grodno	3-4 (2-3,1-1,0-0)

BELFAST GIANTS

As in Second Round except: G – Carsen Chubak replaced Murphy (injured); F – *in* Kevin Westgarth and Kevin Saurette, *out* Garside.

GIANTS' GAME SUMMARIES

21 November 2014

GIANTS-NEMAN GRODNO   1-0 (0-0,1-0,0-0)
Giants' scoring: Kompon 1g; Keefe 1a.
Netminding:
Chubak BEL   10- 9-14 33   *save%* 100.0
Samankov GRO   7-12- 7 26   *save%* 96.15
Pims: Giants 33 (Westgarth 5+game – kneeing), Grodno 8.
Goals/powerplays: Giants 0/4, Grodno 0/4.
Giants' man of match: Chubak.
Referees: Deweerdt BEL, Metsala FIN.
Lines: Furet, Guillaume FRA.   *Attendance:* 214

22 November 2014

ANGERS-GIANTS   2-1 (2-0,0-0,0-1)
Giants scoring: Elfring 1g; Shields, Westgarth 1a.
Netminding:
Aubin ANG   7-15-13 35   *save%* 94.29
Chubak BEL   17- 6- 3 26   *save%* 92.31
Pims: Ducs 14, Giants 10.
Goals/powerplays: Ducs 0/3 (one s/h), Giants 0/5.   *Giants' man of match:* Elfring.
Referees: Metsala FIN, Oskirko RUS.
Lines: Gielly, Pointel FRA.   *Attendance:* 1,064

23 November 2014

SANOK-GIANTS   3-5 (0-1,3-2,0-2)
Giants' scoring: Kompon 1+1; Keefe, Lloyd, Cheverie, McCutcheon 1g; Elfring 2a; Peacock 1a. *Netminding:*
Pitton SAN   12-10-8 30   *save%* 83.33
Chubak BEL   7-15-7 29   *save%* 89.66
Pims: Sanok 22 (Strzyzowski 2+10-check-behind), Giants 10.
Goals/powerplays: Sanok 1/5, Giants 1/5.
Giants' man of match: Lloyd.
Referees: Deweerdt BEL, Oskirko RUS.
Lines: Furet, Pointel FRA.   *Attendance:* 570.

● The Giants picked up several niggly injuries during the weekend's games. As so often in internationals, the opposition iced more lines than the British club. Against the Poles, for instance, Belfast had only 14 skaters to Sanok's 20 with many of the Giants double shifting.

GIANTS' TOP POINTS SCORERS

both rounds	GP	G	A	Pts	Pim
Mike Kompon	6	6	2	8	0
Calvin Elfring	6	2	4	6	2
Darryl Lloyd	6	3	2	5	4
Adam Keefe	6	2	2	4	14
Mark McCutcheon	6	2	1	3	0

THIRD ROUND REPORT

Frustration for the Giants

The golden rule in international ice hockey tournaments is to win every game. No ifs, ands or buts, you have to win 'em all. Ask GB!

Elite League champs Belfast Giants lost two of their six Continental Cup contests. After the first defeat in Germany they got lucky and were able to carry on, but a second beating was pushing their luck, which duly ran out.

The second loss came in France against their hosts, Angers Ducs, who went 2-0 up after only 13 minutes. **Steve Thornton**'s men failed to break down the defence until 59.33 when **Calvin Elfring** tallied one second after Angers returned to full strength.

Despite this defeat, Belfast were still in with a chance of going through to the Super Final after they beat the Poles. All it needed was for favourites Angers to beat Grodno in the final game, a tie, or for Grodno to win by two goals.

When Grodno topped the French by one goal, there was much muttering among the Giants' frustrated fans – especially as the result enabled both Grodno and Angers to move on.

To explain - the Belarusians, the French and the Giants all finished on six points, so the tie-break system counted only the results between these three. With goal difference also level, the Giants lost out as they scored only two goals against their opponents. Angers had five and Grodno four. Like we said, international tournaments are very unforgiving.

That said, some fans sniffed a rodent when Angers used their 21-year-old netminder instead of their 37-year-old ex-NHL keeper in the Grodno battle. But maybe three games in as many days were just too much for the old man.

"It's pretty frustrating the way it ended," said Thornton. "We left it out of our hands with one bad period against Angers. But they were three physical games in three nights."

PAST BRITISH PERFORMANCES

Results since the formation of the Elite League:
2013 NOTTINGHAM PANTHERS *Coach:* **C Neilson**
Third Round in Asiago, Italy: lost 4-3 to **Toros Neftekamsk RUS**; beat Yertis Pavlodar KAZ 2-1; lost 3-2 to **Asiago.**
Second Round in Nottingham: beat **Bipolo Vitoria-Gasteiz SPA 5-3**; beat HYS The Hague NED 7-3; beat HK Juniors Riga LAT 3-1.

2012 **BELFAST GIANTS** *Coach:* **Doug Christiansen**
Second Round in Landshut, Germany: beat Geleen Smoke Eaters NED 11-1, lost to Landshut Cannibals 7-1, beat HSC Csikszereda ROM 4-0.

2011 SHEFF'D STEELERS *Coach:* **Ryan Finnerty**
Third Round in Herning, Denmark: lost to Asiago ITA 4-3 after shootout; lost to Herning 3-0; lost to Dunaujvaros HUN 6-3.

2010 COVENTRY BLAZE *Coach:* **Paul Thompson**
Third Round in Rouen, France: beat Liepajas LAT 6-1, beat Kracow POL 6-1, lost to Rouen 7-3.

2009 **SHEFFIELD STEELERS** *Coach:* **D Matsos**
Super Final in Grenoble, France: beat **Grenoble 5-2**, lost to Salzburg AUT 6-1, lost to Minsk BEL 4-1. *Third Round in Bolzano, Italy:* beat **The Hague NED 4-3**, beat **Maribor SLO 5-4**, beat **Bolzano 4-3** after shootout.

2008 **COVENTRY BLAZE** *Coach:* **P Thompson**
Third Round in Bolzano, Italy: beat **Maribor SLO 6-3**, beat **Dunaujvaros HUN 6-4**, lost to Bolzano 1-0.

2007 **COVENTRY BLAZE** *Coach:* **P Thompson**
Second Round in Aalborg, Denmark: lost to Aalborg 3-0, beat **Salzburg AUT 3-2ot**, lost to Ljubljana SLO 4-2.

2006 **NOTT'HAM PANTHERS** *Coach:* **Mike Ellis**
Second Round in Rouen, France:
lost to Rouen 6-2, lost to Salzburg AUT 5-2, lost to Sonderjyske DEN 4-2.

2005 **COVENTRY BLAZE** *Coach:* **P Thompson**
Second Round in Grenoble, France:
drew with Herning DEN 2-2, beat **Amstel Tigers NED 5-4**, lost to Grenoble 2-0.

2004 **NOTT'HAM PANTHERS** *Coach:* **Paul Adey**
Second Round in Amiens, France:
drew 2-2 with Milan ITA, beat **Ljubljana SLO 1-0**, beat Amiens 3-1.

Earlier results are in The Ice Hockey Annual 2010-11, 2006-07 & 1997-98.

Published every year since 1976

Complete your collection of the sport's 'bible'

Go to www.icehockeyannual.co.uk/backissues

 The Ice Hockey Annual

Follow Stewart on 🐦 @robers45

ROLL OF HONOUR

Winners and runners-up in all domestic club competitions since the start of the Elite League in season 2003-04. Earlier years are in The Ice Hockey Annual 1998-99 and 2007-08.

SEASON	COMPETITION	WINNER	RUNNER-UP	NOTES
2014-15	Elite League Play-off Ch'ship	Coventry Blaze	Sheffield Steelers	Won 4-2 at Nottingham
	Rapid Solicitors Elite League	Sheffield Steelers	Braehead Clan	10-team lge, 2 conferences - Nottingham won Erhardt Braehead won Gardiner
	Elite Challenge Cup	Cardiff Devils	Sheffield Steelers	Won 2-1 at Sheffield
	English Premier Lge Ch'ship	Peterboro' Phantoms	Manchester Phoenix	Won 5-2 at Coventry
	English Premier League	Telford Tigers	Guildford Flames	9-team league
	English Challenge Cup	Teford Tigers	Manchester Phoenix	Won 8-3 agg. (3-1a,5-2h) Incl. Nat'n'l Lge teams.
	Nat'n'l Lge Div 1 South	Chelmsford Chieftains	Invicta Dynamos	10-team division
	Nat'n'l Lge Div 1 North (Moralee)	Blackburn Hawks	Billingham Stars	7-team division
	Nat'n'l Lge Div 2 South-East	Slough Jets	Peterboro' Islanders	6-team division
	Nat'n'l Lge Div 2 South-West	Bristol Pitbulls	Basingstoke Buffalo	5-team division
	Nat'n'l Lge Div 2 North (Laidler)	Solihull Barons	Telford NIHL Tigers	10-team division
	Scottish National League	Kirkcaldy Kestrels	E'burgh SNIHL Capitals	11-team league
	Women's Premier League	Bracknell Queen Bees	Kingston Diamonds	8-team league
2013-14	Elite League Play-off Ch'ship	Sheffield Steelers	Belfast Giants	Won 3-2 at Nottingham
	Rapid Solicitors Elite League	Belfast Giants	Sheffield Steelers	10-team league
	Elite Challenge Cup	Nottingham Panthers	Belfast Giants	Won 7-6 agg. (2-5a, 5-1h)
	English Premier Lge Ch'ship	Basingstoke Bison	Manchester Phoenix	Won 5-3 at Coventry
	English Premier League	Manchester Phoenix	Basingstoke Bison	10-team league
	English Premier Cup	Basingstoke Bison	Milton Keynes Lightning	Won 7-5 agg. (4-1a, 3-4h)
	Nat'n'l Lge South - Div 1	Chelmsford Chieftains	Wightlink Raiders	9-team division
	Nat'n'l Lge Nth - Div 1 (Moralee)	Solway Sharks	Blackburn Hawks	8-team division
	Nat'n'l Lge Nth - Div 2	Oxford City Stars	Slough NL Jets	12-team division
	Nat'n'l Lge Nth - Div 2 (Laidler)	Solihull Barons	Deeside Dragons	8-team division
	Scottish National League	Edinburgh SNL Capitals	Kirkcaldy Kestrels	11-team league
2012-13	Elite League Play-off Ch'ship	Nottingham Panthers	Belfast Giants	Won 3-2ot at Nottingham
	Rapid Solicitors Elite League	Nottingham Panthers	Belfast Giants	10-team league
	Elite Challenge Cup	Nottingham Panthers	Sheffield Steelers	Won 5-3 agg. (4-1a, 1-2h)
	English Premier Lge Ch'ship	Manchester Phoenix	Guildford Flames	Won 5-2 at Coventry
	English Premier League	Guildford Flames	Basingstoke Bison	10-team league
	English Premier Cup	Guildford Flames	Slough Jets	Won 9-5 agg. (4-2a,5-3h)
	Nat'n'l Lge North - Div 1	Solway Sharks	Billingham Stars	9-team division
	Nat'n'l Lge South - Div 1	Chelmsford Chieftains	Wightlink Raiders	9-team division
	Nat'n'l Lge North - Div 2	Nottingham Lions	Deeside Dragons	7-team division
	Nat'n'l Lge South - Div 2	Oxford City Stars	Wightlink Tigers	12-team division
	Scottish National League	Paisley Pirates	Dundee Tigers	10-team league
2011-12	Elite League Play-off Ch'ship	Nottingham Panthers	Cardiff Devils	Won 2-0 at Nottingham
	Rapid Solicitors Elite League	Belfast Giants	Sheffield Steelers	10-team league
	Elite Challenge Cup	Nottingham Panthers	Belfast Giants	Won 10-4 agg. (5-1a, 5-3h)
	English Premier Lge Ch'ship	Slough Jets	Manchester Phoenix	Won 4-1 at Coventry
	English Premier League	Guildford Flames	Manchester Phoenix	10-team league
	English Premier Cup	Guildford Flames	Sheffield Steeldogs	Won 12-5 agg. (6-3a, 6-2h)
	English Nat'n'l Lge North - Div 1	Billingham Stars	Whitley Warriors	9-team division
	English Nat'n'l Lge South - Div 1	Romford Raiders	Chelmsford Chieftains	10-team division
	Eng Nat'n'l Lge North - Div 2	Solway Sharks	Sutton Sting	8-team division
	Eng Nat'n'l Lge South - Div 2	Solent & Gosport Devils	Peterborough Islanders	13-team division
	Scottish National League	Dundee Comets	Paisley Pirates	9-team league

ROLL OF HONOUR

SEASON	COMPETITION	WINNER	RUNNER-UP	NOTES
2010-11	Elite League Play-off Ch'ship	Nottingham Panthers	Cardiff Devils	Won 5-4 at Nottingham
	Elite League	Sheffield Steelers	Cardiff Devils	Tied on pts in 10-team league
	Elite Challenge Cup	Nottingham Panthers	Belfast Giants	Won 4-3 agg. (3-1h,1-2a)
	English Premier Lge Ch'ship	Guildford Flames	Milton Keynes Lightning	Won 5-3 at Coventry
	English Premier League	Manchester Phoenix	Guildford Flames	10-team league
	English Premier Cup	Slough Jets	Basingstoke Bison	Won 7-4 agg. (3-2a, 4-2h)
	English Nat'n'l Lge, North	Whitley Warriors	Nottingham Lions	8-team division
	English Nat'n'l Lge, South	Wightlink Raiders	Chelmsford Chieftains	11-team division
	Eng Nat'n'l Lge, North - Div 2	Solihull Barons	Sutton Sting	7-team division
	Eng Nat'n'l Lge, South - Div 2	Slough Jets 2	Solent & Gosport Devils	13-team division
	Northern League	Fife Flyers	Whitley Warriors	7-team lge; B'ford withdrew. Flyers bt Warriors 6-0 in PO.
2009-10	Elite League Play-off Ch'ship	Belfast Giants	Cardiff Devils	Won 3-2so at Nottingham
	Elite League	Coventry Blaze	Belfast Giants	8-team league
	Challenge Cup	Nottingham Panthers	Cardiff Devils	Won 8-7 agg. (4-2a,4-5h)
	Eng Premier Lge Ch'ship	Slough Jets	Guildford Flames	Won 2-1ot at Coventry
	Eng Premier League	Milton Keynes Lightning	Slough Jets	10-team league
	Eng Premier Cup	Guildford Flames	Milton Keynes Lightning	Won 10-4 agg. (6-1h,4-3a)
	Eng Nat'n'l Lge, North	Whitley Warriors	Nottingham Lions	8-team division
	Eng Nat'n'l Lge, South	Invicta Dynamos	Cardiff Devils	10-team division
	Eng Nat'n'l Lge, North - Div 2	Newcastle ENL Vipers	Flintshire Freeze	7-team division
	Eng Nat'n'l Lge, South - Div 2	Bristol Pitbulls	Swindon ENL Wildcats	11-team division
	Celtic League	Fife Flyers	Dundee Stars	4-team league
	Northern League	Solway Sharks	Fife Flyers	5-team lge; Sharks won PO.
2008-09	Elite League Play-off Ch'ship	Sheffield Steelers	Nottingham Panthers	Won 2-0 at Nottingham
	bmibaby Elite League	Sheffield Steelers	Coventry Blaze	10-team league
	Challenge Cup	Belfast Giants	Manchester Phoenix	Won 6-5 agg. (3-4a, 3-1h)
	Knockout Cup	Belfast Giants	Manchester Phoenix	Won 7-5 agg. 3-3a, 4-2h)
	Eng Premier Lge Ch'ship	Peterboro' Phantoms	Milton Keynes Lightning	Won 5-4 at Coventry
	Eng Premier League	Peterboro' Phantoms	Milton Keynes Lightning	10-team league.
	Eng Premier Cup	Peterboro' Phantoms	Guildford Flames	Won 9-7 agg. (3-4a, 6-3h)
	Eng Nat'n'l Lge, North	Sheffield Spartans	Nottingham Lions	8-team division (INV bt SHE
	Eng Nat'n'l Lge, South	Invicta Dynamos	Bracknell Hornets	8-team division (5-4so
	Eng Nat'n'l Lge Play-offs	Nottingham Lions	Invicta Dynamos	Won 3-2so at Coventry
	Celtic Cup	Fife Flyers	Dundee Stars	6-team league (Flyers won
	Northern League	Solway Sharks	Fife Flyers	5-team league (play-offs
2007-08	Elite League Play-off Ch'ship	Sheffield Steelers	Coventry Blaze	Won 2-0 at Nottingham
	bmibaby Elite League	Coventry Blaze	Sheffield Steelers	10-team league
	Challenge Cup	Nottingham Panthers	Sheffield Steelers	Won 9-7 agg. (6-3a, 3-4h)
	Knockout Cup	Coventry Blaze	Basingstoke Bison	Won 8-6 agg. (2-4a, 6-2h)
	Eng Premier Lge Ch'ship	Slough Jets	Bracknell Bees	Won 4-1 at Coventry
	Eng Premier League	Guildford Flames	Slough Jets	11-team league
	Eng Premier Cup	Bracknell Bees	Milton Keynes Lightning	Won 7-6 agg. (3-4h, 4-2ot/a)
	Eng Nat'n'l Lge, North	Nottingham Lions	Whitley Warriors	12-team lge (NOT bt PET
	Eng Nat'n'l Lge, South	A - Peterboro' Islanders	B - Invicta Dynamos	19-team lge (14-5 agg.
	Eng Nat'n'l Lge Play-offs	Whitley Warriors	Peterboro' Islanders	Won 7-3 at Coventry
	Scottish Premier Lge	Fife Flyers	Edinburgh Capitals	5-team lge; (Fife won
	Northern League	Fife Flyers	Dundee Stars	7-team lge; (play-offs.

SEASON	COMPETITION	WINNER	RUNNER-UP	NOTES
2006-07	Elite League Play-off Ch'ship	Nottingham Panthers	Cardiff Devils	Won 2-1so at Nottingham.
	bmibaby Elite League	Coventry Blaze	Belfast Giants	10-team league
	Challenge Cup	Coventry Blaze	Sheffield Steelers	Won 9-4 agg. (4-3h, 5-1a)
	Knockout Cup	Cardiff Devils	Coventry Blaze	Won 3-0 at Coventry.
	Eng Premier Lge Ch'ship	Bracknell Bees	Guildford Flames	Won 3-2 at Coventry.
	Eng Premier League	Bracknell Bees	Sheffield Scimitars	12-team league
	English Premier Cup	Guildford Flames	Milton Keynes Lightning	Won 7-5 agg. (3-2h, 4-3a)
	Eng Nat'n'l Lge, North	Newcastle (ENL) Vipers	Whitley Warriors	10-team lge. (NEW bt INV
	Eng Nat'n'l Lge, South	Invicta Dynamos	Streatham Redskins	12-team lge. (8-6 agg.
	Eng Nat'n'l Lge Play-offs	Sheffield Spartans	Haringey Greyhounds	Won 4-3 at Coventry.
	Scottish Nat'n'l Lge	Fife Flyers	Dundee Stars	10-team lge; Flyers won PO.
	Northern League	Fife Flyers	Whitley Warriors	7-team lge; Warriors won PO.
2005-06	Elite League Playoff Ch'ship	Newcastle Vipers	Sheffield Steelers	Won 2-1 at Nottingham
	Elite League	Belfast Giants	Newcastle Vipers	9-team lge. (London w'drew).
	Challenge Cup	Cardiff Devils	Coventry Blaze	Won 5-4 agg. after PS.
	Knockout Cup	Sheffield Steelers	Coventry Blaze	Won 2-1 agg. after PS.
	Eng Premier Lge Ch'ship	Milton Keynes Lightning	Bracknell Bees	Won 5-3 at Coventry
	Eng Premier League	Guildford Flames	Slough Jets	13-team league.
	Eng Premier Cup	Bracknell Bees	Hull Stingrays	Won 6-5 on agg. (5-3h,1-2a)
	Eng Nat'n'l Lge Ch'ship	Invicta Dynamos	Billingham Bombers	Won 14-5 on agg. (6-1a,8-4h)
	Eng Nat'n'l Lge, North	Billingham Bombers	Nottingham Lions	8-team league
	Eng Nat'n'l Lge, South	Invicta Dynamos	Cardiff Devils 2	11-team league
	Scottish Nat'n'l Lge	Fife Flyers	Dundee Stars	9-team lge; Flyers won PO.
	Northern League	Fife Flyers	Paisley Pirates	7-team lge; Flyers won PO.
2004-05	Elite League Playoff Ch'ship	Coventry Blaze	Nottingham Panthers	Won 2-1ot at Nottingham
	Elite League	Coventry Blaze	Belfast Giants	7-team league
	Challenge Cup	Coventry Blaze	Cardiff Devils	Won 11-5 on agg. (6-1h,5-4a)
	Crossover Games	Belfast Giants	Cardiff Devils	Inter-league games with BNL
	British Nat'l Lge Ch'ship	Dundee Stars	Guildford Flames	Won best-of-five series, 3-0
	British National League	Bracknell Bees	Newcastle Vipers	7-team league
	Winter Cup	Bracknell Bees	Newcastle Vipers	Win 8-1 on agg. (5-1a,3-0h)
	Eng Premier Lge Ch'ship	MK Lightning	Peterboro' Phantoms	Won 7-2 at Coventry
	Eng Premier League	MK Lightning	Peterboro' Phantoms	9-team league
	Eng Premier Cup	Romford Raiders	Swindon Wildcats	Won 5-3 on agg. (2-0a,3-3h
	Eng Nat'n'l Lge Ch'ship	Sheffield Scimitars	Invicta Dynamos	Won 10-3 on agg. (6-0h, 4-3a)
	Eng Nat'n'l Lge, North	Sheffield Scimitars	Nottingham Lions	9-team league
	Eng Nat'n'l Lge, South	Invicta Dynamos	Oxford City Stars	10-team league
	English Cup	Sheffield Scimitars	Invicta Dynamos	Won 8-3 on agg (4-0a,4-3h)
2003-04	Elite League Playoff Ch'ship	Sheffield Steelers	Nottingham Panthers	Won 2-1 at Nottingham
	Elite League	Sheffield Steelers	Nottingham Panthers	New 8-team league
	Challenge Cup	Nottingham Panthers	Sheffield Steelers	Won 4-3 agg. (1-1h,3-2ot a)
	British Nat'l Lge Ch'ship	Guildford Flames	Bracknell Bees	Won 9-7 on agg. (5-4a,4-3h)
	British National League	Fife Flyers	Guildford Flames	7-team league
	Findus Cup	Newcastle Vipers	Guildford Flames	Won 6-1 at Newcastle
	Eng Premier Lge Ch'ship	MK Lightning	Slough Jets	Won 12-2 on agg. (7-0a, 5-2h)
	Eng Premier League	MK Lightning	Peterboro' Phantoms	9-team league
	Eng Premier Cup	Peterboro' Phantoms	Wightlink Raiders	Won 7-2 on agg. (3-1a,4-1h)
	Eng Nat'n'l Lge Ch'ship	Sheffield Scimitars	Invicta Dynamo	Won 8-5 on agg. (4-3a,4-2h)
	Eng Nat'n'l Lge, North	Flintshire Freeze	Sheffield Scimitars	10-team league
	Eng Nat'n'l Lge, South	Invicta Dynamo	Oxford City Stars	9-team league

GOVERNING BODIES

ICE HOCKEY UK LTD
Chairman: Jim Anderson.
General Secretary: Andy French.
Registered office: Regus House, Malthouse Avenue, Cardiff Gate Business Park, Cardiff CF23 8RU. Tel: 07713-590506.
email: general.secretary@icehockeyuk.co.uk
Media representative: Chris Ellis.
email: media@icehockeyuk.co.uk
Website: www.icehockeyuk.co.uk

The Directors of the Board of the sport's national governing body are:
Jim Anderson (IHUK), Tony Smith (Elite League); Bob Wilkinson, Geoff Hemmerman (English IHA); David Hand (Scottish IH).
Stakeholders: English Ice Hockey Association, Scottish Ice Hockey, Ice Hockey Northern Ireland, Elite Ice Hockey League Ltd.

Ice Hockey Northern Ireland, which was set up in 2011, consists of five recreational teams based in the Dundonald Ice Bowl - Belfast Ice Foxes, Northern Ireland Tridents, Northern Ireland Prowlers, Belfast Spitfires and Castlereagh Spartans.
- from the entry in Wikipedia

ELITE ICE HOCKEY LEAGUE LTD
Chairman: Tony Smith.
Media representative: Chris Ellis.
email: media@eliteleague.co.uk.
Registered office: 53 Chandos Place, Covent Garden, London WC2N 4HS.
Tel: 0207-100-1255 (Mon-Fri 8.30am-6.00pm)
e-mail: office@eliteleague.co.uk.
Website: www.eliteleague.co.uk

ENGLISH ICE HOCKEY ASSOCIATION
Chairman: Ken Taggart.
Secretary: Irene Jones.
email: irene.jones@eiha.co.uk
Registered office: 12 Arnside Avenue, Blackpool FY1 6NB.
Website: www.eiha.co.uk.
Executive Committee: **Ken Taggart** (chairman), **Irene Jones** (secretary), **Charles Dacres, Paul Hayes, Geoff Hemmerman, Bob Wilkinson.**

SCOTTISH ICE HOCKEY
Chairman: David Hand.
email: chairman@siha-uk.co.uk.
Secretary: Samantha Hand, 35 Learmonth Crescent, Edinburgh EH4 1DD.
Tel: 0131-315-4845.
email: generalsecretary@siha-uk.co.uk.
Website: www.siha-uk.co.uk/home

WOMEN'S ICE HOCKEY LEAGUE
Chairman: Geoff Hemmerman
Secretary: Sally Taylor, 22 Foxley Road, Thornton Heath, Surrey CR7 7DS.
Tel/Fax: 0208-684-5382.
email: sally.taylor@btinternet.com
Website: www.eiha.co.uk

GB SUPPORTERS CLUB
Secretary: Annette Petrie, 22 Ashbrook Road, Old Windsor, Bucks SL4 2LS.
Tel/Fax: 01753-851302.
email: gbschq@blueyonder.co.uk.
Website: www.thefifthline.co.uk

ICE HOCKEY JOURNALISTS UK
Chairman: Mike Appleton.
Secretary: Patrick Smyth. Tel: 07740 352 907.
email: secretary@ihjuk.co.uk
Website: www.ihjuk.co.uk

IRISH ICE HOCKEY ASSOCIATION
President: Aaron Guli.
Registered address: Irish Sport HQ, National Sports Campus, Blanchardstown, Dublin 15.
Tel/fax: +353-1-6251157.
General Secretary: Position vacant.
Website: www.iiha.org
Directors: **Gerard Duffy, Alan Fleming, Benjamin Mareil.**
There are currently no ice rinks in operation in the Irish Republic, and their national teams have been dormant since 2013.

CLUB DIRECTORY 2015-16

ABERDEEN
Rink Address: Linx Ice Arena, Beach Promenade, Aberdeen AB24 5NR.
Tel: 01224-655406/7.
Ice Size: 184 x 85 feet (56 x 26 metres).
Spectator Capacity: 1,200.
Senior Team: Lynx (Scottish National League).
Secretary: Arlene Chambers.
email: arlenemaarproj@demon.co.uk.
Website: www.aberdeenlynx.com

ALTRINCHAM (Manchester)
Rink Address: Silver Blades Ice Rink Co. (Altrincham), The Ice Dome, Oakfield Road, Station Site, Altrincham, Cheshire WA15 8EW.
Tel: 0870 085 2929.
Ice Size: 187 x 85 feet (57 x 26 metres).
Spectator capacity: 2,500.
Senior Teams: Manchester Storm (Elite League), Aces (National League).
Contact: Mark Johnson at the rink.
email: info@manchesterstorm.com
Website: www.manchesterstorm.com

AYR
Rink address: Auchenharvie Leisure Centre, Saltcoats Road, Stevenston, Ayr KA20 3JR.
Tel: 01294-605126.
Ice Size: 184 x 98.5 feet (56 x 30 metres).
Spectator Capacity: 132.
Senior Team: North Ayrshire Wild (Scots Nat Lge)
Secretary: Fiona Morton, 46 Auchenharvie Road, Saltcoats, Ayr KA22 5RL.
email: fiomor2000@gmail.com
Website: www.naihc.co.uk

BASINGSTOKE
Rink Address: Planet Ice Basingstoke Arena, Basingstoke Leisure Park, Worting Road, Basingstoke, Hants RG22 6PG.
Tel: 01256-355266.
Ice Size: 197 x 98 feet (60 x 30 metres)
Spectator Capacity: 1,600.
Senior Teams: Bison (English Premier League) and Buffalo (National League).
Contact: Doug Sheppard at the rink.
Website: www.bstokebison.co.uk

BELFAST
SSE ARENA
Address: 2 Queen's Quay, Belfast BT3 9QQ.
Tel: 028 9076 6000.
Ice Size: 197 x 98 feet (60 x 30 metres).
Spectator Capacity (for ice hockey): 7,100.
Team: Giants (Elite League).
Contact: Steve Thornton at the rink.
email: office@belfastgiants.co.uk
Website: www.belfastgiants.co.uk

DUNDONALD INTERNATIONAL ICE BOWL
Belfast Giants' training rink.
Address: 111 Old Dundonald Road, Castlereagh, Co. Antrim BT16 1XT, N Ireland. Tel: 9080-9100.
Ice size: 197 x 98 feet (60 x 30 metres).
Spectator capacity: 1,500.
Senior Team: Belfast SNL Giants (Scottish National League).
Contact: John Sempey. Tel: 07842-148038.
Website: www.theicebowl.com/iceskating/clubs

BILLINGHAM
Rink Address: Billingham Forum Leisure Centre, The Causeway, Town Centre, Billingham, Stockton-on-Tees TS23 2OJ.
Tel: 01642-551381
Ice Size: 180 x 80 feet (55 x 24 metres)
Spectator Capacity: 1,200.
Senior Team: Stars (National League).
Contact: allen@flavellwelding.co.uk.
Website: www.billinghamstars.co.uk

BLACKBURN
Rink Address: Blackburn Ice Arena, Lower Audley, Waterside, Blackburn BB1 1BB.
Ice Size: 197 x 98 feet (60 x 30 metres)
Tel: 01254-668686.
Spectator Capacity: 3,200.
Senior Teams: Hawks & Eagles (NIHL).
Contact: annette_wallbank43@hotmail.com
Website: www.blackburnhawks.com

BRACKNELL

Rink Address: John Nike Leisuresport Complex, John Nike Way, Bracknell, Berks RG12 4TN.
Tel: 01344-789000.
Ice Size: 197 x 98 feet (60 x 30 metres)
Spectator Capacity: 3,100.
Senior Teams: Bees (English Premier League) and Hornets (National League).
email: ben.beeching@precisionsportsmarketing.co.uk
Website: www.bracknellbees.co.uk

BRADFORD

Rink Address: Bradford Ice Arena, 19 Little Horton Lane, Bradford, W Yorks BD5 0AD.
Tel: 01274-733535.
Ice Size: 180 x 80 feet (55 x 24 metres)
Spectator Capacity: 700.
Senior Team: Bulldogs (National League).
Secretary: yvonneroberts@talktalk.net
Website: www.bradfordbulldogs.co.uk

BRAEHEAD (Glasgow)

Rink Address: Braehead Arena, 25 King's Inch Road, Glasgow G51 4BP. Tel: 0141-886-8300.
Ice Size: 197 x 98 feet (60 x 30 metres).
Spectator Capacity (for ice hockey): 3,576.
Senior Teams: Clan (Elite League), Paisley Pirates (Scottish National League).
Contacts: Clan: Andy McLaughlin.
email: andy@braeheadclan.com
Pirates: Jackie Turley.
email: js.turley@btinternet.com
Websites:www.braeheadclan.com,
www.paisleypirates.org.

CAMBRIDGE UNIVERSITY

Home ice 2015-16: Planet Ice Peterborough Arena. (See Peterborough entry).
Senior Team: Cambridge University Blues (British Universities League).
Contact: Prof Bill Harris, Dept of Anatomy, Cambridge University, Downing St., Cambridge CB2 3DYUK. Tel: 01223-333772.
email: harris@mole.bio.cam.ac.uk
Websites: www.srcf.ucam.org/cuihc,
www.buiha.org.uk

CARDIFF

PLANET ICE CARDIFF
Rink Address: Planet Ice, Empire Way, Cardiff Bay, Cardiff CF11 0SP. Tel: 029 2038 2001.
Ice Size: 184 x 85 feet (56 x 26 metres).
Spectator Capacity: 2,300.
Senior Teams: Devils (Elite & National Leagues).
Contact: kris.agland@cardiffdevils.com.
Website: www.cardiffdevils.com

ICE ARENA WALES (opening early 2016)
Rink address: Ice Arena Wales, Olympian Drive, Cardiff CF11 0JS. Tel: TBA.
Ice Size: 60 x 30 metres and 54 x 27 metres.
Spectator capacity: 3,000.
email: info@icearenawales.co.uk
Website: www.icearenawales.co.uk

CHELMSFORD

Rink Address: Riverside Ice & Leisure Centre, Victoria Road, Chelmsford, Essex CM1 1FG.
Tel: 01245-615050.
Ice Size: 184 x 85 feet (56 x 26 metres).
Spectator Capacity: 1,200.
Senior Teams: Chieftains & Warriors (NIHL).
Website: www.chelmsfordchieftains.org

CLEVELEYS (Fylde Coast)

Rink address: Cleveleys Ice Arena, North Promenade, Thornton-Cleveleys FY5 1FF
Tel: 01253-804144.
Ice Size: 118 x 72 feet (36 x 22 metres)
Spectator Capacity: 250
Contact: Pete Bleackley. Tel: 01253-804144
email: hockey@cleveleysicearena.co.uk
Rink website: www.cleveleysicearena.co.uk
Club website: www.blackpooljuniorseagulls.com
Junior and recreational hockey only 2015-16.

COVENTRY

Rink Address: Planet Ice Arena, Croft Road, Coventry CV1 3AZ. Tel: 02476-630393.
Ice Size: 184 x 92 feet (56 x 28 metres)
Spectator Capacity (for ice hockey): 2,616.
Senior Teams: Blaze (Elite & National Leagues).
Contact: Sally Mahers. Tel: 02476-223220.
email: sallymahers@coventryblaze.co.uk
Website: www.coventryblaze.co.uk

DEESIDE (Queensferry)

Rink Address: Deeside Leisure Centre, Chester Road West, Queensferry, Clwyd CH5 5HA. **Tel:** 01244-814725.
Ice Size: 197 x 98 feet (60 x 30 metres).
Spectator Capacity: 1,200 (693 seated).
Senior Team: Dragons (National League).
email: contactus@deesidedragons.com
Website: www.deesidedragons.com.

In season 2015-16, the rink is also home to:
Senior Team: Manchester Phoenix (EPIHL).
Contact: Mags Pullen.
email: mpullen@manchesterphoenix.co.uk
Website: www.manchesterphoenix.co.uk

DUMFRIES (Solway)

Rink Address: The Ice Bowl, King Street, Dumfries DG2 9AN. **Tel:** 01387-251300.
Ice Size: 184 x 95 feet (56 x 29 metres).
Spectator Capacity: 1,000.
Senior Team: Solway Sharks (Nat Lge & Scot NL).
Contact: Les Maxwell.
email: les@hi-engineering.co.uk
Website: www.solwaysharks.co.uk

DUNDEE

Rink Address: Dundee Ice Arena, 7 Dayton Drive, Dundee DD2 3SQ. **Tel:** 01382-455070.
Ice Size: 197 x 98 feet (60 x 30 metres).
Spectator Capacity: 2,300.
Senior Teams: Stars (Elite & Scot Nat Leagues)
Contacts: *Elite League:* Charlie Ward at the rink.
email: office@dundeestars.com
Website: www.dundeestars.com
SNIHL: Andrea Brown.
email: raband.brown@talktalk.net

DUNDEE (CITY) TIGERS - Scottish Nat'l Lge.
Secretary: Paul Guilcher.
email: dundeetigers@hotmail.com.
Website: www.dundeetigers.co.uk

EDINBURGH (Murrayfield)

Rink Address: Murrayfield Ice Rink, Riversdale Crescent, Edinburgh EH12 5XN.
Tel: 0131-337-6933.
Ice Size: 200 x 97 feet (61 x 29.5 metres).
Spectator Capacity: 3,800.
Senior Teams: Capitals (Elite & Scots Nat Lges).
Contact: Scott Neil. **Tel:** 0131-313-2977.
email: scottneil@edinburgh-capitals.com
Website: www.edinburgh-capitals.com

FIFE (Kirkcaldy)

Rink Address: Fife Ice Arena, Rosslyn Street, Kirkcaldy, Fife KY1 3HS. **Tel:** 01592-595100.
Ice Size: 193.5 x 98 feet (59 x 30 metres).
Spectator Capacity: 3,280.
Senior Teams: Flyers (Elite League), Kirkcaldy Kestrels (Scottish National League).
Flyers' contact: allan.paul@fifeflyers.co.uk
Kestrels' contact: Alma Greger.
email: ronn@blueyonder.co.uk
Websites: www.fifeflyers.co.uk, www.kihc.co.uk

GILLINGHAM

Rink Address: Silver Blades Ice Rink Co, The Ice Bowl, Ambley Road, Gillingham Business Park, Gillingham ME8 0PP. **Tel:** 01634-388477.
Ice Size: 184 x 85 feet (56 x 26 metres).
Spectator Capacity: 1,500.
Senior Teams: Invicta Dynamos & Mustangs (National League).
Contact: Jackie Mason. **Tel:** 07710-742427.
email: admin@invictadynamos.co.uk
Website: www.invictadynamos.co.uk

GOSPORT

Rink Address: Planet Ice Gosport Ice Rink, Forest Way, Fareham Road, Gosport PO13 0ZX. **Tel:** 02392-511217.
Ice Size: 145 x 73 feet (44 x 22 metres).
Spectator Capacity: 400.
Senior Team: Solent & Gosport Devils (Nat Lge).
Contact: Alex Murray at the rink.
Website: www.solentdevils.co.uk

GRIMSBY

Rink Address: Grimsby Leisure Centre, Cromwell Road, Grimsby, Lincs DN31 2BH.
Tel: 01472-323100.
Ice Size: 120 x 60 feet (36.5 x 18 metres).
Spectator Capacity: 1,300.
Senior Team: None. *Recreational hockey only.*

GUILDFORD

Rink Address: Spectrum Ice Rink, Parkway, Guildford GU1 1UP. **Tel:** 01483-443333.
Ice Size: 197 x 98 feet (60 x 30 metres).
Spectator Capacity: 2,200.
Senior Team: Flames (English Premier Lge).
Contact: Kirk Humphries. **Tel:** 01483-452244.
email: kirk@guildfordflames.com
Website: www.guildfordflames.com

HARINGEY (London)

Rink Address: Alexandra Palace Way, Wood Green, London N22 4AY. Tel: 0208-365-2121. Ice Size: 184 x 85 feet (56 x 26 metres). Spectator Capacity: 1,250. Senior Team: Racers (NIHL). Contact: Dan Sampson at the rink. Website: www.haringeyracers.co.uk

HULL

Rink Address: The Hull Ice Arena, Kingston Street, Hull HU1 2DZ. Tel: 01482-325252. Ice Size: 197 x 98 feet (60 x 30 metres). Spectator Capacity: 2,000. Senior Teams: Pirates (EPIHL), Jets (NIHL). Contact: Shane Smith. email: contact@hullpirates.co.uk Website: www.hullpirates.co.uk

ISLE OF WIGHT (Ryde)

Rink Address: Ryde Arena, Quay Road, Esplanade, Ryde, I of Wight PO33 2HH. Tel: 01983-615155. Fax: 01983-567460. Ice Size: 165 x 80 feet (50 x 24 metres) Spectator Capacity: 1,000. Senior Teams: Wightlink Raiders & Tigers (NIHL). Contacts: *Raiders*: Heather Jepson. email: raiders@iwrsc.com. *Tigers*: Sean Coleman. Tel: 07590-215650. Websites: www.wightlinkraiders.com, www.wightlinktigers.org

KILMARNOCK

Rink Address: Galleon Centre, 99 Titchfield Street, Kilmarnock, Scotland KA1 1QY. Tel: 01563-524014. Ice Size: 146 x 75.5 feet (44.6 x 23 metres) Senior Team: Storm (Scot Nat League). Secretary: Jacqueline Wright. email: jacque.wright@btopenworld.com Website: www.kilmarnockstorm.com.

LEE VALLEY (London)

Rink Address: Lee Valley Ice Centre, Lea Bridge Road, Leyton, London E10 7QL. Tel: 0208-533-3154. Ice Size: 184 x 85 feet (56 x 26 metres). Spectator Capacity: 1,000. Senior Team: Lions (National League). Website: www.leevalleylions.co.uk *Also home of London Raiders 2015-16 (see entry under Romford below)*

MILTON KEYNES

Rink Address: Planet Ice Milton Keynes Arena, The Leisure Plaza, 1 South Row, Central Milton Keynes MK9 1BL. Tel: 01908-696696. Ice Size: 197 x 98 feet (60 x 30 metres) Spectator Capacity: 2,200. Teams: Lightning (EPIHL) & Thunder (NIHL). Contact: Harry Howton. Tel: 01908-696993. email: howtons.ltd@btinternet.com Websites: www.mk-lightning.com, www.mkthunder.com

NOTTINGHAM

Rink Address: *Capital FM* Arena, Bolero Square, The Lace Market, Nottingham NG1 1LA. Tel: 0115-853-3000. Ice Size: 2 pads each 197 x 98 ft (60 x 30 m). Spectator Capacity (for ice hockey): 6,500. Senior Teams: Panthers (EIHL), Lions (NIHL). Panthers' contact: Gary Moran, First Floor, 4 Stoney Street, Nottingham NG1 1LG. Tel: 0115-941-3103. email: info@panthers.co.uk Lions' contact: Danny Harrison at the rink. Websites: www.panthers.co.uk, www.nottinghamlions.co.uk

OXFORD

Rink Address: The Ice Rink, Oxpens Road, Oxford OX1 1RX. Tel: 01865-467000. Ice Size: 184 x 85 feet (56 x 26 metres). Spectator Capacity: 1,025. Senior Team: City Stars (National League) Contact: Elaine Sutcliffe. Website: www.oxfordcitystars.com

OXFORD UNIVERSITY BLUES

British Universities League. Team Captain: Robert Main Websites: www.oxfordicehockey.com, www.buiha.org.uk

PETERBOROUGH

Rink Address: Planet Ice Peterborough Arena, 1 Mallard Road, Bretton, Peterborough PE3 8YN. Tel: 01733-260222. Ice Size: 184 x 85 feet (56 x 26 metres). Spectator Capacity: 1,500. Senior Teams: Phantoms (EPIHL) & Islanders (NIHL). Contact: carrie@peterboroughphantoms.com. Website: www.gophantoms.co.uk

ROMFORD (London)

(Romford) London Raiders playing home games at Lee Valley Ice Centre in 2015-16, pending completion of a new rink. See New Rinks News.
Senior Team: Raiders (National League).
Contact email: joanne.cahill@ntlworld.com
Website: www.londonraidersihc.com

SHEFFIELD

MOTORPOINT **ARENA**
Address: Broughton Lane, Sheffield S9 2DF.
Tel: 0114-256-5656.
Ice size: 197 x 98 feet (60 x 30 metres)
Spectator Capacity (for ice hockey): 10,000.
Senior Team: Steelers (Elite League).
Contact: Tony Smith.
email: offce@sheffieldsteelers.co.uk
Website: www.sheffieldsteelers.co.uk

iceSHEFFIELD
Address: Coleridge Road, Sheffield S9 5DA.
Tel: 0114-223-3900.
Ice Size: Two pads each 197x98ft (60x30m).
Spectator Capacity: 1,500 (main rink).
Senior Teams: Steeldogs (English Premier Lge), Spartans and Senators (National League).
Steeldogs' contact: Shaun Smith.
email: contact@sheffieldsteeldogs.co.uk.
Websites: www.sheffieldsteeldogs.co.uk,
www.sheffieldspartans.co.uk,
www.sheffieldsenators.co.uk
Also home of Sutton Sting 2015-16. See entry for Sutton-in-Ashfield below.

SLOUGH

Rink Address: Absolutely Ice, The Ice Arena, Montem Lane, Slough SL1 2QG.
Tel: 01753-894810.
Ice Size: 184 x 85 feet (56 x 26 metres).
Spectator Capacity: 1,200.
Senior Team: Jets (National League).
Contact: Steve English. **Tel:** 01753-821171.
email: senglish@jetshockey.co.uk
Website: www.jetshockey.co.uk

SOLIHULL

Rink Address: Ilobs Moat Road, Solihull B92 8JN. **Tel:** 0121-742-5561.
Ice Size: 185 x 90 feet (56 x 27 metres).
Spectator Capacity: 1,500.
Senior Team: Barons (National League).
Contact: solihullbarons@gmail.com
Website: www.solihull-barons.net

STREATHAM (London)

Rink address: Streatham Ice Arena & Leisure Centre, 390 Streatham High Road, Streatham, London SW16 6HX. **Tel:** 020 8677 5758.
Ice Size: 200 x 100 feet (60 x 30 metres).
Spectator Capacity: 1,000 approx.
Senior Team: Redskins (National League).
Contact: Graham D'Anger at the rink.
Websites: www.streatham-hockey.co.uk.

SUTTON-IN-ASHFIELD

Rink Address: Lammas Leisure Centre, Lammas Road, Sutton-in-Ashfield, Nottingham NG17 2AD. **Tel:** 01623-511177.
Ice Size: 120 x 60 feet (36 x 18 metres).
Senior Team: Sutton Sting (National League).
Team plays home games at iceSheffield.
Contact: Gary Apsley. **email:** gary@apsley.net.
Tel: 07852-570517.
Website: www.suttonsting.co.uk

SWINDON

Rink Address: Swindon Ice Arena, White Hill Way, Swindon SN5 7DL. **Tel:** 01793-445566.
Ice Size: 184 x 85 feet (56 x 26 metres).
Spectator Capacity: 1,650.
Senior Teams: Wildcats (English Premier and National Leagues).
Contact: Steve Nell. **Tel:** 07771-863674.
email: steve.nell@swindonwildcats.com
Website: www.swindonwildcats.com

TELFORD

Rink Address: The Ice Rink, St Quentins Gate, Telford TF3 4JQ. **Tel:** 0845-155-9966.
Ice Size: 184 x 85 metres (56 x 26 metres).
Spectator Capacity: 1,200.
Senior Teams: Tigers (Eng Premier & Nat Lges).
Contact: Paul Thomason/James Shaw.
email: contact@telfordtigers.co.uk
Website: www.tigershockeyuk.com

WHITLEY BAY

Rink Address: The Ice Rink, Hillheads Road, Whitley Bay NE25 8HP. **Tel:** 0191-291-1000.
Ice Size: 186 x 81 feet (56.5 x 24.5 metres).
Spectator Capacity: 3,200.
Senior Team: Warriors (National League).
Secretary: Colin Edwards.
Website: www.whitleywarriors.net

WIDNES

Rink Address: Silver Blades Ice Rink, The Hive Leisure Park, Earle Road, Widnes, Cheshire WA8 0GY. **Tel:** 0151-420-7930.
Ice Size: 56 x 26 metres.
Spectator capacity: 1,000 approx.
Senior Team: Wild (National League).
Contact: Mick Caunce.
email: info@widneswild.co.uk
Website: www.widneswild.co.uk

Late addition

ELGIN (Scotland)

Rink Address: Moray Leisure Centre, Borough Briggs Road, Elgin, Moray IV30 1AP.
Tel: 01343-550033.
Ice Size: 147.5 x 82 feet (45 x 25 metres).
Spectator Capacity: 200.
Senior Team: Moray Typhoons (Scots Nat Lge).
Club Secretary: Suzanne Green.
email: sgreenstevie@tiscali.co.uk
Facebook Page: MorayTyphoons.

The Ice Arena Wales which is scheduled to open during the 2015-16 ice hockey season.

photo: www.icearenawales.co.uk

Hot tubs, Swim spas, Gazebos, Accessories

...relax ...workout ...soak
live ...love ...laugh

The natural way to relax and unwind
When you enter your Canadian spa you will enter a world of soothing relaxation that will help relieve the stress and tension of the fast paced world we all live in.

You deserve to get only the best for your relaxation - so come and experience the soothing hydrotherapy massage benefits of a hot tub and the only place where you can find the best products is the Canadian Spa Company.

The Canadian Spa Company is the leading manufacturer when it comes to quality swim spas and hot tubs in the market today. Our products are manufactured using only the finest quality components and state of the art digital control systems.

Come and talk to us today: 01293 824094

 www.canadianspacompany.com